A GUIDE TO THE BALTIC STATES

Edited by Ingrīda Kalniņš

Note

While every effort has been made to ensure that factual information
is accurate, the publisher does not take responsibility for any
changes, omissions or typographical errors found by readers of this
guide. Reader comments are welcomed.

Published by: Inroads, Inc.
                     P.O. Box 3197
                     Merrifield, VA 22116-3197

ISBN 0-9626502-0-X

Library of Congress Catalog Card Number: 89-81868

CONTRIBUTORS

Lithuanian Section:

Rasa Avizienis - author

Contributors:

Rita Datkus, Aldona Kaminskas, Algimantas Kezys, Ginta Remeikis, Emilija Sakadolskis, Darius Suziedelis, Saulius Suziedelis, Rūta Virkutis, and the contributors in Lithuania.

Latvian Section:

Ingrīda Kalnins - author

Contributors:

Andris Cerbulis (photos), Ojārs Kalniņš, Ināra Punga, Vitauts Sīmanis (photos), American Latvian Youth Association, and the contributors in Latvia.

Estonian Section:

Contributors:

Krista Areng, Liivi Jõe, Ojārs Kalniņš, Liina Keerdoja, Maria Pedak-Kari, and Toomas Tubealkain.

Maps:

Kristīna Putenis

Cover Design:

The Idea Department
St. Louis, Mo.

A special thanks to Bill Hough for the idea, and to Kārlis Cerbulis, Ojārs Kalniņš and Vita Tērauds for their overall help and support in making it a reality.

CONTENTS

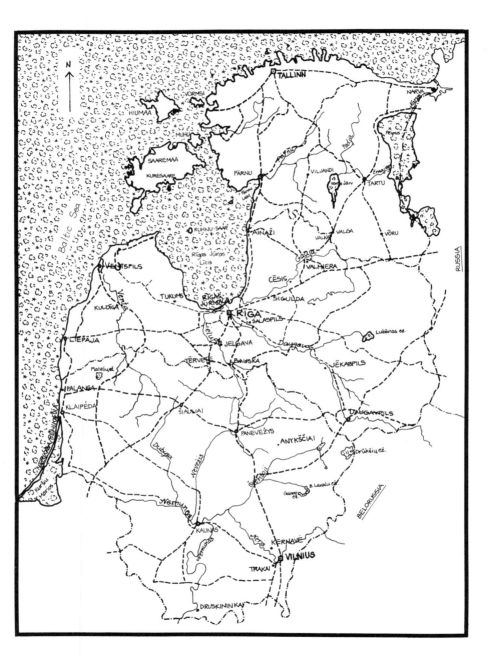

INTRODUCTION

Until just recently, a tour guide to the Baltic States was hardly necessary. Among the few tourists to enter the Soviet-ruled republics of Estonia, Latvia, and Lithuania between the end of World War II and the late 1980's, the vast majority were natives of the three countries returning to visit friends and relatives in their homelands. The remainder were members of tour groups, for whom a visit to Tallinn, Riga or Vilnius was simply a brief stop along a pre-packaged Intourist tour of the Soviet Union. The natives didn't need a tour guide, and the Intourist travelers were told all they needed - and were allowed - to know by Intourist guides.

What they were usually told was that the formerly independent republics of Estonia, Latvia, and Lithuania had willingly given up their independence and joined the Union of Soviet Socialist Republics in 1940. What they learned on a Soviet tour of Tallinn, Estonia, for example, was Soviet Estonian history, Soviet Estonian culture, Soviet Estonian art, and Soviet Estonian architecture. In other words, they were exposed to mostly Soviet, and very little Estonian.

The fact is, the term "Soviet" was imposed on everything Estonian, Latvian, and Lithuanian in 1940. And what many people - Mikhail Gorbachev included - are realizing today, is that it never took.

A visitor to the Baltic States today is an eyewitness to a remarkable unraveling process, as five decades of encrusted Soviet rule is rapidly being peeled away to reveal three very unique, independent-minded Northern European cultures in a dramatic process of national rebirth and rediscovery. The social and political upheavals unleashed by Gorbachev's policies of glasnost and perestroika have dramatically changed the face of Eastern Europe. And now these same forces are breaking down the Soviet Union itself.

A trip to the Baltic States today is not just an opportunity to visit a long-neglected part of European cultural history, but rather an extraordinary opportunity to see modern history in the making. Changes in the Baltic States are literally taking place on a daily basis. Events are occurring at such a break-neck pace, that it has been almost impossible to incorporate all of the most recent ones into this guide. (For instance, Gorbachev's historic December, 1989 visit to Lithuania, during which he unsuccessfully tried to persuade the Lithuanians from following a path which would lead them to breaking with the Soviet Union.)

The Baltic States are in a state of transition. There is a distinct de-Sovietization taking place in all three of the countries. The national flags of independent Estonia, Latvia, and Lithuania have

1

replaced Soviet-created flags. Street names, changed by the Soviets in the 1940's, are reverting back to the originals which existed during the years of independence. (In the Latvian section of the guide, for instance, independence era street names are used exclusively, but Soviet names are given in parenthesis to avoid confusion.) Churches, converted to museums and concert halls by the Soviets, are again holding weekly services for resurgent local congregations.

The Balts are slowly reclaiming their ancestral homelands. It is not an easy task as the effects of five decades of Soviet rule have taken their toll on the Baltic environment, society and psyche. But the Balts have suffered through foreign occupation before, and have managed to survive them with their sense of national identity intact. It appears that the same is true of this latest occupation.

This guide book, like developments in the Baltic States, is unique, in that it attempts to provide visitors with something more than just a tour of historical sites and architectural landmarks. To really appreciate the richness of the Baltic cultures, the beauty of their lands, and the complexities of their societies, a visitor must also have an insight into their histories, and the events that are reshaping the very nature of everyday life in present-day Estonia, Latvia, and Lithuania. This book is an attempt to provide those insights.

Ingrīda Kalniņš
Falls Church, Virginia

GETTING THERE

Organized Tours

The easiest way to get to the Baltics is on an Intourist sponsored tour. Many US travel agents offer package tours to one or more cities in the Baltic. Tours typically include travel from the United States to a gateway city such as Helsinki, Leningrad or Moscow, and then on to Rīga, Tallinn or Vilnius. Packages include first class accommodations in Intourist hotels, meals, and organized sightseeing expeditions to the most popular tourist attractions. In the 1989 season, package tours ranged from 7 to 14 days and cost between $1650 and $2800. Recent changes in the Soviet Union have also opened up alternatives to the Intourist monopoly on organized tours. For example, options for travel to Latvia in 1989 included group tours from Helsinki offering 10 days in Rīga for only $650. For names and addresses of some agencies offering tours to the Baltic, see the individual country sections.

Individual Travel

For the more adventurous souls, individual travel is also possible to the Baltic area. Any travel agent working with Intourist can make arrangements for travel to the Baltic, accommodations in Intourist hotels, and even access to Intourist led sightseeing tours. For the even more adventurous (or less financially secure), glasnost has opened up homestay opportunities, that offer travelers a low-cost, highly personalized, meet-the-people way to see the Baltic. Inroads, Inc. of Merrifield, VA, currently offers such a program in Latvia. See the Latvia section for more details.

TRAVEL ROUTES

By Air

Direct flights to the Baltic capitals have until 1989 been available only through Moscow or Leningrad. By the end of 1989, Swedish airline SAS will offer direct flights from Stockholm to Tallinn, and in May, 1990, Finland's airline Finnair will have direct flights from Helsinki to Tallinn and Rīga. These flights would be the most direct, convenient method of travel to the Baltic, eliminating the necessity for overnights in Leningrad or Moscow, and the extra hours of flight time generated by traveling east of the Baltic and then back west again. The time-tested routes, however, are still through Leningrad and Moscow. Flight time from Moscow to the Baltic capitals is approximately 1 hour 45 minutes.

By Train

Train travel to the Baltic is possible either from West Germany through East Germany and Poland, or from Helsinki, through Leningrad. Both trips are relatively inexpensive, but very time-consuming and uncomfortable. For example, the Berlin-Rīga train trip takes 40 hours, while the Helsinki - Vilnius ride would be approximately 17 hours. For the budget conscious or the adventurous traveler, the slow approach to the Baltic can be rewarding.

Train travel between the Baltic countries, however, is the preferred mode of travel. Overnight trips from Tallinn to Rīga last 7 hours, from Rīga to Vilnius 6 hours. One can make reservations in advance through Intourist and pay in hard currency for the trips, or take care of travel arrangements on the spot and pay in rubles.

By Boat

By far the most popular route to Estonia and Latvia has been the ferry from Helsinki to Tallinn, with land travel on to Rīga. The Soviet ferry, Georg Ots, makes the Tallinn/Helsinki round trip once a day during the summer season, and several times a week during the off-season. The ferry is in dry dock for several weeks every January. Taking advantage of the ferry entails flying to Helsinki and spending the night, as incoming flights from the U.S. do not arrive in time for the 10:30 am departure. Arrangements can be made to overnight on the ferry itself. Prices for the ferry are approximately $60.00 one way. It is possible to purchase a one-way ticket, and make the return trip purchase in Tallinn, paying in rubles (17 rubles at 1989 prices). Those traveling on to Rīga can take either the train or the bus on the afternoon of arrival, or spend the day in Tallinn and catch an overnight train or bus to Rīga. Most group tours are met in Tallinn by a bus for travel on to Rīga. Individual travelers can often hook up with these tour groups on the spot in Tallinn for a convenient, fast way to travel on to Rīga.

By Car

Motor routes to the Baltic were opened to foreign tourists on January 1, 1988. There is one major highway, the M-12, going up from Minsk through Vilnius, on to Rīga, Tallinn and Leningrad. Individual travelers can make arrangements for car travel to the Baltic, including hotel accommodations in Intourist hotels, or in the summer, at camping facilities along the way.

Car travel through the Baltic, while still relatively new, is becoming increasingly popular as a less expensive way to see more of the Baltic than the typical Intourist tour group allows. Car travel in the Baltic is not without restrictions, however. These include a ban on travel off of the major highway M-12, and a severely limited number of areas open to foreign travelers (see individual country sections for listings of open areas).

Car travel also requires a great deal of preparation, such as bringing along spare parts for Western make cars, and arranging for insurance and special travel documents. Cars rented in Europe come with travel insurance covering travel in almost all parts of Europe, except the Soviet Union. Special insurance must be purchased either in the U.S., in Europe, or on the Soviet border from the Soviet insurance agency Ingostrakh. Necessary travel documents include an international driver's license, transit visas for East European countries on your travel route, and a Soviet visa specifying travel by car. You must advise the Soviet embassy on your visa questionnaire about your travel plans, travel route and point of destination, so that the proper information appears on your travel documents. For motorists, it is also vital that the visa states "car travel". If this does not appear on the visa, you will not be allowed to enter the Soviet Union with your vehicle. The Russian notation for "motorist" as it should appear on your visa is (in Cyrillic): "АВТОТУРИСТ".

Some things to be aware of while traveling by car in the Baltic: auto parts are a deficit item, and therefore, local practice is to remove windshield wipers and other "removables" from the car while it is parked; there are few good quality road maps available; sporadic gasoline shortages are a distinct possibility; and the Soviet Union has very strict drunk driving laws.

Companies renting vehicles to the Soviet Union include the major renters: National, Dollar, and Inter-Rent among others.

ENTRY FORMALITIES

Passport and Visa

A valid passport as well as a Soviet visa are necessary for travel to the Baltic. A Soviet visa can be obtained from the Soviet embassy in Washington, D.C. There are three types of visas: tourist, business and private. Most will travel to the Baltic on a tourist visa arranged by a travel agency working with the official Soviet travel agency Intourist. Individuals traveling on business, or upon the invitation of an organization in Estonia, Latvia or Lithuania, will be traveling on a business visa. Individuals with invitations from friends or family will be traveling with a private visa. Travel agencies providing travel services to the Baltic can supply visa questionnaires for tourist and business visas. Others need to request proper forms for private visas from the:

Consular Division of the Soviet Embassy
1825 Phelps Place NW
Washington, DC 20008
(202) 332-1483

Note that it is next to impossible to reach the Consular Division of the Embassy by telephone, therefore we suggest contacting the Embassy by mail. Visa questionnaires must be submitted to the Soviet Embassy along with 2 copies of the information pages on your passport as well as 3 black and white photographs. Your travel agent will usually take care of the visa application process for you.

Customs Regulations

Visitors must complete customs forms upon entering and leaving the Soviet Union. Customs authorities are interested in foreign currency and valuables. They will leave you a customs form that you must produce every time you change money. Monetary transactions will be recorded, and the form must be produced upon leaving the Soviet Union. Travelers may bring in duty-free personal possessions, 1 liter of spirits or 2 liters of wine, 250 cigarettes or 250 grams of tobacco.

Customs regulations forbid the importing or exporting of rubles. It is forbidden to bring in literature that can be classified as pornographic or anti-Soviet.

Travelers are allowed to export all items bought in hard currency stores, if the proper receipts are retained. The export allowance for alcohol and tobacco is: 0.5 liters of alcohol, 1 liter of wine, 250 cigarettes or 250 grams of tobacco. It is illegal to export hard currency which was not accounted for on the customs declaration upon entering the Soviet Union. Art items must be accompanied by an official document from the Ministry of Culture permitting export.

MONEY

As they are Soviet occupied countries, the Baltic States use Soviet currency. There has been a lot of discussion about reverting to independence era monetary systems, along with economic changes in general, but at present nothing concrete has emerged from these discussions.

The fall of 1989 saw a major change in the Soviet currency exchange rate as it applies to tourists. The official rate has been revised from $1.00 = 63 kopeks, to a much more realistic $1.00 = 6.26 rubles. It is an attempt by the authorities to undercut the expanding black market rate which has gone as high as 15 rubles to a dollar. It is not clear at this time to what extent foreign tourists will benefit from the new exchange rate in terms of hotel rates, meals, etc.

Currency Regulations

A visitor may bring an unlimited amount of foreign currency into the Baltic States, but the sum must be declared upon entry. Be sure to keep all receipts from exchange transactions and purchases. These will be needed to document the difference between the amount of foreign money you brought into the country, and the amount which you are taking out of the country. Rubles cannot be taken in, or brought out. Unspent rubles must be reconverted to foreign currency before departure. Rubles are not convertible on world markets and they have little value outside the Soviet Union, other than as a souvenir.

Local Currency

Bank notes are issued in denominations of 1, 3, 5, 10, 25, 50 and 100 rubles. A ruble is worth 100 kopeks. Coins are issued in denominations of 1 ruble, and 1, 2, 3, 5, 10, 15, 20, and 50 kopeks.

Changing Money

The only place to legally exchange foreign money for rubles is at the Intourist Service Desk in your hotel or at the state bank. Keep all receipts from exchange transactions. You may be approached by locals with offers to exchange money at extremely advantageous rates. It is illegal to do so, and penalties for transgressing this law are severe. If you are heading outside of Vilnius, Riga or Tallinn, be sure you have enough rubles with you before departing. It can be difficult, indeed impossible, to exchange money outside the capital cities.

Foreign Currency

Foreign currency can only be used at hard currency stores and bars. Some of the better restaurants will also accept it, if you have made a reservation in advance through your hotel. To avoid hassles, check it out before you go. Credit cards may also be used, as well as traveler's checks. But purchase the latter in small denominations as change can be hard to come by in most places.

Tipping

Although officially frowned upon, modest tipping will go a long way in building goodwill with service providers, such as taxi drivers, waiters, hotel porters, etc. Besides money, you might want to consider giving little souvenirs, such as Western cigarettes, disposable lighters and pens, etc.

USEFUL FACTS

Time

In 1989, the time zone in the Baltic States was switched to coincide with Helsinki time. Previously they were on Moscow time. As we go to press, air and train schedules still follow Moscow time, which can be confusing. For instance, if a plane is scheduled to arrive at 6PM, it will actually arrive in the Baltic States at 5PM local time.

When it is 10PM in Tallinn, Rīga and Vilnius, comparable times are:

9PM	Bonn
8PM	London
3PM	New York
12 Noon	Los Angeles

Climate and Clothing

Summer in the Baltic States is moderately warm. Daytime temperatures average in the mid-70's° F., with cooler evening temperatures. A light weight jacket or sweater will come in handy, as will a raincoat and/or umbrella. The summer months are blessed with a lot of daylight. In June and July the sun doesn't set until close to midnight, and rises before 6AM.

Winter sets in around November. The coldest months tend to be

January and February. Average temperatures hover in the 15-20° F. range, although they can drop down to -20° F. Heavy winter clothing, including a warm winter coat, gloves, hat, scarf, and boots are essential. If you plan on spending a lot of time outdoors, long underwear and layered clothing are advised.

Spring and autumn tend to be wet due to melting snow and rainfall, and temperatures can be erratic. Waterproof footwear will add to your comfort, as will layered clothing and raingear.

Electricity

Baltic current is 220 volts, 50 cycles. You will need an electrical converter if you plan on using an American hair dryer, shaver, etc.

Health

Vaccinations

Not necessary for travelers from western countries.

Medicine

If you take any medication on a regular basis, be sure to bring enough with you for the length of your stay. Non-prescription drugs, such as aspirin, antacids, etc., are not readily available.

Water

To avoid stomach upsets, do not drink tap water and avoid ice in your drinks. Bottled water is readily available.

Weights and Measures

The Baltic States use the metric system of measurement, and temperatures are measured in Centigrade.

Length

centimeters (cm)	cm or in	inches (in)
2.54	= in 1 cm =	0.394
5.08	2	0.787
7.62	3	1.181
10.16	4	1.575
12.70	5	1.969
15.24	6	2.362
17.70	7	2.756
20.32	8	3.150
22.86	9	3.543
25.40	10	3.937
50.80	20	7.874
76.20	30	11.811
101.60	40	15.748
127.00	50	19.685

Distance

kilometers (km)	km or m	miles (m)
1.609	= m 1 k =	0.621
3.219	2	1.243
4.828	3	1.864
6.437	4	2.485
8.047	5	3.107
9.656	6	3.728
11.265	7	4.350
12.875	8	4.971
14.484	9	5.592
16.093	10	6.214
32.187	20	12.427
48.280	30	18.641
64.374	40	24.855
80.467	50	31.069

Temperature

32	50	70	85	105	212	°F
0	10	20	30	40	100	°C

Mass

kilogram (kg)	kg or lb	pounds (lb)
0.454	= lb 1 kg =	2.205
0.907	2	4.409
1.361	3	6.614
1.814	4	8.819
2.268	5	11.023
2.722	6	13.228
3.175	7	15.432
3.629	8	17.637
4.082	9	19.842
4.536	10	22.046
9.072	20	44.092
13.608	30	66.139
18.144	40	88.185
22.680	50	110.231

Volume

liters (l)	l or gal	US gallons (gal)
3.79	= l 1 gal =	0.26
7.58	2	0.52
11.37	3	0.78
15.16	4	1.04
18.95	5	1.30
22.74	6	1.56
26.53	7	1.82
30.32	8	2.08
34.11	9	2.34
37.90	10	2.60
75.80	20	5.20
113.70	30	7.80
151.60	40	10.40
189.50	50	13.00

USEFUL ADDRESSES

Intourist Offices

Soviet Consulates

United States:

630 Fifth Av. Suite 868
New York, New York 10111
(212) 757-3884

1825 Phelps Pl. NW
Washington, DC 20008
(202) 332-1483

2790 Green St.
San Francisco, CA 94123
(415) 922-6642

Canada:

1801 McGill College Av.
Montreal, Quebec H3A 2N4
(514) 849-6394

52 Range Rd.
Ottawa, Ontario K1N 8G5
(613) 236-7220

3655 Ave. du Musee
Montreal, Quebec H3G 2E1
(514) 843-5901

Great Britain:

292 Regent St.
London, England W1R 7P0
(01) 631-1252

5 Kensington Palace Gdns.
London, England W8 4Q2
(01) 229-3215 or 3216

West Germany:

Stephanstr. 1
6000 Frankfurt am Main
West Germany
(069) 28-5776

Waldstrasse 42
53 Bonn 2
West Germany
(0228) 31-2086

Because the United States and most Western countries do not recognize the illegal incorporation of the Baltic States into the Soviet Union, they do not have embassies or consulates in Estonia, Latvia or Lithuania. The nearest ones are in Leningrad and Moscow.

Western Embassies in Moscow	**Western Consulates in Leningrad**

United States:

19-23 Ul. Chaykovskogo
252-2451-9

15 Ul. Petr Lavrova
274-8235

Canada:

23 Starokonyushenny Pereulok
241-9155, 3067 or 5070

Great Britain:

14 Naberezhnaya Morisa Toreza
231-8511 or 8512

West Germany:

Ul. Bolshaya Gruzinskaya
252-5521

39 Ul. Petr Lavrova
273-5598

Finland:

15-17 Kropotkin Pereulok
246-4027

71 Ul. Chaykovskogo
273-7321

LITHUANIA

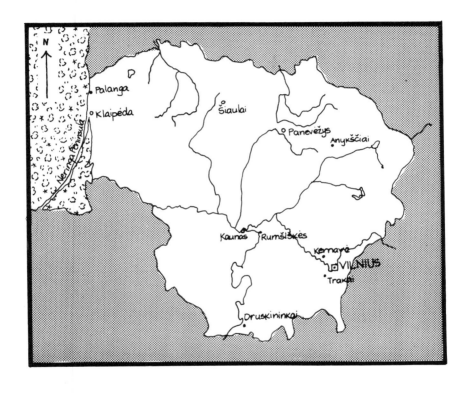

LITHUANIA

A picturesque country of rolling hills, numerous forests, rivers, streams and lakes, Lithuania is the largest and southernmost of the Baltic States. It is home to 3.5 million people of whom 80% are Lithuanian, the rest being mostly Russian and Polish.

The Lithuanians are a group of the Indo-European family of nations, distinct from both the Slavic and German branches, with a unique culture and language. They lived here on the shores of the Baltic Sea long before the Christian era, and at the dawn of European history had attained a level of civilization equal to that of many other European peoples of that age.

Lithuania was established as a state in the 14th century under its only king - Mindaugas. In the 15th century the Grand Duchy of Lithuania attained the height of its existence, reaching from the Baltic Sea to the Black Sea. The subsequent union with Poland lasted over 200 years until Russia gained control over Lithuanian lands at the end of the 18th century. Lithuania enjoyed a brief period of independence between 1918 and 1940. This experience allowed Lithuanians to develop cultural and political institutions which were vital in preserving and strengthening their national consciousness and will to persevere, despite overwhelming odds and hostile, powerful neighbors. Thanks to the independence period, Lithuanians managed to survive the worst of the Stalinist horrors and emerge as a compact, nationally-conscious people determined to regain their rights to self-determination.

Under Soviet leader Gorbachev's policy of "glasnost", Lithuanians have been able to express their long-buried national sentiments and desires to control the destiny of their homeland. The present atmosphere in Lithuania is in some respects truly revolutionary, thus making travel there all the more fascinating and informative.

GEOGRAPHY

Natural Formations

Lithuania is characterized by gently rolling hills, flat plains, many forests, rivers and streams, and clear lakes.

The country lies on the eastern shores of the Baltic Sea approximately at the same latitude as Denmark, Scotland and southern Canada. A relatively small country with an area of 26,173 sq. mi., it is nonetheless the largest of the three Baltic States and also larger than Denmark, Switzerland, the Netherlands and Belgium. Its neighbors are: Latvia to the north; Byelorussia to the east and south; Poland and the Kaliningrad region of the Russian Republic (historically Lithuania Minor) to the south-west.

The territory of Lithuania is an extension of the western part of the great East European plain. Retreating Ice Age glaciers formed the rolling landscape and left chains of moranic hills. Glacial deposits contain natural resources such as clay, dolomite, sand, gravel, chalk, gypsum and limestone.

Lithuania is criss-crossed by more than 700 rivers and creeks, the largest being the river Nemunas. Historically the Nemunas was an important shipping route through Lithuania and therefore of strategic importance. A string of fortresses and castles was built along the river. East of the town of Jurbarkas in central Lithuania are the 16th-17th century castles of Raudonė and Panemunė, and the two castle hills of Veliuona, which offer the traveler a beautiful vista. Today the Nemunas is still important as a transport route, a source of energy at the Kaunas hydro-electric station and as a recreation resource.

Lakes are numerous in Lithuania as well. Of the approximately 3000 lakes found in the country, the majority are in eastern Lithuania. The district of Ignalina is also the location of Lithuania's first national park. Most lakes are shallow, gradually spreading into surrounding marshes or swamps. In southern Lithuania lies the Žuvintas wildlife preserve. Lake Žuvintas is ringed by large swamps which are home to more than 200 species of birds including herons, sea gulls, grouse, ducks, geese and swans, the pride of Žuvintas.

The Baltic Coast

The Baltic coastline of Lithuania extends about 55 miles. The sandy beaches attract many tourists, especially to the resort of Palanga. The Neringa peninsula makes up more than half of the coast, separating the Kuršių Marios, a large Baltic lagoon, from the Baltic Sea. Neringa is exceptionally beautiful with majestic dunes and extensive pine forests. The fishing villages of Nida and Juodkrantė on the lagoon's shores have become favorite summer vacation spots.

The Kuršių Marios is the largest inland body of water in Lithuania. The river Nemunas flows into the Kuršių Marios, whose semi-fresh waters are rich in fish. The lagoon is connected to the Baltic Sea by a narrow strait, where the Baltic port of Klaipėda (Memel in German) is situated.

"Lithuanian gold" or amber is cast out by the sea onto the shores of Lithuania. Baltic amber, an organic gemstone formed over millions of years from fossil resin, is usually found in shades of yellow with tints of orange and brown. Fossilized insects and plants are sometimes visible inside. A piece of this "Lithuanian gold" is a beautiful souvenir from "The Land of Amber".

Climate

Lithuania's climate is moderate. Summer brings temperatures of 65-70° F. and plentiful rain, with July being the warmest month. The winters can be cold and foggy, with average temperatures of 20° F., but the sea tends to moderate local climatic conditions somewhat. Average annual rainfall amounts to 26 inches.

Flora and Fauna

Plant life in Lithuania is varied and rich. Woodlands cover one-fourth of Lithuania's territory, of which 41% is pine, 20% spruce, 18% birch and 12% alder and maple. Oak, ash and linden are also found. The Stelmužė oak tree, the oldest oak in Lithuania and one of the most ancient in Europe, measures 39 feet in circumference and is said to be approximately 1500 years old.

In southern Lithuania forests make up about one half of the territory. This is the area where several natural treasures are located: the Varėna-Druskininkai pine forests, the Čepkeliai swamp, the largest swamp in Lithuania, and the historic Rudininkų Forest. This forest, now an historic landscape preserve, was the favorite hunting ground for Lithuania's dukes and lesser aristocracy. The rebels of the 1831 and 1863 uprisings against Tsarist rule operated out of these woods. Rudininkų Forest covers an area of 40,000 hectares and is the largest forest in Lithuania. A variety of animals, including elk, beaver and wild boar, make this and other forests of Lithuania their home.

Berry and mushroom picking is a popular pastime for many Lithuanians. Wild strawberries, raspberries, chanterelles, and the extremely popular European mushroom, the steinpilze, can be found in the woods. Mushroom picking is best left to those who are acquainted with the art. Others can simply take a leisurely stroll and enjoy the beauty of Lithuania's many forests.

A large area of the country is covered by meadowland and grassland, which is used for the country's important livestock sector.

The forests, plains and waters of Lithuania are home to 60 species of mammals and 300 species of birds. Elk and bison, fox and wolf, wild boar and deer, beaver and mink are all a part of the wildlife found in the country. Aside from the already mentioned birds found in the Žuvintas preserve, owls, hawks, falcons, nightingales, and the great white stork are frequently seen. The white stork is the most popular bird in Lithuania, which according to the locals, never roosts at the home of an evil man. The cuckoo, by contrast, foretells misfortune.

Various frogs, toads and snakes make their home in the extensive swamplands. Approximately 50 types of fish, including the eel, which is a delicacy found in the Kuršių Marios, inhabit the inland waters of Lithuania.

Thus the wildlife of Lithuania, although not unique, is diverse and numerous. Conservation is of utmost importance in the minds of Lithuanians, and has found prominent expression in the program of the popular Sąjudis and Green movements.

ECONOMY

Historically the Lithuanians have been a farming people. The soil is fertile and 40% of Lithuania's land is arable. During the years of independence the productivity of private agriculture at least doubled.

The Soviet occupation altered the course of economic growth. The Soviets forced the collectivization of agriculture and industrialization during the 50's and through the 60's. This was a brutal period coinciding with the continuing guerilla war and deportations.

Today agriculture remains important with 1/3 of the economically active population engaged in farming. Livestock breeding is the primary branch of agriculture with an emphasis on dairy farming and pig raising. Leading crops are rye, oats and wheat. Flax, sugar beets, potatoes and fodder crops are also cultivated.

The dominant sector in industry is food processing which includes pork, dairy products, beet sugar, confectionery and liquors. The machine building industry is the most rapidly growing sector. Other industries include textiles, knitwear, furniture, plywood and paper.

Lithuania produces enough electrical power for export. Electrical power is produced by peat-fueled power stations, long-haul coal burning, and a hydro-electric station on the Nemunas river. Situated in eastern Lithuania is the controversial Ignalina nuclear power plant. Built next to a national park known for its scenic forestland and lakes, it was planned to be the largest nuclear power plant in the world, with four reactors of the Chernobyl type. It is a major environmental concern for Lithuanians as well as the Latvians, Swedes and other neighbors. The Chernobyl accident dramatically heightened concern about its safety. Following major public demonstrations in 1988, the Lithuanian authorities cancelled plans to build a 4th reactor at the site and ceased funding for the construction of the 3rd block. The second reactor had been shut down in 1988 for safety reasons.

93% of all industry is controlled by Moscow-based ministries. Under perestroika there is a drive to expand considerably decision-making powers by republic authorities and local enterprises, designated officially as republic economic accountability and sovereignity. Western journalists also report that, unlike in most other parts of the USSR, the number of privately-run cooperatives was growing rapidly as of the beginning of 1989. Privately-run businesses now include cafes, food stores, food catering, taxi service and art galleries.

GOVERNMENT

Nominally the highest legislative body of the republic is the Supreme Soviet, whose membership is selected by the Communist Party and then automatically elected for 4-year terms. The Supreme Soviet then appoints a Presidium to function when it is out of session. A Council of Ministers, also appointed by the Supreme Soviet, is in charge of administering the government. Under the influence of the Gorbachev reforms, this electoral system has been undergoing significant change, with many of the legislative seats opened to multi-candidate elections in which the popular Sajudis won overwhelming victories. It is too early to tell what effect these changes would have on questions of real political authority inside the country, but party control, exercised through Moscow, still enjoys many institutional guarantees and appears well-entrenched for the foreseeable future.

RECENT HISTORY IN LITHUANIA

In approximately the past year, independent organizations in Lithuania, previously relegated primarily to underground operation, have increased their activity tremendously in scope and variety. As in the other Baltic republics, movements focusing on national rights have grown to be truly grass-roots political organizations. In large part due to Gorbachev's campaign of glasnost, these groups have found it possible to operate in the public eye and to draw large numbers of people previously afraid to participate in political life.

In order to attach a time frame to these changes, August 23, 1987 would be a good place to start. In Lithuania, as in Latvia and Estonia, Molotov-Ribbentrop Pact commemorations on this day were among the first large-scale public demonstrations to take place in the Gorbachev era. The Lithuanian rally attracted over 500 people to Gediminas Square. This however, still being early in the game, elicited KGB harassment of the organizers of the demonstration following the event.

As far as public actions are concerned, things then remained relatively quiet in Lithuania until February 16, 1988, when commemorations of the 70th anniversary of the Independence Act of 1918 drew between 10-15,000 people. Militia violence was reported in numerous cases against peaceful demonstrators. Continuing through the spring of 1988, public demonstrations were held on several occasions to mark significant dates in Lithuanian history. These actions were not officially condoned, and harassment was the order of the day for the demonstrators and the organizers.

On June 3, 1988, a group of 500 academics met at the Academy of Sciences in Vilnius for the formation of a new organization, designated the Movement to Support Perestroika (Sajudis). The official program of Sajudis advocates working within the present system for greater economic and cultural autonomy for Lithuania. Sajudis is an organization officially tolerated by the government and numbers Communist Party members among its activists.

During the summer of 1988, Sajudis began organizing public rallies of its own, and was successful in drawing huge crowds. On August 23, 1988, a demonstration organized by Sajudis in Vilnius' Vingis Park to commemorate the Molotov-Ribbentrop Pact was attended by 200,000 people. Official permission had been granted by the government for this event.

On July 3, 1988, another group appeared on the scene. Their efforts were not quite as successful. The Lithuanian Freedom League, founded in 1978, emerged from underground activity and made public its program, which calls for the immediate withdrawal of Soviet occupation forces and independence for Lithuania within the European Community. The political actions staged by this group continued to experience harassment by militia and KGB officials. At a peaceful demonstration sponsored by the League on September 28, 1988, participants were brutally beaten by militia in riot gear.

Although the two groups differ in their philosophies, they rallied together to protest this act of violence, which resulted in a switch in top Party leadership in Lithuania. First Secretary Rimgaudas Songaila, said to have been among those who ordered the violence, was replaced by Algirdas Brazauskas on October 20, 1988 after a lengthy period of public outcry.

The founding Congress of Sąjudis was held on October 22-23, 1988, and was marked by the return of the Vilnius Cathedral, which had been converted to an art gallery, to religious use. The Congress elected a 220-member parliament and a 35-member executive council to leadership.

Though refusing to consider a measure on sovereignty similar to that adopted by the Estonian Supreme Soviet, the Lithuanian government has made some concessions to the movements: the return of the flag and national anthem of independent Lithuania to official use; the designation of February 16 as a state holiday and the granting of permission for commemorations organized by Sąjudis for this day; the adoption of Lithuanian as the official language of the republic; and the return of Vilnius Cathedral as well as several other churches.

In a departure from their accepted program, the national assembly of Sąjudis, venturing into murkier waters, on February 16, 1989 adopted a declaration calling for a "free, democratic and neutral Lithuania existing in a de-militarized zone". The statement stops short of a demand for immediate independence, but clearly states that this is a long-term goal. This action indicates a far-reaching change in Sąjudis, a radicalization of their original program, which some believe may be the straw which breaks Gorbachev's back and elicits a crackdown from Moscow. For the time being however, this remains speculation and the push for change in Lithuania continues at an astounding pace.

Lithuania still has far to go in the quest for independence, but the changes seen in just the past year show that some headway has been made - more so than at any other time since the Soviet occupation began - and this gives hope to the Lithuanian people that the next year will bring them even closer to their dream of an independent nation.

THE LITHUANIAN LANGUAGE

Lithuanian, a Baltic language similar only to Latvian, is one of the oldest living Indo-European languages in the sense that it has retained many archaic forms that other related languages have long since abandoned. The Lithuanian written (literary) language dates back from the 16th century, the first documents being a translation of the Lord's Prayer and Ave Maria (1525). The modern language is written in a 32-letter alphabet and is based on the High West Lithuanian dialect (Suvalkiečių). This dialect was declared the official language of independent Lithuania in 1918.

During the years of Soviet occupation Russian increasingly displaced Lithuanian in Lithaunia's cultural, economic, administrative and political life. Lithuanians were becoming alarmed that, increasingly, major government insitutions were operating exclusively in Russian. The greater part of recent Russian-speaking immigrants to Lithuania, guaranteed full access to Russian-language schools, cultural amenities and social services, was reluctant to acquire even a minimum working knowledge of Lithuanian. In mixed working enterprises, for example, even where Russian-speakers formed a minority, the authorities required the use of Russian. Analogous language safeguards for Lithuanian minorities in Byelorussia or the Kaliningrad region are virtually nonexistent.

But in 1989, in an effort to keep in step with the ongoing national reawakening in Lithuania, the government reinstated Lithuanian as the official language of the republic, requiring, among other things, that officials staffing public institutions and economic enterprises develop a working knowledge of the language within several years. The general idea apparently is to ensure that Lithuanian speakers have the right to use their language in local government offices, cultural institutions and workplaces, without, however, discriminating against non-Lithuanian speakers. Under the new language law, Russian speakers, for example, would retain the right to be served in government offices in their own language, while retaining the existing network of Russian-language schools and cultural institutions. It is too soon, however, to determine how energetically the regime will implement this vital (for Lithuanians) legal act.

LITERATURE

Initial signs of reform and openness in Lithuania appeared in the official press and literature before they made any actual breakthroughs in Lithuanian life, and changes in these areas were late in coming. It was only in December of 1986 that an article in the weekly newspaper "Gimtasis Krastas" (Native Land) appeared in the spirit of openness, causing more than a little controversy. The article contained an overview of customs followed during the traditional Lithuanian Christmas Eve dinner. Christmas celebrations had been banned since the annexation of Lithuania into the Soviet Union.

Even though censorship has mostly been lifted (Soviet writers still cannot directly speak out against the Communist Party as a concept), this question still has not been answered since most literature is in a stage of transition, being in many cases focused on writing about issues which had been hushed up for nearly 50 years.

Even though at present readers in Lithuania focus on the press and documentary material which was earlier forbidden, literature itself has taken giant strides forward. To a lesser degree, this is also true of poetry and drama.

Literature first appeared in a new light in December, 1986 in the official literary magazine "Pergalė". A story called "Gyvenimas po klevu" (Life under the Maple Tree) by Romualdas Granauskas recounts the life of an old woman in Lithuania and her painful reflections during post-war events and forced collectivization of farms. The story is written as an objective representation of reality, not a show of sentimental emotion, making it all the more painful as readers recall their own past in black and white.

This story seemed to open doors for the publication of literary works of a more politically sensitive nature. Works of prose gained widespread popularity because of their taboo material. The novel "Žuvys nepažįsta savo vaikų" (Fish Don't Recognize Their Children) by Juozas Požėra is written as a documentary account of realities in the Siberian wilderness. The story is based on a man who goes to Siberia expecting great hunting opportunities and adventure, and who, ironically, learns how to survive in Siberia from a Lithuanian exile.

It is no surprise that stories concerning life in Siberia would find an appreciative audience in Lithuania. Two more writers, Ričardas Gavelis and Eugenijus Ignatavičius, succeeded in publishing short story anthologies which had for years been blocked by censorship. The stories with the greatest impact deal with Siberia. In Gavelis' book "Nubaustieji" (The Punished), the hero Berankis (Handless) reflects about his past in Siberia. Berankis, along with 25 other men, were banished to the taiga and left to fend for themselves. As a means of seeking help, Berankis cuts off his hand, ties it to a raft, and floats it downriver hoping it will signal their distress. The story is written in a harshly realistic style. The grim atmosphere is established in the very beginning: "Winter in that land lasted eight months. Four were left for the rest of the seasons."

In "Upė į šiaurę" (River to the North) from "Chrizantemų Autobuse" (In the Bus of Chrysanthemums), Ignatavičius touches on a reality experienced by hundreds of thousands of Lithuanians in the post-war years. A mother, having been exiled to Siberia, hides her children in empty herring barrels and sends them off to freedom in a boat, knowing she will never see them again and expecting to be put to death for this act. Three weeks later she realizes her children must be free because soldiers begin interrogating her as to their whereabouts. As she is led away, her neighbors look on in horror, but she turns to them and shouts: "You don't know how happy I am!".

Juozas Aputis, a well-known master of the short story, also made his contribution to literature in the new period of openness. In his story, "Vargonų balsas skalbykloje" (The Voice of the Organ in the Laundry), published in the literary magazine "Nemunas" in May, 1988, he gives a realistic picture of the Lithuanian armed resistance in the early post-war period through accounts of the experiences of three high school boys.

All the authors mentioned here are solid writers, although it is evident that their popularity is drawn significantly from the subject matter, which only a few years ago was forbidden fruit. More than likely the most interesting stage of post-glasnost literature is yet to come, when the period of transition comes to an end and literature can settle into its function of articulating reality rather than being outdistanced by it, as had been the experience in Lithuania and the Baltic States heretofore.

ART

Twentieth-century Lithuanian art has not forgotten that the present is rooted in the past. Lithuanian artists have often sought to extract from their national cultural heritage that which uniquely expresses the national consciousness, a primeval ethnic world view, so as to infuse a powerful expressiveness and originality into their art, which has increasingly come under the influence of modern art. Whereas early in the century various European artists found new means of expression in the "primitivism" of the Middle Ages, Oceania, or African art, artists in Lithuania sought inspiration and new forms from early Lithuanian folk art, folk lore, in general from archaic, often not wholly finalized ethnic cultural strata.

The passage of time, together with the everchanging existential and artistic situation of the Lithuanian nation understandably perfected, expanded, and brought about changes in this tendency. In present-day art there are numerous examples illustrating that this reflection on the archaic and primitive is no longer narrowly ethnocentric. Lithuanian artists incorporate a variety of international cultural traditions and motifs into their works, and are making use of widespread iconographic prototypes. It is not uncommon to come across mythical world views, including an anthropocentric cosmos, the juxtaposition of living and non-living objects, the demoniacal, sacralized ritualistic scenes, anthropomorphic figures, and so on.

Lithuanian artists seek to express the universality of being through various means: the use of parallels to well-known myths, newly created myths or a myth-like interpretation of present-day reality, etc. In these aspects Lithuanian art retains genetic contact not only with the archetypes of mankind's collective consciousness, but also reflects the problematical, and often catastrophic condition of modern man - his dramatic and paradoxical sense of self. The viewer will notice that in such instances, the means of self-preservation and source of spiritual strength in Lithuanian art is the unity between Man and Nature.

MUSIC

The Lithuanian musical scene ranges from the most archaic forms of folk music to highly innovative 20th century expressions. These two extremes are not mutually exclusive, but rather interrelated in new and unexpected ways. Visitors to Lithuania should not pass up the opportunity to experience the wide spectrum of musical offerings.

Music accompanied the life of the Lithuanian peasant from dawn to dusk. Folk songs were sung on holidays and they accompanied daily tasks such as reaping, herding, ploughing, milling, spinning and weaving. Weddings, Christenings and funerals had their own repertoires, including beautiful laments, lullabies and ballads. Most are lyrical, restrained, modal pieces with very irregular rhythms and free meters. The texts are poetic gems: imagery often metaphorically likens events in nature with characters. Young maidens take the form of a snow-white lily, while their young suitors might be compared to falcons.

Although Lithuania covers a small geographic area, each region has developed its own unique style. Southeastern Dzūkija is known for its intricately ornamented, melodic monodic songs. Songs of northwestern Žemaitija are improvisatory and rhythmically free. Northeastern Aukštaitija features a unique form of polyphonic rounds, called "sutartinės", which are not found in any other region of Lithuania or in neighboring countries. The individual voices of these songs interact contrapuntally and imitatively, often resulting in major seconds, sevenths and tritones, defying traditional harmony and sounding very dissonant. The rhythms are syncopated. These "rounds" represent the most original and ancient in Lithuanian folklore.

Instrumental folk music is not as rich as the vocal tradition, but it is also very interesting. Unfortunately, research in instrumental music came late, many of the instruments have been lost, and few musical examples have been written down. The "kanklės" (psaltery) is one of the oldest Lithuanian string instruments. According to pagan legends, the kanklės melody is the voice of a dead soul. They are constructed from wood in the form of a trapezoid. The oldest ones contained as few as five strings. The "birbynė" is a hollowed out wooden pipe with an animal horn attached to the end as a resonator.

27

Other wind instruments include various size wooden trumpets of up to 2 1/2 meters ("daudytes"), a flute-type pipe ("lumzdelis"), clay whistles in the shape of animals ("molinukai"), the buckhorn ("ožragis") made from a goat's horn, and pan-pipes ("skudučiai") of the Aukštaitija region which mainly performed the polyphonic "sutartinės". Each of these pan-pipes produces a single pitch which necessitates a group of performers. Percussion instruments are quite numerous. Of note are tuned wooden troughs called "skrabalai" and "tabalai" which are various sized planks producing different pitches.

The cultural and political isolation of Lithuania probably accounts for the slow start of "serious" composed music. The introduction of Christianity in the 14th century brought its musical influences. Polish music was prominent in the life of the nobility. Many early composers were trained in Russia and Germany, which left its mark on Lithuanian music for a long time. Romanticism was the mainstay of Lithuanian music well into this century, also due to the fact that this was the style espoused by the Soviets. While there were some notable earlier attempts to free Lithuanian music from these traditions, breakthroughs did not come until the 60's and 70's. Although late in coming, Lithuanian contemporary music has matured quickly. Serialism, texture music, chance music, minimalism, synthetic modality and other styles are expressed in very original ways, often quite clearly employing Lithuanian folk traditions. But not merely as quotations, but rather as sophisticated, structural elements.

Until recently Lithuanian young people have had to rely on imports for popular entertainment. This was not easy since Western influences, especially in popular art forms, were frowned on by Communist authorities. Early home-grown attempts range from the blase to the unintentionally humorous. Today, however, there is a wide array of original and interesting work in jazz, rock, musical theater, and even Lithuanian-style country/western or Bob Dylan inspired balladeering.

Visitors to the capital, Vilnius, will find musical activities taking place almost every day of the week. The Academic Opera and Ballet Theater features the classics and works by Lithuanian composers. Under the auspices of the Philharmonic Society you can hear the National Symphony orchestra and a wide array of smaller ensembles. Of particular note is the high quality of Lithuanian chamber music. Some of the best contemporary works are for small ensembles. Concerts take place in the State Philharmonic Society hall, the Art Workers' Palace, at the Conservatory, in churces and other cultural centers.

Kaunas boasts the newly renovated Musical Theater which was the center of pre-World War II musical activity. Carillon concerts in the garden of the Kaunas History Museum are a popular pastime. Chamber music is a frequent event at the castle of Trakai. Druskininkai, the birthplace of composer and painter M.K. Čiurlionis hosts many pianists. The seaport city of Klaipėda is fast becoming another major cultural center. Panevežys, Šiauliai and other cities should not be overlooked for interesting musical events.

Probably the best way to experience Lithuanian music is through festivals. Folk music enthusiasts can immerse themselves in the week-long "Skamba kankliai" celebrations of vocalists, instrumentalists and dancers which takes place in old-town Vilnius every May. The massive song and dance festivals are held every five years in summer, and they showcase rich choral traditions and folk dances. The next one is scheduled for 1989. Jazz festivals in Birštonas and the popular "Baltic Youth" music festival in Palanga draws performers from Lithuania and elsewhere. Lovers of classical music may be fortunate enough to catch a festival of string quartet or chamber orchestra music, commemorations of various composers, or performances of children's music. Not to be underestimated are performances by amateur choirs, folklore ensembles and instrumentalists affiliated with universities, cultural institutions, even factories!

Lithuanian music offers something for everyone. So give a listen and don't pass up the rich musical traditions which go back centuries.

Gediminas square

VILNIUS

The capital city is situated at the confluence of the Neris and Vilnelé rivers in south-eastern Lithuania. Vilnius is over 180 miles from the Baltic Sea and only 21 miles from Byelorussia, a neighboring republic. The city covers an area of 100 sq. miles of which approximately 1/3 is forests, parks and gardens ; 1/3 is covered by buildings; and the rest by roads, rivers, tributaries and lakes. It is surrounded by scenic wooded hills.

On the southern left bank of the Neris river is the old quarter as well as the city's modern center. The impressive old town with its narrow streets and small squares is located here, as are most of the points of interest. On the right bank is the hotel Lietuva, the large Žalgiris Sports Arena and several new housing complexes.

Vilnius is the heart of Lithuania's political, economic, cultural and public life. The over 400 year-old University of Vilnius, the very center of learning in Lithuania, has 13 faculties and is attended by 16,000 students. Other institutions of higher learning include the Pedagogical Institute, the Art Institute, the Civil Engineering Institute and the Conservatory. The latter also have an enrollment of approximately 16,000 students. About half of the entire student population of Lithuania studies in Vilnius.

Vilnius is a fast-growing city with a population of 650,000, which is increasing by about 12,000 yearly. One seventh of the entire population of Lithuania lives in the capital.

Historically Vilnius has always been a multi-ethnic city. Before World War II, Vilnius and its surrounding region were under Polish rule and a large percentage of the population was Jewish, Byelorussian and Polish. With 30% of its inhabitants of Jewish background, Vilnius was known as the "Jerusalem of Lithuania". In fact, Vilnius was considered one of the most important centers of Jewish culture in the world. At that time, Lithuanians were in the minority.

Today people of 92 nationalities live in Vilnius. Nearly half of the poplulation is Lithuanian, and over a fifth is Russian; the majority of the rest are Poles and Byelorussians. A walk around town will definitely acquaint the visitor with the international flavor of this fascinating and beautiful city.

HISTORY OF VILNIUS

The emergence of Vilnius as Lithuania's major city and capital is linked to Gediminas, under whose rule the country entered the political arena as a powerful state to be reckoned with. He was the founder of the Gediminas (also known as the Jogaila or Jagiellonian) dynasty which ruled Lithuania and later Poland for 250 years. A legend about the founding of Vilnius has been passed down through the centuries.

...Gediminas, who lived in the castle at Trakai, loved to hunt in the massive woods covering the area on which Vilnius stands today. Once, after a successful hunt, he and his entourage set-up camp on the shores of Neris and Vilnelė and reveled late into the night. After falling asleep Gediminas had a strange dream. High upon the hill by the river Vilnelė stood a huge iron wolf howling as loudly as a hundred wolves.

Upon awaking Gediminas sent for the pagan priest Lizdeika, guardian of the sacred flame, to interpret the dream. The priest read into the dream a message from the gods, "You must build a castle on the hill where the wolf was howling. The castle will be as awesome as the wolf and soon a powerful city will emerge around the fortress. The city will be beautiful and its glory will ring out like the howl of one hundred wolves..." So Gediminas did as Lizdeika had said and the city of Vilnius was born.

Written documents confirm the city's founding date to be 1323, although archeological findings suggest that the area was inhabited well over two thousand years ago. The hills and rivers provided protection for the people who settled there, and the Neris gave access to the Nemunas and hence the Baltic Sea as well as to rivers flowing to the Dnieper basin and the Black Sea. Thus the site was perfect for establishing trade routes, and also well situated strategically against the intensifying struggle with the Crusaders.

The fortress built on the hill served defensive purposes and was called the Upper Castle. During the mid-14th century when the Crusaders began to penetrate deeper into Lithuania, the town along the river banks at the foot of the hill was fortified by ramparts and towers. This fortified town became known as the Lower Castle and contained the homes of merchants and craftsmen, the Duke's residence as well as the living quarters of feudal lords.

Although the Crusaders never overcame the walls of Vilnius' castle, the Teutonic aggression drew Lithuania and neighboring Poland closer together. The Krevo Act of 1385 granted Jogaila, the Duke of Lithuania, the hand of Polish Queen Jadwiga and the throne of the

Polish King. Abiding by this treaty Jogaila placed Lithuania and Poland under the same dynasty in 1386 and converted the country to Christianity in 1387.

That same year, 1387, Vilnius was granted a charter of self-rule. Three domains existed in Vilnius: the castles belonged to the dukes, the bishops controlled part of the town, and the townspeople who lived south of the castles, where the old town is situated, were ruled by the magistracy.

In 1392, Vytautas the Great, Jogaila's cousin, won a long-lasting struggle with Jogaila and gained control of Vilnius and the Grand Duchy of Lithuania. After the defeat of the Crusaders at the Battle of Grunwald, led by Vytautas in 1410, Vilnius' cultural and trading ties with Western and Eastern Europe expanded and large numbers of merchants and craftsmen came to settle in the city.

Bust of Vytautas the Great in Gediminas Castle

The town grew - Gothic churches and monasteries sprang up, stone buildings replaced wooden structures. At the end of the 15th century a huge stone defense wall was constructed in response to a threat from the Crimean Tartars. Begun at the Lower Castle, the wall together with the castle ramparts encompassed the town. In places the wall reached 36 ft. high and 6-9 ft. thick. Nine gates and several defense towers were contructed where roads entered Vilnius. Within these walls the city developed over the next three centuries.

Vilnius flourished during the 1500's. Population grew to 30,000 and trade continued to evolve. The first printing press and glass workshop were opened, in 1536 a stone bridge was constructed across the Neris and in 1579 the Jesuit acedemy, forerunner of Vilnius University, was founded. The Renaissance style was prevalent at this time and many churches, palaces and administrative buildings were built.

Unfortunately, with the death of Žygimantas Augustas in 1572, who had overseen much of Vilnius' expansion, the Gediminas or Jagiellonian dynasty ended. In 1569 the Union of Lublin had more closely joined Poland and Lithuania into an entity known as the Polish-Lithuanian Commonwealth. Vilnius lost its significance as the capital because the elected Polish kings, who were also Grand Dukes of Lithuania, no longer frequented the city.

The 17th and 18th centuries brought many calamities. The 1655 war against the Russians, the Northern War (1700-1712), recurrent fires and plagues reduced the population by half, crafts and trade declined and Vilnius was plundered by its enemies.

Construction continued during this period and was mainly in the Baroque style, which was characteristically majestic, ornate and dynamic, with interiors rich in frescos, bas-reliefs and sculpture. The aristocracy built luxurious palaces and generously financed the construction of churches and monasteries, often inviting Italian Baroque masters to Vilnius to work. One of the first Baroque buildings constructed in Vilnius was the Church of St. Casimir, followed by the chapel of St. Casimir inside the Cathedral and the Church of St. Theresa. A Baroque style unique to Vilnius had evolved by the middle of the 18th century. Verticality, a harmonious blending of horizontal and vertical lines and two graceful towers, replacing the typical cupola, define the Baroque style of Vilnius.

The Jesuits figured prominently in the cultural and educational life of the city and often organized festivals for the townspeople. Sometimes feuds between the noble families would erupt and endanger residents' lives as well.

During the Northern War the Polish-Lithuanian state was severely weakened and in 1772 and 1793 Russia, Prussia and Austria carried out the first two divisions of the commonwealth. In 1794 an uprising against the new rule started in Poland and was led by Thaddeus Kosciusko, a general from the Lithuanian Grand Duchy who had fought in the American Revolution. During this revolt the Vilnius city walls and towers were used for the last time for defensive purposes. But the uprising, which lasted approximately eight months, was crushed and the Commonwealth was partitioned for the third time in 1795. Most of Lithuania was joined to Russia and this occupation was to last for 121 years.

Vilnius' vital statistics in 1795 were:

Population: 17,690 - 2,471 of which constituted nobility, 675 clerical, 238 teachers and professors.

Churches: 32 Roman Catholic, 15 monasteries, 5 Uniate, 1 Russian Orthodox, 1 Evangelical Reformed, 1 Lutheran.

There were 10 palaces, a university complex, a teacher's institute, 12 shelters and 4 printing presses.

During this period of occupation Vilnius was the center of a guberniya (or province) annexed by the Russian empire. The nobility, which was by then almost completely Polonized, maintained a high profile in society, had extensive rights and elected guberniya and district officials. The townfolk were governed by magistrates and had their own courts, both of which were also elected. Peasant serfs were dominated by the nobility and their conditions continued to worsen. Only the peasants working on the state manors had separate courts established in the districts.

At the turn of the century the Baroque style of architecture gradually gave way to that of neo-Classicism. In 1793 an architecture department was established in Vilnius academy, which was under the direction of prominent neo-Classical architect Liudas Stuoka-Gucevicius. The Vilnius school was characterized by simplicity and elegance. It was during this period that the Town Hall (1799), the new Cathedral (1785-1801) and the Verkiai Palace were built.

In 1812 Napoleon marched into Vilnius on his way toward Russia. Hopes were high then that Lithuania would free itself and the nobility began to seek ways of recreating the Polish-Lithuanian Commonwealth. A conference of noblemen, which declared a desire to reunite the Commonwealth's lands, took place in Warsaw and received an enthusiastic response in Vilnius as well as elsewhere in Lithuania. But this was not to be. Napoleon was defeated and his withdrawing armies ravaged and plundered Lithuania and especially Vilnius, leaving behind the sick, injured and several thousand corpses. The cost to the Vilnius guberniya of the Napoleonic offensive and defeat was approximately 20,000,000 rubles.

By the time of the Russian occupation the aristocracy and higher education in Lithuania were thoroughly Polonized. Falling under Russian rule brought them closer to Poland, uniting them against a common enemy. The Tsarist regime began to use more repression to control the population and implemented an unsuccessful attempt to Russify education. In response, various semi-legal organizations were formed, among them the Masons, who wanted to better the economic and cultural life of the country, several student organizations, who sought to raise public awareness and propagate values such as knowledge, morality and patriotism. A severe Russian backlash against this movement led to the arrest and deportation of the leaders, including poet Adam Mickiewicz.

Despite this, a revolt against the regime was brewing and only a spark was needed to ignite a conflagration in Lithuania. The spark was provided in 1830, when another uprising flared in Warsaw. Upon receiving word of this, an organizational group was formed in Vilnius, but the time was not ripe for a successful revolt. The most capable leaders had been deported, people were not prepared and weapons were not available. Although revolt gripped most of Lithuania, the Russian army was able to squelch the uprising in the fall of 1831, before it reached Vilnius.

The result was more repression. People were deported to Russia and Russians were brought to settle in Lithuania. Monasteries were closed and Catholic churches (such as the Church of St. Casimir) were converted to Russian Orthodox ones. The University of Vilnius was closed in 1832, at which time the contents of the library, teaching materials, etc. were brought to the newly founded Russian University in Kiev. And finally in 1840 the Lithuanian Statute, which had been the country's legal code for nearly three centuries, was suspended.

Nevertheless, Poland and Lithuania again revolted in 1863-64. This uprising had its roots in somewhat liberal and nationalistic revolutionary movements, which began in Poland and spread to Lithuania. Although serfdom had been abolished in Russia in 1861, the revolutionary committee in Lithuania sought the support of peasants by proclaiming that they would be liberated and acquire ownership of the lands they were working in return for their support of the uprising. This proved to be effective because many more peasants participated in the revolt in Lithuania than in Poland.

The aristocracy also supported the uprising because they wished to be rid of the Russian yoke. Thus, armed with hunting rifles, scythes and other simple weapons, the rebels gathered in the forests and, led by military officers, priests and noblemen, attacked the Russians, stopped transportation, seized food and munition transports. The uprising spread throughout the country and the Russian army retained only large cities, such as Vilnius.

The Tsarist government sent a new governor-general, M. N. Muraviev, aptly nicknamed "The Hangman," to Vilnius to crush the revolt. Upon his arrival, he immediately ordered the execution of two priests and a nobleman. And to further scare the rebels, gallows were set up in the marketplace (presently Lenin Square) and many rebels were hanged. The hangings took place during the day so that more people could witness the fate of the rebels. A country-wide organization was established to capture, try and punish anyone participating in the uprising.

These savage measures took their toll, and, by the beginning of 1864, the revolt was over. Thousands of people had been killed or deported, hundreds more emigrated abroad, entire villages were cleared out and burned. But the repercussions of the uprising were yet to come.

The government took extreme measures to attempt to Russify Lithuania. All parochial schools were shut down and eventually Russian schools with only Russian teachers replaced them. Social organizations were banned and the Church was also severely repressed. Strict censorship was instituted. And in 1865 the printing of Lithuanian publications using the Latin alphabet was outlawed. It would remain banned for 40 years, during which books would be smuggled into Lithuania from Prussia and children would secretly be taught Lithuanian in underground schools, or by their parents at home.

The goal of the regime was not only to crush the sprouting nationalist movement of Lithuanian intellectuals. The repressive policies had a direct impact on the lives of peasants as well, especially on their religious faith. But all of this only strengthened the budding national awakening, which spread through the latter part of the 19th century and ultimately led to complete independence for Lithuania.

Meanwhile, Vilnius expanded quite rapidly during the second half of that century. In 1860 a railway was completed, which linked Vilnius with Warsaw and St. Petersburg, and later with Baltic ports as well as other Russian cities. Industry expanded and, as the demand for labor increased, the population boomed. Vilnius became Lithuania's main industrial center and railway junction. The city's boundaries expanded and a new center formed along Jurgis Ave. (now Lenin Prospect). Administrative buildings and large suburbs were built.

Neo-Classicism in the city's architecture gave way to eclecticism (an example of this being the Main Concert Hall of the State Philharmonic on Aušros Vartų St.)

Vital statistics for Vilnius at the turn of the century were:

Population: 138,600 (63,000 Jews)

Churches: 22 Catholic; 6 chapels; 11 Russian Orthodox; 6 Jewish synagogues; 2 Lutheran; 1 Mosque.

10 cemeteries, 2 seminaries, 2 male and 2 female high schools, 2 teacher's institutes, 26 primary schools (not including Jewish schools), and 90 factories.

During the decade before the war Lithuanian activity blossomed: the press ban was abolished in 1904 and cultural organizations were once again allowed. Russia at the same time became involved in an unsuccessful war with Japan which significantly undermined an already shaky confidence in the Tsarist government. In 1905 a revolution broke out, its socialist leaders demanding a democratic republic. It soon gripped the entire country, and the occupied nations also began demanding autonomy.

In Lithuania the Great Assembly of Vilnius, the first modern Lithuanian political convention, convened in December of 1905. A resolution was accepted, which demanded autonomy for Lithuania with a democratically elected parliament, called the Seimas, to reside in Vilnius. It urged Lithuanians to avoid paying taxes to the Russian government, close down monopolies of alcohol producers, boycott Russian schools, evade army service and disregard all former government agencies. It also demanded that schools teach all subjects in Lithuanian and that all public matters be handled in Lithuanian. This was a turning point in the Lithuanian national movement.

Although the revolt was again stifled by the government and many people, especially the intelligentsia, were repressed, the national movement continued. Scores of Lithuanian publications began being printed, cultural and educational organizations were formed and the social and cultural life of Vilnius and Lithuania blossomed.

When World War I broke out in 1914, a Committee to Assist War Victims was established, which eventually assumed a key role in Lithuanian political activity. In 1915, Vilnius was occupied by the German army and suffered severe repression for three and a half years. The

Conference of Vilnius took place September 17-22, 1917 and chose the Lithuanian National Council, which led the fight for independence. Finally on February 16, 1918 the Council proclaimed Lithuania's independence and, in the fall of that year, an independent government was formed and began functioning.

Wars for independence were fought against the interventions from Soviet Russia, Poland and an army of reactionary German and Russian volunteers known as the Bermondtist (named after the Russian adventurer Bermondt-Avalov who commanded the troops). Eventually freedom was attained and Lithuania was recognized as a sovereign state by the community of nations and became a member of the League of Nations in 1922.

Unfortunately the historic Lithuanian capital of Vilnius met a different fate. Retreating from the Bolsheviks, the government of Lithuania was moved to the provisional capital of Kaunas in January of 1919. Vilnius changed hands many times between the Poles and the Russians. On July 12, 1920 a peace treaty was signed with the Soviet Union with Vilnius specified as belonging to Lithuania. Four days later the Soviets drove the Poles out of Vilnius and turned the city over to the Lithuanians.

Just a few months later, Polish troops led by General L. Zeligowski reoccupied Vilnius, thus violating the Suwalki Treaty, signed two days earlier. Poland claimed that the troops occupying Vilnius were renegades and that the government had nothing to do with Zeligowski's actions. A supposedly "independent" government was set up in Vilnius.

Two years of debating in the League of Nations could not resolve the Vilnius Issue. The city and the region remained under Polish occupation until World War II and Lithuania refused to have any relations with Poland during this time. The borders between the neighboring countries remained closed for 17 years.

Vilnius became a provincial town which received little attention or funding from the Polish government. Growth of industry and trade was minimal. More Polish settlers were brought in further diluting the already weak Lithuanian presence in Vilnius. The Lithuanian people of Vilnius and its environs were persecuted and Lithuanian culture was repressed.

In August of 1939, Hitler's Germany and Stalin's Soviet Union signed the infamous Molotov-Ribbentrop pact and divided between themselves Poland and the Baltic States. In October of that same year, the Lithuanian government signed a treaty with the Soviets, whereby Vilnius was returned to Lithuania. But it was forced to accept Red Army bases on its territory. From these bases on June 15th of 1940 the Soviets occupied Lithuania, in complete violation of international law and mutual treaties with respect to sovereignty. A puppet administration was quickly formed and the forcible incorporation of independent Lithuania into the USSR was concluded August 3, 1940.

Large-scale repression and deportations to Siberia took place during this occupation. As many as 40,000 people were deported. The people lived in constant fear, their lives in total upheaval under Soviet oppression.

On June 22, 1941 Hitler's Germany invaded its former partner, the Soviet Union. The Lithuanians attempted to revolt against the Soviets at this time and re-established an independent Lithuania. But the Germans had a different plan and on August 5 initiated an occupational regime.

The German occupation lasted for three years and was also tragic and brutal. Fully 1/3 of Vilnius' population was exterminated. Mass executions of 100,000 people took place in the nearby suburb of Paneriai, where most of the Jewish population was murdered. Unlike the Jews and Gypsies, most of whom perished in the Holocaust, the Lithuanian people were not exterminated en masse; however, thousands of Lithuanians were killed by the Nazis and tens of thousands of young people were deported to the Reich for labor. Despite their loathing of Stalinist Russia, many Lithuanians resisted the Germans. Lithuania was the only European nation which refused to sponsor an ethnic SS legion.

As the advancing Red Army drove the Nazis back West, it reoccupied Vilnius on July 13th, 1944. At the end of the war only 110,000 people were left in the city, half of the pre-war population. Entire streets and buildings had been turned to rubble. All industrial enterprises had been destroyed, including the electric power station and gas producing factory. The city had no water or electricity, no means of transport or communication. 42% of the city's dwelling houses and 80% of its architectural monuments lay in ruin.

But Lithuania's suffering did not end. The Soviets again sought to mold Lithuania into a Soviet republic and used terror extensively to deal with resistance. From 1944 to 1952 resistance fighters waged a guerilla war against the Soviets in which nearly 100,000 lives were lost. Massive deportations again took place; at least a quarter million people were deported from Lithuania, primarily to the Far North, Siberia and Central Asia. Many never returned. Forced industrialization and collectivization of agriculture, which were brutally carried out with no regard to the population took their toll. During the last few years the Soviet Lithuanian press has confirmed the worst of the Stalinist horrors and a new commission is preparing to study the mass repressions as well as compensate the victims.

During the Soviet occupation Vilnius has been rebuilt. New industries have been established and huge apartment complexes, like Žirmunai and the more modern Lazdynai, have been erected. Despite new construction a severe housing shortage still exists and parts of the city are in disrepair. Nonetheless today Vilnius is the political, educational and cultural center of Lithuania, attracting many people to live and to visit.

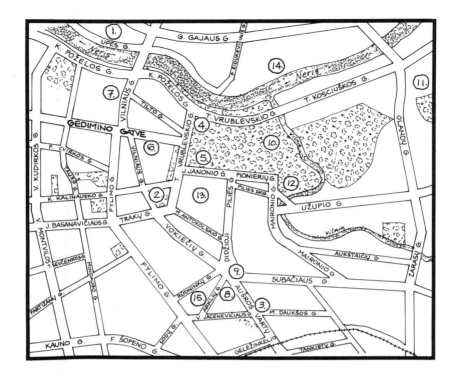

OLD TOWN VILNIUS

1. Hotel Lietuva
2. The Palace of Art Workers
3. The Gates of Dawn
4. Museum of History and Ethnography
5. The Cathedral
6. The Academic Drama Theater
7. The Academic Opera and Ballet Theater
8. The State Philharmonic Society Building
9. The Art Museum
10. Gediminas Tower
11. The Church of Saints Peter and Paul
12. The Church of St. Anne and the Church of the Bernardines
13. The University of Vilnius
14. The Sports Palace
15. The State Youth Theater of Lithuania

THE OLD TOWN

The old town of Vilnius is one of the most sizable in Eastern Europe and the largest in the USSR. It encompasses 74 quarters, 70 streets and lanes and over 1200 buildings which were constructed over the course of five centuries. Artists and craftsmen of diverse cultures blended the mainly Western European architectural traditions of various periods to create a unique urban ensemble.

Thus a walk through the old town is like a lesson in architectural history. Vilnius is often said to be a Baroque city because of the many Baroque facades which a visitor is likely to notice at first. But art historians have determined that the quarters of the old town, formed during the 15-16th centuries, reflect Gothic principles of construction.

Let's start the walking tour of Old Town Vilnius at the only remaining gate of the 1-1/2 mile long Gothic defense wall that once surrounded the city.

Walking Tour Starting Point: Ausros Vartai (Gates of Dawn)
        formerly Medininku Gates, at
        crossing of Ausros Varty St. &
        Jaceneviciaus/M. Dauksos Sts.

Ausros Vartu Street

The Gates of Dawn, built in the 16th century on the road to Medininku Castle, are an example of Gothic and Renaissance architecture. The rectangular wall above the arch has 2 rows of rounded openings, which served defensive purposes. An attic, decorated with reliefs depicting griffins and the crest of Lithuania is topped off by a cornice.

The gates house a chapel (seen from the inside of the gate) built in the neo-Classical style with doric pillasters and a portico. Climb up the stairs through a gallery on the right to see the Renaissance painting of Our Lady of Vilnius. This work of art is believed to be miraculous and draws a steady stream of worshippers.

The chapel is connected by a gallery on the right to the Church of St. Theresa. Built in 1635-1650, it is an example of early Baroque in which the horizontal lines and flat planes of Renaissance unite with the curved lines and dynamic form of Baroque. The interior, which was repaired in the latter half of the 18th century, acquired late Baroque features tending toward Rococo. It has a large number of paintings, sculptures and bas-reliefs. Ceiling frescos depict scenes from St. Theresa's life.

Aušros vartai - The Gates of Dawn

Continuing on Aušros Vartų St. at #86 is the Church of the Holy Spirit, the main Russian Orthodox church of Vilnius and Lithuania. It stands in the middle of a large courtyard surrounded by a convent and belfry. Constructed in the mid-17th century, the facade is modest, consisting of two towers and a dome. The Rococo interior is light and spacious with many reliefs and valuable icons.

#84, which has brightly patterned walls, houses the Medininkų restaurant. Inside the courtyard there is a small sculpture exhibition.

On the left at #73 you will find the gates to the Bazilian Monastery. The gates seem to have been carved without any sharp lines, flat surfaces or superfluous elements. The soft curved lines, multi-tiered cornices and intricate contours exemplify the richness of the late Baroque period.

The large Main Concert Hall of the State Philharmonic (#69), built in 1902, is eclectic yet aesthetically appealing.

Didžioji St.

Here at the Philharmonic, Aušros Vartų St. becomes Didžioji St. Continuing along this thoroughfare on the right at #74 is the Church of St. Casimir, the oldest Baroque church in Vilnius (1604-1615). As is typical of the churches built during this period, the building's outline is defined by a dome, the largest in the city. In 1837 the church was taken over by the Russian Orthodox Church and acquired orthodox characteristics, including an onion-shaped dome.

In 1925 the church underwent reconstruction, but it was only in 1942 that the crown atop the dome, symbolizing the royal lineage of St. Casimir, replaced the onion dome. Inside, a long nave is crossed by a trancept with the dome rising above the crossing.

In 1966, the authorities took it upon themselves to convert the church into the Museum of Atheism. Since St. Casimir is revered as the patron saint of Lithuania, this act represented an especially painful affront to the faithful. In the past year as the government seemingly began to rethink its policy of religious persecution, it decreed that St. Casimir's be returned to the believers.

Crossing the street you will notice the Astoria Hotel (59/2) and the narrow Arklių St. nearby, which leads to an 18th century palatial building that houses the Youth and Puppet Theaters (Arklių St. 5).

Here, Didžioji St. broadens markedly and forms the large triangular Muziejaus Square. Formerly named Rotušés (Town Hall) Square, it appears to have originated in the 15th century following the war against the German Order. A market appeared here at the junction of trade routes linking Moscow, Riga, Polotsk and Cracow. The market place was a logical location on which to build the Town Hall.

The first Town Hall, probably constructed in the late 15th century, was a two-story Gothic building with a dome and a tall clock tower. It stood in the middle of the square and played a significant role in the life of the town: the clock chimed the time of day, tolling bells announced the arrival of a king or foreign emissary, a dignitary's death, the outbreak of a war, or any other important event. Sundays and holidays, a band played on the Town Hall's balcony and various festivities took place in the square. Weekdays the open space was filled with the stands of merchants noisily selling their wares. Laborers, offering their services for the day would also gather here. Until the second half of the 17th century, a pillory stood in the square where lawbreakers were tied and flogged. This was also the site where gallows would be set up for a public execution.

The town council met in the Town Hall every Thursday. The magistry personnel kept up accounts, collected taxes and investigated lawsuits. It also maintained the town's armed guard, public criers, a hangman, a watchmaker to look after the clock, bell ringers, etc. Archives, the treasury, the armory, specimen weights and measures were also housed in the Town Hall, while the cellar served as a prison.

In the 18th century fires severely damaged the building. Attempted restoration efforts failed and, between 1785-1799, the new Town Hall was constructed in the prevalent style of architecture, neo-Classicism. It is a square, monumental building with a six-doric column portico designed by Laurynas Stuoka-Gucevičius, Vilnius' finest neo-Classical architect. Today the Art Museum of Lithuania is in this building (Didžioji St. 55).

The modern building behind the old Town Hall (Vokiečių St. 2) houses the Art Exhibition Hall, a branch of the Art Museum, which was built specifically for this purpose. Inside there is a cafe and a Daile Arts and Crafts shop.

From the Art Exhibition Hall proceed along Vokiečių St. towards the Neris River. Here, in the area generally bounded by Garelio, Traku and Vokiečių streets, the Nazis set up the Vilnius Ghetto for countless numbers of their Jewish victims. By the end of World War II, the Nazis had virtually destroyed Vilnius' Jewish community of over 60,000, which was one of the most important Jewish cultural centers in the world.

Returning to Didžioji St., notice the building at #24. The bottom floor has Gothic-style windows, while the 2nd and 3rd floors retain neo-Classical elements. The 4th floor was only added early in this century, but it nicely completes the composition. It was in this building, now known as the Narutis Hotel, that the Lithuanian National Council declared Lithuania's independence on February 16, 1918 (the country's national holiday). For decades after the Soviet occupation, commemorating this occasion was considered a serious political offense subject to prosecution. All of this changed, however, after the advent of Sąjudis in 1988. Thanks to skillful pressure exerted by Sąjudis, the authorities relented and Lithuanians were able to joyfully celebrate this holiday in 1989, without fear of official harassment. After some searching, a plaque commemorating the spot where independence was proclaimed was recently found and affixed to the front of the building. It had originally been created in the late 1930's, but never hung there for political reasons.

The University of Vilnius

The next point on our walking tour is the architectural ensemble of the University of Vilnius, which begins with the Church of St. John at the crossing of Didžioji and Sruogos Streets. Founded in 1579 by the Jesuits under the auspices of King Stefan Batory, it is the oldest university in the USSR.

As the university expanded over the years, new buildings were constructed and nine unique squares were eventually formed. All of the architectural styles that are seen in the old town, from Gothic to neo-Classicism, are represented in the halls and buildings of the University of Vilnius.

Let's start by taking a look at the Church of St. John. The southern side of the church, which we see from Didžioji St., acquired neo-Classical elements - a portico with four Corinthian columns - during reconstruction in the 19th century.

Originally St. John's was a small Gothic church begun in 1387. When the Jesuits took it over in 1571, it was extended to Didžioji St. and acquired Renaissance features. (Enter the University's main P. Skarga courtyard through the large gates between the church and the belfry.) After the fires of the 18th century, the edifice was restored in the Baroque style (architect J.K. Glaubicas). Baroque features are clearly recognizable in the dynamic lines, forms and decorative elements of the main facade seen from inside the square.

Inside the church, note the main altar, which is an exquisite composition of eleven small altars arranged in a semicircle on two levels. There are seven side chapels and numerous busts, monuments and memorial plaques to eminent people whose names are linked to Vilnius and the University: poet Adam Mickiewicz, general Thaddeus Kosciuszko and composer Stanislaw Moniuszko (who was the Church organist from 1840 to 1858). Notice the stained-glass windows in the presbytery and the vast 18th century frescos on the vaults depicting some of the University's more prominent academics.

The Church of St. John now houses the Museum of Science and a concert hall, which are sources of considerable unhappiness among Lithuanian believers. (See museum section.)

The belfry provides an important vertical accent for the Old Town. It was built at the beginning of the 17th century, while the top tier was added in the mid-18th century and is Baroque in shape and design. From the tower there is a splendid view of Vilnius.

The University's oldest buildings appear opposite the church and to the right of the courtyard entrance. The arcades surrounding this and other courtyards give the University a Renaissance feel.

Go through the arches opposite the church into the small M. Pocobuto courtyard, which has a 17th century astronomical observatory (now inactive). The facade is interesting because the architect aimed to

Interior of the Church of St. John

replace the Baroque style with that of neo-Classicism. The facade constructed at the end of the 18th century has two cylindrical pilasters and a wide relief depicting the twelve zodiacal signs.

Return to the main courtyard and pass to the left of the church into a third courtyard (Sarbievijus). The buildings here are also counted among the oldest. Enter the University's Littera Bookstore to view the unique frescos by prominent Lithuanian artist and sculptor Antanas Kmieliauskas.

17th century astronomical observatory in Vilnius University

Sarbievijus courtyard, Vilnius University

Continue through the gates which are topped by a plaque to the poet Mykolas Sarbievijus into Universiteto St. Under the arch of the four story building you can see a statue of the poet and Protestant pastor, Kristijonas Donelaitis, considered the father of Lithuanian literature.

If time permits, it is worthwhile to explore some of the University's halls. Just a few highlights are:

- Frescos by the contemporary artist Petras Repšys in the vestibule of the Center for Lithuanian Studies. Some of them were inspired by remote pagan and early Renaissance motifs.

Frescos by Antanas Kmieliauskas in the University Council Hall

- Frescos depicting fragments of man's life and moments of Lithuania's history by Antanas Kmieliauskas in the University Council Hall convey a Renaissance feeling.

- The main library, especially Smuglevičius Hall, which houses an ancient manuscript reading room. The hall was decorated by the foremost Lithuanian painter of the 18th century, Pranciskus Smuglevičius.

- The fresco Nine Muses in the Philology Faculty's vestibule, represents the antique muses of art and science. The artist, Rimtautas Gibavičius, found a balance between modern forms and Greek classicism while successfully integrating the fresco with the architecture of the stairway.

Daukantas (formerly Kutuzov) Square

On the other side of Universiteto St. appears Daukantas Square and the Palace of Art Workers, a two story building which once served as the residence of Vilnius bishops. At the end of the 18th century, the architect L. Stuoka-Gucevičius reconstructed the palace which later became the residence of the Tsar's vice regents in Lithuania. At this time it was redesigned again in the late neo-Classical or Empire style. The facade consists of three two-story blocks joined by two rows of Doric columns. An impressive classical courtyard and park decorated beautifully with colonnades are added features of an already attractive architectural ensemble.

At Daukantas Square 1 you see the small Church of the Bonifratrians dating back to the Baroque period. It is now called the small Baroque Hall and plays host to chamber and organ music concerts. The church has an attractive interior and excellent acoustics.

A monument to architect Laurynas Stuoka-Gucevičius stands beside the square.

Gediminas Square

From Daukantas Square walk up Tallat-Kelpšos St. (about 1-1/2 blocks) to Gediminas Square. (The Central Telegraph Office is located at Tallat-Kelpšos St. 3.) The square is situated on part of the territory where the lower castle once stood. You will see the public gardens and Castle Hill behind the square.

Gediminas Square (until 1951 called Cathedral Square) originated in the 19th century, where markets and the famous fairs of St. Casimir were held. Early in this century the markets were moved and the southern end of the square was turned into a public garden. In 1931 the Neris river flooded the square, prompting the authorities to undertake restoration work to raise the square slightly.

A neo-Classical cathedral built in 1784 dominates the square. The history of the building dates back to ancient times, when, according to recent excavations, a pagan temple dedicated to Perkūnas, the god of thunder, stood on this site. It is now believed that there was a cathedral on this spot during the reign of King Mindaugas (who died in 1263). In 1387 another cathedral was built. After it was destroyed by fire, Grand Duke Vytautas ordered the construction of a new cathedral, this time in the Gothic style and on a much larger scale. Over the next three centuries the cathedral underwent repeated reconstruction changing from Gothic to Baroque. The cathedral closed in 1769 when one of the Baroque towers collapsed. A reconstruction design contest was won by the master of Lithuanian neo-Classical architecture, Laurynas Stuoka-Gucevičius.

The main facade of the cathedral is dominated by a six-Doric column portico, while the side facades are symmetrically decorated with six-column colonnades. The niches on the southern side of the building contain seven Baroque sculptures of Lithuania's dukes. On the northern side the niches shelter sculptures of apostles and saints.

The relief on the main facade's pediment depicts a sacrificial thanksgiving offering by Noah's family after the great flood. The five reliefs above the main entrance door represent scenes from the apostles' lives. These reliefs, executed by Italian sculptor Tommaso Righi (1727-1802) in the Baroque style are dramatic and dynamic, seemingly contrasting with the simplicity and majestic tranquility of Stuoka-Gucevičius' neo-Classical design. The niches also have Baroque statues of Abraham, the four evangelists and Moses.

Two cupolas complete the exterior. The south-eastern Baroque cupola covers the chapel of St. Casimir. The north-eastern cupola above the sacristy was designed in the Baroque style by Stuoka-Gucevičius over 150 years later.

Inside, two rows of rectangular pillars divide the cathedral into three naves, an arrangement that has remained unchanged over the centuries. Stuoka-Gucevičius decorated the walls with pilasters and the doors to the side chapels with new portals.

Notice the painting "Polish King Boleslov the Brave killing Archbishop Stanislaw of Cracow" behind the central altar. This, and the paintings of the twelve apostles, are works by Pranciškus Smuglevičius (1745-1807).

The chapel of St. Casimir is of great artistic value as an example of early Baroque art in Vilnius. The square chapel is covered by a large cupola decorated with frescos depicting the saint's life. The walls are finished in marble and granite, while the structural ornaments and reliefs of the cupola, arcades and main altar are executed in white stucco. Of further note are two large frescos on the side walls: "The Opening of St. Casimir's Tomb" and "The Miracle at St. Casimir's Tomb" by Italian painter Angelo Palloni.

During excavation work in 1931, the remains of royalty, high clergymen and noblemen were uncovered and then transferred to a mausoleum built to house them. It is located under the chapel of St. Casimir. Also worthy of interest are the Baroque chapel of the Valavičius Family and the Renaissance style tombs of the Goštautas Family chapel.

From 1956 to November, 1988, the cathedral building served as the Art Museum of Lithuania. The reconsecration of the cathedral early in 1989, widely reported in the world press, was a joyous celebration for the believers of Lithuania. Daily services are now held there.

The cathedral's detached bell tower standing in Gediminas Square appears to have been built in three stages. The round base dates back to the 13th century and was once a part of the Lower Castle's defense wall. The circumstance that the foundation was discovered to lie 12 feet underground, shows that the ground level of Gediminas Square was 15 feet lower than today. The octangular top was added in the 16th century, with two sections for the bells and the top story for the clock. Since its beginnings, the tower has undergone many restorations, the last being in the early part of the 19th century, when the top was covered by a tin dome. The 17th-century clock still functions. The offices of the Vilnius Excursion and Travel Bureau are located in the bell tower.

The structures surrounding the square are occupied by mostly administrative institutions, including the Presidium of the Supreme Soviet. In the southeastern corner of the square a memorial stone with the inscription "Vilnius 1323-1973" was emplaced as part of the city's celebration of its 650th anniversary.

The tour up to this point lasts about 3 hours.

We continue our excursion on foot from the public gardens at the base of Castle Hill located to the left of the cathedral. The four story building you will see here, known as the New Arsenal of the Lower Castle, houses the Museum of History and Ethnography of Lithuania (see section on Museums).

Towering overhead, Castle Hill and Gediminas Castle at the confluence of the rivers Neris and Vilnele dominate the skyline of Vilnius. In a dramatic turn of events on October 7, 1988, the yellow, green, and red national flag of independent Lithuania was raised above Gediminas tower in place of the Soviet republic banner. This was a particularly memorable celebration for the estimated 50,000 gathered at the foot of one of Lithuania's best-known symbols of her medieval statehood. For even as late as June of 1988, merely having the pre-war flag in one's possession was considered to be a grave anti-Soviet offense punishable by imprisonment.

A path runs up the southern slope of the hill from the cathedral. The hill rises to a height of 144 feet above Gedimino Square and 426 feet above sea level. Atop the hill are the ruins of a 14th century Gothic castle with the most prominent part being the octangular defense tower known as Gediminas Tower. It measures 60 feet from top to bottom. Inside there is a modest museum devoted to the history of Vilnius. Climb up the spiral staircase to the observation platform for a spectacular view of Vilnius. (See the Vilnius History section for an account of the history of Gediminas Castle.)

To return to street level, take the path leading down towards the public garden with a monument to the Russian poet Alexander Pushkin.

From here you will enter Maironio St., named after the beloved Lithuanian poet of the early 20th century. Nearby, at Maironio St. 8, stands a superb Gothic architectural ensemble made up of the churches of the Bernardines and St. Anne. The latter, finished in 1580, represents the finest achievement of the Lithuanian Gothic style during the 250 years of its existence.

When Napoleon first caught sight of St. Anne's during his march to Moscow, he reportedly was so captivated by its appearance that he exclaimed: "I want to carry this church back to France on the palm of my hand." Whether the great conqueror really said this cannot be verified, but the church is truly beautiful and has been lovingly photographed and painted by Lithuanian photographers and painters countless times. Thirty-three different forms of small red and yellow bricks were used to create a graceful, harmonious and ornate facade. Its general lines emphasize upward thrusts, while the numerous towers and pinnacles lend a sense of delicacy and elegance.

The most intricate and original section is the center of the facade. Four narrow windows, with those of the middle reaching higher than the side windows, are outlined by sharp, angular borders. They are intersected by a wide ogee arch from which rises the dainty middle tower. Two triangular turrets with diminutive windows which are interposed between the middle and side towers complete the facade. Architectural forms such as the ogee arch are repeated and thereby unify the whole composition. The Church of St. Anne is open for worship.

Standing further away from the street is the Church of the Bernardines. The Bernardine monks who built the church arrived in Vilnius from Poland in 1469, and were granted this plot of land by Casimir IV the Jagiellonian (Kazimieras Jogailaitis). The present structure arose after the first 2 buildings were destroyed (one by fire, and the other by design to prevent its collapse). Completed in 1520, it became, and remains one of the largest buildings in the old quarter. The church also apparently served a defensive purpose. Its thick walls were fortified by buttresses and corner towers, and several gunports were built into the northern wall facing Castle Hill. Dominating the center of the facade are tall narrow windows as well as ornamented arch-shaped niches which are crowned by a relief of ogee arch motifs. Subsequently Baroque elements were added to the pediment and side towers.

Upon entering, the visitor is immediately struck by the church's soaring interior. Three naves of identical height are traversed by 4 pairs of octangular pillars. An impressive sight are the vaults of the side naves and the sacristy. The Baroque altars, pulpit, choir and tombstones with their curved lines enliven the linear Gothic structure.

The gothic Churches of the Bernadines and St. Anne

Perhaps the most attractive element of the whole composition is the three-tier bell tower standing at the southern side of the church. Decorated by a pattern composed of 10 different kinds of bricks, the octangular upper tiers are especially intricate, containing niches outlined by braided curves, multi-tiered arches and a terra-cotta relief.

A medieval monastery of the Bernardine order is located on the northern side of the church. It was closed in 1864 and today houses the Art Institute of Lithuania. Every element of this Gothic architectural ensemble is uniquely beautiful and contributes to an impressively harmonious whole.

Across Maironio St. stands the Church of St. Michael, which was begun in 1594 and experienced subsequent additions and restoration work in the next century. Although Gothic characteristics such as buttressed windows are still evident, the dominant elements are Renaissance, including the semi-circular doorways and windows as well as the horizontal lines of the cornices. The shallow niches are embellished by friezes and pilasters decorated with stylized rue leaves instead of the traditional acanthus. The rue, or "rūta", is the traditional flower of Lithuania.

Decidedly Renaissance features characterize the interior. The building has one nave with a cylindrical vault with lunettes, embellished by a series of relief patterns consisting of rozettes, flowers and stars. The main altar, constructed of marble, was built in the 17th century. Especially noteworthy are the tombstones of the noble Sapieha family.

The Church of St. Michael, like many other churches in Lithuania, was desecrated by the Soviet authorities, who converted it into the Museum of Architecture.

From the small square facing the church, several small lanes lead off in different directions. The last leg of our walking tour leads us down the unique Pilies Skersgatvis (Castle Lane), a narrow, winding and picturesque passageway which returns you to Pilies St. near Gediminas Square. At every step a new perspective comes into view, alternately narrow and wide, light and dark.

Curved walls reminiscent of former ramparts and contrasting Baroque portals look down on the passerby, while two-story houses dating from the 17th and 18th centuries line both sides of the lane. A narrow sidewalk runs along only one side of the street, which is paved with red brick.

Many of the houses have interesting stories to tell. As you move along the lane notice No. 11 on the left. A plaque on the outside wall notes that Adam Mickiewicz, Poland's greatest Romantic poet, lived in this building in 1822. Inside the small courtyard on the western facade there is a wooden gallery. The Mickiewicz Memorial Apartment is located inside.

Pilies Lane No. 8 is called the Olizar Palace. Built in 1748, it had many owners, including the Bishop of Vilnius and the family of Count Olizar (hence the name). The palace is a blend of Baroque and neo-Classical styles. Today it houses the Communist Party Central Committee's publishing houses and the editorial boards of various publications.

From the late 1500's, the Pilies Lane area fell under the jurisdiction of the Vilnius episcopate. Building and restoration were strictly controlled, particularly after 1698, when a law was passed stipulating that special permission was required for all construction work. Perhaps this is why the buildings on this street remained almost untouched during the massive reconstruction efforts of the 18th century.

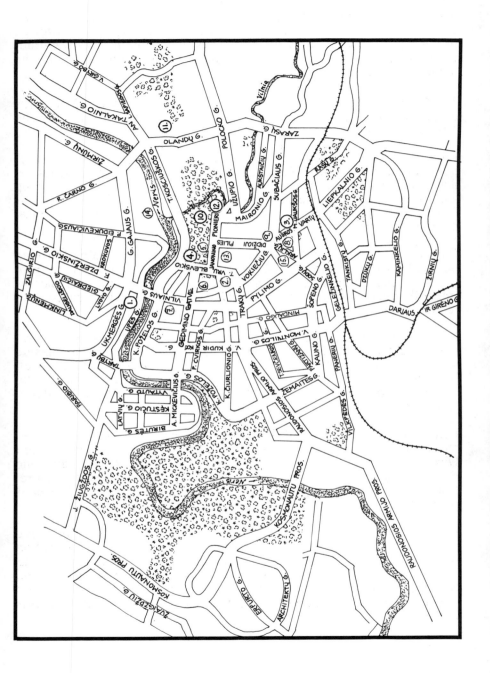

VILNIUS

1. Hotel Lietuva
2. The Palace of Art Workers
3. The Gates of Dawn
4. Museum of History and Ethnography
5. The Cathedral
6. The Academic Drama Theater
7. The Academic Opera and Ballet Theater
8. The State Philharmonic Society Building
9. The Art Museum
10. Gediminas Tower
11. The Church of Saints Peter and Paul
12. The Church of St. Anne and the Church of the Bernardines
13. The University of Vilnius
14. The Sports Palace
15. The State Youth Theater of Lithuania

Pilies skersgatvis - Castle lane

MUSEUMS

Museum of History and Ethnography
Vrublevskio St. 1 (near Castle Hill) tel. 45-19-33.
Hours: Daily from 11:00-19:00, closed Tuesdays.

Originally opened in 1855 and called the Museum of Antiques, it is now one of the richest museums in Lithuania. About 300,000 exhibits acquaint the visitor with Lithuania's archeology, ethnography, folk art and history.

Art Museum
Didžioji St. 55, tel. 62-86-79.   Folk department: Rudninku St. 22/2, tel. 61-74-14.
Hours: Daily from 12:00-18:00, closed Mondays.

A collection of paintings, drawings, and sculpture by Lithuanian artists.   It includes a valuable collection of Lithuanian folk art: linens, ceramics, wood carvings, sculpture, and extensive information about the history of art and architecture in Vilnius.

Palace of Art Exhibitions
Vokiečiu St. 2, tel. 61-70-97.
Hours: Daily from 11:00-19:00, closed Mondays.

This modern building (the 1973 USSR Council of Ministers award for architecture went to the architect Vytautas Cekanauskas) contains many halls accommodating various exhibitions of art.   It also has a cafe, the Daile Arts and Crafts Shop and an auditorium.   There is a permanent open-air sculpture garden in the courtyard.

Museum of Architecture (Church of St. Michael)
Svietimo St. 13, tel. 61-64-09.
Hours: Daily from 11:00-19:00, closed Tuesdays.

The visitor is acquainted with Lithuanian architecture and the construction and reconstruction of historic monuments.

Gediminas Tower
Castle Hill, tel. 61-11-33.
Hours: Daily from 09:00-21:00 in summer; 12:00-18:00 in winter, closed Tuesdays.

A small exhibition containing models of 14th century and 17th century castles, samples of building materials, old maps and drawings of Vilnius and its castles.

The Church of St. John belfry

Museum of Scientific Thought
Didžioji St. 21, (Church of St. John), tel. 61-17-96.
Hours: Daily from 12:00-18:00, closed Tuesdays.

The visitor is acquainted with the history of Vilnius University and the development of science and education in Lithuania. Occasional concerts are held here.

Photographic Society Exhibition Hall
Didžioji St. 45.
Hours: Daily from 11:00-20:00, closed Mondays.

Adam Mickiewicz Memorial Apartment
Pilies Skersgatvis 11
Hours: Daily from 12:00-18:00, closed Mondays and Tuesdays.

Under the control of Vilnius University, the museum contains paintings, sculptures, photos, and documents from the time the poet lived here (several months in 1822), books he read, and the first works he published in Vilnius. His study has also been recreated.

Museum of Applied Art
Kosciuškos St. at the confluence of the Neris and Vilnelé rivers.

A popular new museum.

NOTE: The Cathedral housed the Art Gallery, which contained 2 exhibitions of Lithuanian painting from the 16th to early 20th century and Western European painting from the 15th to the 19th century. Since the Cathedral has been reconsecrated, the collections have been removed. Inquire at Intourist as to where these collections can be viewed.

CONCERTS AND THEATERS

The State Youth Theater of Lithuania, Arkliu St. 5, tel. 62-67-32, is housed in the impressive 17-18th century Count Oginsky Palace. The restored building is decorated with frescos, tapestries, and the courtyard serves as a pleasant diversion during intermissions. The Youth Theater, which has had sell-out crowds in Lithuania for quite some time, won critical acclaim in the West during its 1988 tour to the U.S. and Europe. Highly innovative stagings by Eimuntas Nekrošius and others present works by classic and contemporary authors.

The Academic Opera and Ballet Theater (Vienuolio St. 1, tel. 62-07-27) opened its doors in 1974. It continues to carry on the tradition of the Kaunas City Theater, which raised the curtain for "La Traviata" on December 31, 1920. The New Year's Eve staging of this Verdi classic continues to be a popular and frilly affair. From September to June audiences can hear the standard Russian and Western classics with a few excursions to contemporary works. The acoustics are horrible, but the high-backed seats are the most comfortable around. The eclectic architecture of the building is interesting, as is the curious tradition of walking arm-in-arm in a circle during intermission.

The State Philharmonic Society Building (Aušros Vartų St. 69, tel. 62-71-65), formerly the city's Public Hall, was built in 1902. It houses the Symphony Orchestra and is also the umbrella organization for many chamber groups, a mixed choir, popular music ensembles, individual instrumentalists and vocalists. Guest artists from other countries are often featured.

The Academic Drama Theater, Gedimino St. 4, tel.62-97-71, presents many familiar works in a traditional, realistic style. Innovation is an exception and recent years have provided no exciting theater on the main stage. Hopefully this will change. Not so in the small experimental theater in the back which provides intimate, interesting performances. The reconstruction of the building is Scandinavian and inviting. Don't miss the sculpture of the muses over the entrance.

The Lėlė (Puppet) Theater is a great deal of fun if you can deal with the kids, although there are some shows for adult audiences. Well-crafted sets, dolls, puppets and masks come alive through talented actors and technicians. Lėlė is right next door to the Youth Theater, tel. 62-86-78, in the Count Oginsky Palace.

The Palace of Art Workers, Daukantas Sq. 3/8, tel.61-69-68, is housed in the former Bishop's Palace, later to become the Russian Governor's Mansion. Napoleon is reported to have stayed here in 1812. It is an ornate, neo-Classical building next to Vilnius University and the intimate Baroque Hall (formerly a church which is also the site of many excellent concerts) and hosts many fine artists and ensembles in its elegant rooms.

Tickets (exceptionally inexpensive) for the performances of these theaters are readily available through Intourist.

MOVIE THEATERS

Vilnius has 25 movie theaters ("kino teatrai" in Lithuanian). Most of the films playing are in Russian, with a few in Lithuanian. The film industry in Lithuania has produced some excellent films such as "Moteris ir keturi jos vyrai" ("A Woman and her Four Men"), but the number of films produced has been very modest, because of a lack of funds. In general, the quality of the cinema offerings leaves much to be desired. If your time is limited, you would do better to attend the live theater performances or a concert!

A listing of movies playing around town can be found in the daily paper Tiesa (The Truth), the Lithuanian version of Pravda. Here is a listing of some centrally located movie theaters:

Aušra - Pylimo St. 50

Vilnius - Gedimino St. 7, tel. 61-26-76

Lietuva - Pylimo St. 17a, tel. 62-34-22

Maskva - Didžioji St. 68a, tel.62-78-47

Planeta - Požėlos St. 34, tel.61-14-03

Pergalė - Gagarino St. 1, tel. 62-35-67

Kronika - Pylimo St. 22, tel. 61-74-35

SPORTS FACILITIES

Sports Palace - Eidukevičiaus St. 1, tel. 75-23-21, 75-89-42

Track and Field Arena - Žemaites St. 6, tel. 66-00-55

Žalgiris Stadium - Eidukevičiaus St. 3/11. tel. 73-12-26

POOLS AND SAUNA

There are several pools and sauna facilities in Vilnius. It is best to inquire at the Hotel Service Bureau, if you are staying at a large hotel such as the Lietuva, or at the front desk. They should be able to make arrangements for you.

AROUND TOWN

Church of Saints Peter and Paul- Antakalnio St. 1 (Open 10am to 5:30pm.) This 14th century building, rebuilt in 1668-1684 in the characteristically Lithuanian Baroque style of architecture, is truly a gem. Although the main facade is rather simple, the interior is renowned for its splendor and is one of the most outstanding Baroque monuments in Lithuania. Thousands of sculptures and stucco bas-reliefs decorate the vestibule, central nave, transcept, side chapels and dome. Various themes - religious, secular, mythological and the ordinary - have been created by 200 artists under the direction of the Italian masters Pietro Peretti and Giovanni Maria

Church of Saints Peter and Paul, interior detail

Galli (1677-1685), Andrea Capone and Giovanni Pensa (1691-1704). Each of the more than 2000 human figures and faces is unique, but has a role in the overall composition. The reliefs of animals and plants show great knowledge and respect for the natural world. Together the images produce a harmonious ensemble which seems to be in constant, exalted motion.

The Opera and Ballet Theater - The large modern structure at Vienuolio St. 1 was completed in 1974 and accommodates 1,150 spectators. Concrete and marble were the primary building materials, although liberal quantities of red tile, brass, copper, wood and glass were also employed for the decorations. Through the large glass panels one can view an interesting assemblage of curves, stairs and chandeliers of the interior. In the evening the theater shimmers a golden amber color and is quite attractive.

Church of Saints Peter and Paul, interior detail

Lenin Square (formerly Lukiškių Square), Gedimino St. and V. Kudirkos St.   This is not one of the gayest spots in the capital, for it was here that the leaders of the 1863 uprising against Russian rule were executed. Various government buildings ring the square, including the headquarters of the KGB. It is said that three levels of KGB cellars extend right underneath the square.   The students of the State Conservatory of Lithuania, located next door, like to refer to the headquarters as "the percussion section".

The small square nearby contains a memorial to the Lithuanian classical   writer,   Žemaitė   (1845-1921).   Žemaitė   (Julija Beniuševičiūtė-Žymantienė) was born into an impoverished noble family which had adopted a predominantly Polish outlook, but learned Lithuanian as a child by playing with her peasant neighbors' children.   She later taught herself how to read and write Lithuanian.   Her writings are realistic, depicting the country existence and the social, moral and family problems of the peasants. Žemaitė took active part in the national rebirth movement and the struggle for Lithuania's freedom. She enjoys an honored place in Lithuania's history and in the hearts of its people.

Palace of Weddings - Atop Tauras hill at Kalinausko St. 21. The structure is a good example of modern architecture in Vilnius. A long stairway leads up to the spacious vestibule. To the left are the wedding rooms, while the accommodations to the right are used for a kind of Soviet version of Christening ceremonies. (Both ceremonies attempt to mimic religious rites and are designed to exhalt the place of the Soviet government in family life.) The wedding hall has a large window adorned with crystallized glass and the birth registration room is decorated with a panel of stained glass.

Žalgiris Sports Complex - P. Eidukevičiaus St. 1-3. This large sports complex of several buildings is another example of modern Lithuanian architecture. The main structure is the Sports Palace which stands at the very edge of the Neris river channel. It was opened in 1971 and is one of the largest community buildings in Vilnius. The curved main facade looks onto Castle Hill and the river. From the first floor of the Palace there is a splendid view. The main hall is used for sporting events as well as meetings, concerts, etc.

The Žalgiris Stadium is smaller and older, having been built in 1950. The Sports Complex also includes an indoor ice skating rink and a rowing base on the Neris.

Republic Library of Lithuania - Gedimino St. 51. Situated in a small square, the library building was built in 1963 and houses over 3,500,000 volumes.

Verkių Palace Ensemble - Turistų St. 19. A stately 18th century manor designed by the two foremost neo-Classical architects Laurynas Stuoka-Gucevičius (the Cathedral and Town Hall are also his works) and Martynas Knakfusas, a professor of architecture from the end of the 18th century. The ensemble is characterized by a unified composition, elements of neo-Classical architecture, and a typical Lithuanian manor's planned structure, which nevertheless possesses elements of originality and distinction. The ensemble blends well with the surrounding landscape marked by rolling hills and a stream. The landscaped grounds (which include driveways, footpaths and a fountain) all harmonize delicately with the overall architectural structure of the Verkių Palace. Tours can be arranged. A branch of the Art museum is housed here, and the Academy of Sciences of Lithuania has offices and meeting halls.

Vingis Park - Vilnius' main park is situated in a picturesque bend of the Neris, which surrounds the park on three sides. The main entrance is from Ciurlionis St. Proceed up the walk to the center of the park for a view of the huge grass field next to the giant concert stage. This is the location of the mass folksong festivals held every five years. The stage was designed by Estonian architects and accommodates 20,000 singers, but it can also be quickly transformed to seat an audience of that size, with a platform on the lawn serving as a stage.

During the past year hundreds of thousands of Lithuanians have gathered here to take part in rallies for national sovereignty. One mass meeting, called to commemorate the Molotov-Ribbentrop Pact, which opened the way for the brutal Soviet occupation of Lithuania, drew over 200,000 people.

On the shores of the Neris River near Vilnius

Historically the area where Vingis Park is now belonged to the aristocratic Radziwill family. Later it passed to the Jesuits who built a palace and planted gardens on the grounds. At the end of the 18th century the Bishop of Vilnius took over the property. But Vingis Park's claim to fame is its owner, Count Benigsen, the Governor General of Vilnius in the early 1800's. Leo Tolstoy mentioned the count in his novel "War and Peace" in connection with the visit of Tsar Alexander I to Vilnius, shortly before Napoleon's attack on Russia. "Count Benigsen, a landowner of the Vilenskaya gubernia, offered his country house for this occasion, and June 13th was set aside as the date for a dinner, a ball, boating excursions and a fireworks display at Zakreta, the Count's country house."

In 1920 the park was donated to the University of Vilnius, and the Botanical Gardens were established there. They are found near the children's railway on the sloping bank of the Neris. The outdoor Lakštingala Cafe is located behind the stage in the park.

WHERE TO STAY

Most Western tourists usually stay in the new Lietuva, a good Intourist hotel with a wide variety of services, several restaurants and bars as well as a nightclub. Address: Hotel Lietuva, Ukmergės St. 20, tel. 73-60-16.

The smaller hotels such as the Neringa (Lenin Prospect 23), Vilnius (Gedimino St. 20), Draugystė (M. K. Čiurlionio St. 84) and Astorija (Didžioji St. 59 /2) are satisfactory. The older Intourist hotel, Gintaras, is undergoing renovation at present.

When booking an individual trip you can request a particular hotel, although chances of getting it are slim if there are vacancies in Hotel Lietuva. Prices for individual bookings are quite high - 89 rubles ($150) per night for a double, breakfast included.

Group trips organized through a travel agency are much less expensive (During high season approximately $2500 for 12-13 days, including air fare, hotel costs and meals.) Travel agencies that arrange group trips to Lithuania are:

Chicago -   American Service Travel Bureau
            9727 S. Western Ave.
            Chicago, IL 60643
            (312) 238-9787

G. T. International
10401 Roberts Road
Palos Hills, IL 60465
(312) 430-7272

New York -   Union Tours Inc.
79 Madison Ave.
New York, N.Y. 10016
(212) 683-9500

Massachusetts - Baltic Tours
77 Oak St. Suite 4
Newton, MA 02164
(617) 965-8080

Canada - Audra Travel Corporation
2100 Bloor St. W.
Toronto, Ontario M6S 1M7
(416) 763-6279

Hotel Services: Most hotels which accomodate foreign tourists have Hotel Service Bureaus which can arrange for various tours, theater and concert tickets, make reservations for restaurants and saunas and order European and overseas phone calls for you.   Ask at the reception desk if you need a cab, a wake-up call, luggage transport or general information.   In case of a medical emergency seek assistance at the front desk as well.

EAT, DRINK AND BE MERRY

Lithuanian Cuisine

The Lithuanian cuisine developed over many generations and is deeply rooted in the countryside where it was closely linked with the common people's life style and customs.   Most festivities, private and public, center around a table, where good food and good company go hand-in-hand. Locals seldom patronize restaurants, preferring instead the familiar comforts of home.   Moreover, going out tends to be quite expensive for most local inhabitants, although Western travelers will find the prices very reasonable, even in the better quality restaurants.   If invited to a Lithuanian's home, be prepared to spend the entire evening at a heavily-laden table, where the hosts (Lithuanians pride themselves on their hospitality) will relentlessly urge you to "have a little more" ("Dar truputį!").

Hors d'oeuvres are popular, including various salads (mišrainė), marinated mushrooms (grybai), herring (silkė), cold meats and sausages. Skilandis is an excellent smoked sausage which is to be eaten with the local dark rye bread. A variety of soups are also served, a specialty being the cold beet soup (šaltibarščiai), which is especially popular, and refreshing, during the summer.

Potato dishes are common and prepared in a variety of ways. These include the following: cepelinai - grated potato dumplings stuffed with meat, cheese or mushrooms topped with fried bacon bits (the name means zeppelin, which is appropriate, given their cylindrical shape); vėdarai - a type of potato sausage; potato pancakes; and kugelis - a potato pudding which came to Lithuania from Germany. Boiled potatoes also accompany many of the chief entrees, such as šaltibarščiai, rūgusis pienas (sour milk), varškė (cottage cheese) and pasukos (buttermilk).

Another popular dish is virtinukai - small dumplings stuffed with meat, cheese or mushrooms. Lithuanian farmer's cheese comes in many tasty permutations: fresh, dried, sweet or flavored with caraway seeds. It is still the custom in some rural areas to welcome an unexpected visitor by serving farmer's cheese accompanied with honey. Later the hosts bring out ham, sausage and scrambled eggs, often with a bottle of "something stronger". Because Lithuania was traditionally an agrarian country, the dishes tend to be on the heavy side (to provide enough energy for field work), but also appetizing and prepared with care.

For dessert try a kompotas (fruit compote), kisielius (a type of fruit pudding, especially popular around the Christmas holidays), pyragas or tortas (cake). Locals are especially fond of the ice cream sold by street vendors, which, though delicious, comes in only a few basic flavors. Lithuanians take pride in their confectionary, which although not quite up to the standards of the finest Swiss chocolate, nevertheless is genuinely of high quality. Ask for the Baltoji meška (Polar Bear) or Paukščių pienas (Bird Nectar) varieties.

Also worth a try are gira (a refreshing beverage made by fermenting grains or fruit), and midus (mead). Lithuania also produces several decent liquors, including Palanga and Dainava (both of which are similar to brandy) as well as Žagarės (a cherry liqueur). But beware of samagonas, a powerful and often nasty-tasting home brew or cheap wine!

Restaurants

(** indicates higher quality establishments.)

In the Old Town:

Amatininkų Užeiga (Artisans Inn) - Antokolskio St. 2

Astorija - Arklių St. 4

Bistro - Universiteto St. 2

Bočių (Forefathers Inn) - K. Giedrio St. 3

Lokys (The Bear) - Antokolskio St. 8. This restaurant is famous for its old town Gothic surroundings and occasionally serves moose and boar meat.

Medininkai - Aušros Vartų St. 84. Housed in a building with brightly colored walls Medininkai restaurant has a distinctive, cozy old fashioned atmosphere.

Palanga - Vilniaus St. 10/16

** Senasis Rūsys (The Old Celler) - Garelio St. 10/16. One of the most popular restaurants in Vilnius; its ceiling is vaulted and it is decorated with original lamps, forged-metal fixtures and stained-glass windows.

Žemaičių Alinė (Žemaičių Beerhall) - Vokiečių St. 24

Around town:

** Draugystė (Friendship) - M. K. Čiurlionio St. 86 (In Hotel Draugystė)

Erfurtas - Architektų St. 19 (In the Lazdynai district). Separate from the main dining room is also the Erfurtas nightclub, one of the first in Lithuania.

Šaltinėlis - Žirmūnų St. 106 (In the Žirmūnų district). Also a nightclub.

** Vilnius - Gedimino St. 20

Žirmūnai - Žirmūnų St. 67 (In the Žirmūnų district.)

**Seklyčia - Hotel Lietuva, lower level. Try it for ethnic food.

**Panorama - Hotel Lietuva, 22nd floor

TV and Radio Tower bar - sip delicious but formidably potent kokteliai while you spin around town. Best view during the day--not much to see at night.

Cafes

Literatų Svetainė - Gedimino St. 1

Neringa - Gedimino St. 23 (In hotel Neringa)

Nykštukas Children's Cafe - P. Cvirkos 14

** Stiklių Cafe - near Garelio and Antokolskio Streets. This is one of the first privately-run eating establishments to have begun operating during perestroika. The locals say it is pleasant and Western visitors say it is very good.

Hotel Lietuva - Lobby and Outdoor Cafes

Lakštingala (The Nightingale) - Vingis Park

Night Clubs and Hard Currency Bars

Food is served in nightclubs. The programs are, for lack of a better term, amusing. Las Vegas-style dancing performed to loud disco and Lithuanian estradine (pop music) are standard fare.

Dainava - Vienuolio St. 4

Erfurtas - Architektų St. 19

Šaltinėlis - Žirmūnų St. 104

Šviesioji Salė (The Light Hall) - Hotel Lietuva

Juodasis Baras (The Black Bar) - Hotel Lietuva

WHERE TO SHOP

Foreign Currency Stores (Dolerinė)

The main foreign currency store in Vilnius is at Konarskio St. 17, tel. 63-79-02. Hours are USUALLY from 10am to 7pm Mondays through Saturdays, closed for lunch 2 to 3pm. It is wise to call ahead to make sure the store will be open. There are branches in Hotel Lietuva and in the Karolinškiu district (Merkurijus). Foreign currency stores apparently have opened in Kaunas and Klaipeda.

Among the things you can purchase at the dolerine are automobiles, electrical appliances, linens, clothing, alcoholic beverages, cigarettes, coffee, tea, amber, folk art objects, books and souvenirs. The limit on credit card purchases is 500 rubles (300 rubles on Mastercard). But only cash or travellers checks are accepted for imported electronic equipment.

Souvenir and Specialty Shops

Central Department Store - Ukmergés St. 16 (73-05-59)

Central Book Store - Gedimino St. 13 (62-16-09)

Records - Gedimino St. 33 and Vilniaus St. 17 (62-01-68)

Antiquariat Rare Book Store - Garelio St. 6 (62-95-10)

Tourist Book Store - Pilies St. 10 (61-63-81)

University Book Store - B. Sruogos St. 12 (61-34-60)

For Arts and Crafts:

Dailé - Gedimino St. 1 (61-38-27)
  - Cvirkos St. 5/13 (62-45-52)
  - Vokiečiu St. 2 (61-95-16)
  - Žydu St. 2 (61-40-01)

Klumpe - Antokolskio St. 6 (62-88-26)

Suvenyrai - Gedimino St. 31

Dailés Parodu Rūmai (Art Exhibition Palace) - Pilies St. 2

Unlike the Dailé and other smaller souvenir shops, this store carries original art works, as well as the mass-produced folk art and craft articles.

Confectionary:

Vilnius Central Foodstore - Gedimino St. 24

Svajonė Confectionary Shop - Gedimino St. 15

Confectionary Shop - Vokiečių St. 12

Best Buys

Amber, linen and folk handicrafts are high on the list of good buys. Art books are beautifully published as are photography books such as "Daina Lietuvai" (A Song to Lithuania) and "Vilniaus Architektūra" (The Architecture of Vilnius").

No permission is needed to take items bought in foreign currency stores out of the country, nor for mass-produced articles of craft art and souvenirs. KEEP receipts and DO NOT remove tags.

Permission is needed for: works of art, antiques, etchings, porcelain, ceramics, articles of wood or leather, precious and semiprecious stones, metalwork, original folk handicrafts, tapestries, rare books, manuscripts, musical instruments and other articles of artistic, historical, scientific or cultural value.

Permits to transport the above-mentioned items out of the country can be obtained by applying to the Lithuanian SSR Ministry of Culture's Artwork Control Department located at Basanavičiaus St. 20, tel. 61-63-81.

Items must be brought in to be documented and photographed. A service fee will be charged and an export permit will be issued. The permit and photographs must be presented at customs, and payment of the excise duty is to be made at this time. This sum equals the value of the article indicated on the permit.

GETTING AROUND

Moving about the city is relatively easy. You have your choice of busses, trolleys, or taxis. Coupons are required to ride the buses and trolleys and can be obtained at newspaper stands (kiosks) and in foodstores at the low price of 4 kopeks. The coupons are good for a single ride and must be inserted into the validating machine upon boarding. Buses and trolleys operate from 6am to 12:30-1am (depending on the route). Maps and route descriptions are sometimes available at newspaper kiosks.

The main bus station is at Sodų St. 22 (next to the train station), tel. 66-04-81. It is the only inter-city and local bus depot in Vilnius.

Taking the taxi is the simplest way of getting around. Private taxis, plenty of which have sprung up since the advent of perestroika, and state-owned cabs are inexpensive, costing approximately 1 ruble per 5 kilometers (watch the odometer if there is no fare meter). Note that the "express" taxis can be obtained without waiting, but cost two or three times the fares of regular taxis. To take a cab, wait at one of the taxi stands scattered throughout the city. Flagging down a taxi in the middle of the street is not easy. Here is a listing of centrally located taxi stands:

- Vienuolio St. 1 (near Gedimino St. and Hotel Neringa)
- Gediminas Square
- Didžioji St. 60 (Muzeum Square)
- Geležinkelio St. 10 (Train station)
- J. Paleckio St. 2 (near the Lietuva and Turistas hotels)
- Pylimo St. 21
- Pylimo St. 58 (near Hotel Gintaras)
- S. Konarskio St. 7
- Olandų St. 1 (near the Church of St. Peter and St. Paul)
- Partizánų St. 50
- Partizanų St. 74
- Subačiaus St. 62
- Ukmergės St. 12 (near the hotels Lietuva and Turistas)
- M. K. Čiurlionio St. 84 (near Hotel Draugystė)
- P. Eidukevičius St. (near the Sports Palace)

To order a taxi by phone call 77-29-29. Inquiries about taxi service can be directed to 77-48-88.

The Vilnius Railway Station is located at Geležinkelio St. 10. Call 63-00-86 for train information. To buy train tickets in advance go to the Ticket Sales Office, Aušros Vartų St. 69, tel. 62-30-44.

Vilnius' airport is five miles from the city center. Bus #2 serves this route; bus #1 runs from the airport to the train and bus stations. A minibus service is also available, as are taxis. There is an Intourist branch office at the airport.

The Aeroflot ticket office is located at Ukmergės St. 12, tel. 75-25-85. For airport information dial 63-02-01, 63-55-60 or 66-94-65.

GAS STATIONS (AZS)

AZS-1 3 Valakampių St.

AZS-2 44 Tarybų St.

AZS-3 18 Putnos St.

AZS-4 272 Raudonosios Armijos Ave.

AZS-6 at beginning of Vilnius-Minsk main road.

AZS-7 119 Raudonosios Armijos Ave.

AZS-8 4 Gegužės 1-osios St. Naujoi Vilnia

AZS-51 153 Dzeržinskio St.

FOR SERVICE AND REPAIR

Station #1: 217 Raudonosios Armijos Ave.

Station #2: 34 Eišiškių Highway

Station #3: 41a Kirtimų St.

Vilnius City Automobile Inspection: 20 Algirdo St.

TELEPHONES, TELEGRAMS AND POST OFFICES

If you wish to make a local call from a pay phone, deposit a 2 kopek coin, listen for the tone and then dial the number. When the party answers, wait for the coin to drop and then start speaking.

Calling overseas is very complex and costs approximately 6 rubles per minute for a call to the USA. It is NOT possible to dial direct. You can order a long-distance call through the Hotel Service Bureau (if there is one in your hotel) or by dialing 07.

USEFUL TELEPHONE NUMBERS:

Vilnius directory inquiries: 09

Long distance calls: 07

Long distance directory inquiries: 05

Telegram ordering by phone: 06

Long-distance telephone, postal and telegraph services are available at these locations:

The Central Post Office - Gedimino St. 9, tel. 62-54-68. The Post Office is open 8am-8pm M-F; telegraph and long distance calling service hours are from 8am to 10pm weekdays, 11am to 7pm weekends and holidays. (**As with everything, call ahead to confirm the hours of operation.)

Communications Center - Vilniaus St. 33, tel. 62-59-85. Post office hours are 9am-8pm M-F, 9am-5pm Sa-Su; long distance calling service is available around the clock (Hall A is open from midnight to 8am, Hall B from 8am to midnight); and the telegraph office is open 8am-11pm daily.

The Central Telegraph Office - Tallat-Kelpša St. 3

USEFUL ADRESSES AND TELEPHONE NUMBERS

Intourist - in Hotel Lietuva, Ukmergės St. 20, tel. 73-60-16

Vilnius Travel and Excursion Bureau: Ukmergės St. 1, tel. 75-20-40, and the Belfry Tower on Gediminas Square, tel. 61-24-26

Foreign Currency Exchange: USSR Bank For Foreign Trade, Totorių St. 1, Hours: 8:30am-12:30pm, M-F and at the Hotel Lietuva, Ukmergės St. 20, tel. 73-60-16. (Call for hours.)

To avoid problems, remember to exchange money before going to other cities in Lithuania.

City Information Bureau - Gedimino St. 54, tel. 62-64-24. Hours: open daily 8am-8pm.

The Tėviškė Society - Tilto Lane (skersgatvis) 8/2, tel. 61-35-80.

Tėviškė (Motherland) is an organization which fosters cultural relations with persons of Lithuanian decent residing outside of Lithuania and has its own newspaper "Gimtasis Kraštas" (Native land). It is possible to enlist Tėviškė's assistance in mailing books bought or received during your visit (to reduce the weight of your baggage), although you must pay the price of postage. Keep in mind the regulations governing transport of items out of the country.

PERSONAL SERVICES

Laundry, dry cleaning, hairdressing, tailoring, clothing repair, and other services can be obtained by inquiring at your hotel's front desk or Service Bureau office. Copying and translating services are available at Intourist offices.

WHERE TO TURN FOR HELP

Emergency Phone Numbers:

Fire: 01
Police (milicija): 02
Ambulance: 03
Auto accidents: 45-85-64

Lost property: 62-46-06 or 62-18-53

Hospitals, Pharmacies and Medical Attention

In case of a medical emergency, it is best to inquire at the hotel reception desk or call an ambulance. It is VERY IMPORTANT to bring with you any medication you regularly use, or may require, because medicines are NOT readily available here (not even something as simple as aspirin can be reliably obtained).

Centrally located pharmacies:

- Vilniaus St. 22
- Lenin Prospect 27 (on duty 24 hrs.)
- Didžioji St. 63

DAY TRIPS

The following day trips through the Lithuanian countryside are a must for travelers to Vilnius, as many treasures lie within a few hours of the city. Prior to the 1980's, tourists were generally confined to urban centers. Glimpses of village life were only available through carefully prearranged tours. Travel is somewhat less restrictive these days, so take advantage and check out one of the following areas, each easily accomplished in one day.

These trips are easiest for those travelers who have access to a car, or by bicycle. Be sure to bring all of your personal documents with you. While officials in Vilnius may encourage you to set out on your own, local officials may request some kind of identification. Take only the valuables you will need - leave the rest in your hotel room. Cars - especially Western models - are a curiosity in the countryside. Adequate maps aren't always readily available, but bookstores in Vilnius or Kaunas will usually have something in stock.

Wooden folk sculptures are scattered throughout the countryside

Dzūkijas's Villages

This trip will take you into the heart of Lithuania's song country. The dzūkai (residents of Dzūkija) have a distinct dialect and love to sing. Head west out of Vilnius, following Raudonosios Armijos prospekt. Follow signs to Druskininkai, the capital of the region, which is also a popular resort town. The road soon enters dense forests and the famed Dzūkija sands come into view. This sandy region offers ideal places for a picnic beneath the towering pines.

About an hour into the trip, watch for signs to Merkinė, the historic stronghold of princes on the Nemunas River. Founded in the 12th century, one of the main attractions in Merkinė is the castle hill which overlooks the Nemunas. The first Lithuanian fort was built on this hill as early as 1377. The view is exquisite. The beautiful church in town is thought to have been built by Grand Duke Jogaila in 1388, when he christened Lithuania.

From Merkinė you can head out into the forests of Dzūkija, and happen upon one of the area's forest villages, where an entire village might be situated in a grove of pines. A word of caution: road conditions are spartan. Forest villages and other small townships in the area are representative of an older, simpler village lifestyle. Most homes do not have plumbing, a few even lack electricity. But a warm smile to the locals, and a polite request to pose for a picture may just be enough to get you invited into their homes for a taste of the local moonshine - samagonas.

Heading back to Vilnius along the Druskininkai-Vilnius road, turn off into Perloja, which is 30 minutes from Vilnius. Here you will find one of the few remaining statues of Vytautas the Great, built in the independence period. This impressive monument draws patriots from all over eastern Lithuania. Wedding parties are a common sight here, showing a respect for history on such a joyous occasion.

The Castle Road

Leave Vilnius via the Kaunas road, which follows the Nemunas River along some of its widest, and most breathtaking points. From Kaunas follow the signs to Jurbarkas. You will be driving on the right (northern) bank of the Nemunas River, which formed the boundary between the Grand Duchy of Lithuania and the territory controlled by the Teutonic Knights in the 15th century. The well-fortified castles on the cliffs were controlled off and on by both powers. The castles remaining today have been rebuilt through the centuries.

About 15 km. from Kaunas you will find the Raudondvaris ruins. The castle is open at strange times, and renovation seems to be an on-going, constant situation. A friendly smile, and a few words in English will probably get you into the castle even if it is closed when you arrive.

Your next stop is Veliuona, some 45 km. from Raudondvaris. This is home to another rare statue of Vytautas the Great. Though smaller and more modest than that in Perloja, it nonetheless attests to the pride locals have for the famed Lithuanian ruler. Drive into the village, which sits on a beautiful bluff overlooking the river. This is a great spot for picture taking, as the Nemunas valley is at its most majestic at this point.

A few minutes drive from here is the castle at Raudoné. It, too, is undergoing renovation. But the adventurous and polite tourist will be able to climb into the impressive towers of the castle for a fantastic view of the surrounding countryside. The castle is believed to stand on foundations first laid in the 1340's. In the 1600's a stone fortification was erected, and the towers are part of that construction. During the First World War, the castle served as a German concentration camp. During the independence years, it was to be the summer residence of the Lithuanian Republic's president, but the Second World War ended those plans.

From here you can head into Jurbarkas, a medium sized town, where you can get a bite to eat at a number of small establishments. To return to Vilnius you can retrace the castle route. Another option is to head south to Vilkaviškis, in the Suvalkija region, then east to Kaunas and on to the capital. Be advised that you will be near the Kaliningrad District, formerly Prussia. This area is highly restricted to foreigners, so think twice before heading into this district. Although the old German architecture still standing in this region is fascinating, its not worth the trade-off of encountering irate Russian militia.

Žemaitija

This is a slightly longer trip than the previous two, but for the folk culture enthusiast, it is a must. From Vilnius, follow the signs to Ukmergė and Panevėžys, then turn west to Šiauliai. Be sure to stop at the Hill of Crosses north of the city. (See Šiauliai section for details.) Heading west, follow the signs to Telšiai and Plungė, the capitals of the Žemaitija region. After passing Plungė, watch for signs to Salantai. It will take about 2 hours to reach this point.

On the road to Salantai, watch for a small rise in the fields to your right (east). Immediately before entering the town, you will see a grove of trees to the east. This is the locally famous Orvydų Sodyba

(Garden of Orvydai). A small access road brings you to the site.
Park near the grove and enter the garden.

This garden is in fact a fantastic collection of woodcarvings and
sculptures occupying an area roughly the size of a town square. The
Orvydas family began working on the pieces immediately after the
Soviet occupation of Lithuania, and since then have created a
wonderland of imagination.

You will pass under low archways formed by strategically placed
fallen trees, squeeze between huge boulders to examine small huts
where every corner is adorned by several woodcarvings and
sculptures. A swing hangs over a green grotto, a carving of Jesus
stares out from a bush, a small room is carved out of a thick tree
base. Its almost impossible to count the works of art exhibited
here, but you may well want to try!

It is worth noting that the Orvydas family has suffered persecution
under the Soviet regime for their individuality and carving of
religious sculptures. Today, however, Mr. Orvydas is a prospering
local businessman, producing custom stone sculptures and
gravestones. His workshop is behind the garden.

Continuing north from Salantai, you will reach Mosėdis. Here you
will find the Akmenų muziejus (Rock museum), which demonstrates the
local tradition of keeping rock gardens. The outdoor Rock museum is
on the north side of this beautifully maintained town. The focus of
the museum is a pit dubbed the crater. According to the creator, you
can enter only after "forgetting the usual". The locals believe that
the obelisk in the middle of the crater is a monument to the
Lithuanian partisans, who resisted the Red Army from 1944 to the
1950's. This locale saw a great deal of partisan activity in the
post-war years, and several partisans are known to be buried in the
area. Although there is no proof as to the meaning of the obelisk,
this remains an appropriate place to honor the memory of the valiant
freedom fighters.

You can return to Vilnius by back-tracking along the same route. The
quickest route back to the capital is accomplished by heading south
to the port city of Klaipėda. From there it is less than 3 hours to
Vilnius via the new highway.

DRUSKININKAI

Located in the south of Lithuania on the banks of the Nemunas river
among scenic pine forests is Druskininkai, a well known Lithuanian
spa. It began its career as a health resort as early as 1837, when

Girios aidas - The Echo of the Forest, Druskininkai

the salty mineral waters of the springs were investigated and found to have curative properties. (The Lithuanian word for salt is "druska", hence the name of the spa.) The city has nine sanatoriums which can accomodate 4,000 people at one time.

Druskininkai takes pride in being the home of Mikalojus Konstantinas Ciurlionis (1875-1911). Although he was actually born in nearby Varéna, the painter and composer spent his childhood here, drawing aesthetic inspiration from the folksongs, legends and tales of the Dzūkija region. His family lived in the house at M. K. Ciurlionis St. 41, where there is a memorial museum to the artist. During the summer chamber music and piano concerts are given in the garden. A monument to Ciurlionis also stands in a small square at the end of Kirov St.

Do not miss Saulés Takas (The Sun Path), a beautiful nature trail winding through the nearby pine forests along the Ratnyčia brook to an old water mill in Jaskoniu village. The 3.5 mile route originates in the health park of the spa near the Palace of Health. As you follow the path note the arbors and whimsical cottages made of branches as well as their carved wooden benches. The air is pure and fragrant.

Girios Aidas (The Echo of the Forest) is an imposing three story wooden house that stands on a single supporting pedestal. The rooms are finished in different varieties of wood: oak, birch, pine and fir. Local foresters have established a Museum of Forestry here which acquaints the visitor with this occupation and its tools.

The three carved columns near the Girios Aidas are part of the M. K. Ciurlionio Road running from Varéna to Druskininkai. On the 100th anniversary of Ciurlionis' birth, folk art masters carved more than 20 wooden columns depicting scenes from the great artist's life and set them up along the road. They are a beautiful monument to one of Lithuania's greatest artists.

The picturesque surroundings of Druskininkai, its clear lakes, extensive wetlands, fragrant woodlands and historic castle hills make this one of the most attractive holiday destinations in all of Lithuania. And nowhere can a mushroom lover find so many mushrooms as in the forests of southern Lithuania.

ŠIAULIAI

Šiauliai (sometimes known as Saulés miestas, or city of the sun) in northwestern Lithuania is the country's fourth largest city with a population of 143,000. Although there is some evidence that a settlement may have existed here 2500 years ago, historical chronicles date its founding to 1236 A.D., when Lithuanians routed the invading Knights of the Livonian Order in the Battle of Saulė (sun). Unfortunately most of Siauliai was destroyed in the great fire of 1872, and has been rebuilt since then. To celebrate the 750th birthday of Siauliai, the statue Saulys (Golden Archer) by sculptor Kuzma was constructed on a central column and since then functions as a sundial in the city square. The Battle of Saulė is commemorated in a stained glass panel inside one of the city's movie theaters.

Siauliai boasts of an old pedestrian mall, Vilniaus St., where one finds the Art Exhibition Hall, Clock Tower Square (a favorite meeting place) and the Museum of Photography.

The Church of St. Peter and Paul was built during the late 16th and early 17th centuries and is an important monument of the Lithuanian Renaissance period. The building is finished in white plaster and has one of the highest spires (210 ft.) in Lithuania. As is apparent from the small gunports, the building also served a defensive function. The church's interior is characterized by a long nave and rich Renaissance decorations.

The Church of St. George was built in 1909 by the Tsarist government for the Russian army's troops stationed in Siauliai. After the war the church was taken over by the Catholic Church of Lithuania. In 1976 a fire almost destroyed the building and the underground periodical"Chronicles of the Lithuanian Catholic Church" got word out to the West that firemen purposely did not attempt to put out the fire properly. After a large outcry both in Siauliai and in the Lithuanian emigre communities, the Soviet government restored the church. The architecture of the building is Russian Byzantine with a tower and an onion dome.

Siauliai is the home of a teacher's college and a branch of the Kaunas Polytechnical Institute. Its industry produces TV sets, precision lathes, personal computers and bicycles. The city hosts a bicycle festival yearly in late May.

Hill of Crosses

Six miles north of Siauliai on the road to Meskuciai stands the Hill of Crosses, one of the most revered shrines in the country for Lithuanian Catholics. The hill, which earlier accommodated a defensive fortification, is covered by a multitude of crosses planted into the ground by local believers. After the Soviet occupation, numerous attempts were made by the government to destroy this symbol of Christian prayer.

Crosses (many of them valuable examples of folk art) were torn down and burned, but they sprouted up again and again. The last major attempt at leveling the shrine was in 1975. Since then, Lithuanian believers have placed thousands upon thousands of crosses on the hill. Newlyweds often come here after their wedding ceremony to ask for God's blessing. It is customary for any visitor to the Hill of Crosses to leave behind a cross and a prayer. The eerie atmosphere of this holy place draws thousands of believers and pilgrims each year, but is also well worth a side trip by the casual traveler.

PANEVĖŽYS

Situated in northern Lithuania on the river Nevėžis, Panevėžys is a smaller and younger Lithuanian city primarily famous for its Drama Theater. Founded in 1940, the widely acclaimed theater was long headed by director Juozas Miltinis. Its performances often attract audiences from as far away as Leningrad and Moscow.

Panevėžys is primarily an industrial city producing cathode-ray tubes, cables, compressors and glass. The largest linen textile mill of the Baltic states is located here.

The local museum has a large collection of insects and butterflies as well as an extensive exhibit of coins and metals.

ANYKŠČIAI

Anykščiai lies at the confluence of the Anykšta and Šventoji Rivers in a beautiful corner of Lithuania directly north of Vilnius. Its picture-perfect forests and river banks, scenic brooks and historical monuments draw thousands of visitors each year. Anykščiai was renowned for its fruit wines, although Gorbachev's anti-drinking campaign forced local management to convert production to fruit juices. Anykščiai was immortalized by the 19th century Lithuanian poet A. Baranauskas in "Anykščių šilelis" (The Forest of Anykščiai).

Anykščiai is probably best known as the home of some of the most prominent authors of Lithuania. Visit the homestead and final resting place of A. Vienuolis-Žukauskas (1882-1957), a short-story writer. One of his most famous stories, "Paskenduolė" depicts the tragic fate of a young girl whose lover leaves for America to seek his fortune and leaves her with child. In "Paskenduolė" Vienuolis achieved a masterpiece of the Lithuanian language. Inside the house is a memorial museum to Vienuolis and Baranauskas and nearby is the simple kletele (barn), where "Anykščių šilelis" was written.

Home of writer Jonas Biliūnas in Niūronys, a village near Anykščiai

Near Anykščiai is the Liūdiškiu castle hill where another prominent Lithuanian author, Jonas Biliūnas (1879-1907), is buried. Biliūnas' lyrical short stories are beautifully written and philosophical. Few children in Lithuania can forget Biliūnas' tale of a little boy, who dreams of becoming a brave hunter and then kills a cat with his bow and arrow, but suffers deep pangs of remorse. The writer's birthplace is nearby in the quaint village of Niūronys, where the traveller can visit a small memorial museum.

But Anykščiai is not only a must for literature lovers. The scenic countryside with its small villages and their friendly inhabitants makes the trip unforgettable for everyone.

TRAKAI

Trakai, the medieval capital of Lithuania is nestled in a beautiful region of lakes, forests and hills 18 miles southwest of Vilnius. Once the stronghold and residence of the Grand Dukes of Lithuania, it serves now as a magnificent monument to the past glory of the medieval Lithuanian state. The complex of defensive works and castle stands on a peninsula and an island.

Trakai - on the shores of Lake Galvė

In the town park of Trakai (located on a peninsula), you can see the ruins of the old castle, presumably built by Gediminas' son, Duke Kęstutis, between 1362 and 1382. This castle was repeatedly attacked by the German Order, and in response to intensifying aggression, Grand Duke Vytautas constructed another fortress a short distance away on an island of Lake Galvė. The latter stronghold (completed towards the end of the 14th century) was larger and in a more easily-defensible location.

To reach the island castle (impressively restored in recent decades), cross the first bridge from the peninsula to the small Karaimų (Karaite) islet, and then continue on the bridge linking it to the Castle island itself. You will enter a large courtyard past the main gates which is surrounded by high walls with round towers in the corners. This courtyard is separated from the main building by a moat which is crossed by a bridge (formerly a drawbridge). The main ensemble consists of a watchtower, which is 100 ft. high, and two three-story structures which served as the residence of the royal family. Guests were received in the large vaulted hall located in the right wing. The Trakų History Museum is now housed in the main rooms. From the observation points and windows of the castle the visitor has a fine view of the surrounding landscape: crystal-clear lakes dotted with islands and rolling hills in the distance.

Trakai is a small town consisting of old wooden buildings and some modern structures. Melnikaitės St. (Vytauto-Melnikaitės St. is the main axis road of Trakai) is notable for the wooden houses built by the Karaites, a tribe of Turkic people who were brought to Lithuania by Grand Duke Vytautas in the late 14th century and served as bodyguards to the dukes. A kinessa, an active house of prayer of the Karaites, is located here as well as the Ethnography Museum of the Karaites (Melnikaites St. 22).

International boating events, such as the rowing competitions for the Amber Oars Prize, take place in the Trakai region. There is also a training school for rowing and canoeing as well as two water sports centers on Lake Galvė.

There are various ways of getting there. Electric trains run daily from Vilnius Train Station to Trakai several times a day. Call 63-00-44 in advance for train schedules and other information.

Buses depart daily from Vilnius' main bus depot to Trakai approximately every 40 minutes, starting at 5:30 am. The number to call for schedule information is 66-04-81.

By car take Raudonosios Armijos (Red Army) Prospect southwest to Galvės St., which leads to the Vilnius-Trakai highway.

The inner courtyard of Trakų Castle

A typical farmhouse

RUMSISKES

On the scenic shores of the man-made Kaunas Sea (Kauno Marios), about 50 miles west of Vilnius, is the small town of Rumšiškės. The original site of the town lies at the bottom of the Kaunas Sea, flooded when the Kaunas hydro-electric power plant was built. Rumšiškės was then relocated to a picturesque site near a forest on the highest terrace of the Nemunas banks. The modest church and bell tower of Rumšiškės are well-known having appeared in many photographs and travel brochures ever since the years of independence. Unfortunately the church lost some of the original folk wood carvings in the move. Rumšiškės is the administrative center of the Kaišiadoriu district and a collective farm.

Situated next to the town is the impressive open-air museum of 18th-20th century Lithuanian peasant life. Although Lithuania is a small country, it is rich in its regional folk culture. The country is divided into four ethnographic regions, each with quite distinct customs: Žemaitija (Lowlands), Aukštaitija (Highlands), Dzūkija and Sūduva. Appropriately enough, the museum groups its exhibits according to these four ethnographic regions.

Typical country structures were brought to Rumšiškės from all over Lithuania. Entire farmsteads and fragments of villages have been recreated to form a truly representational exhibit of Lithuanian country life.

You could begin your tour of Rumšiškės with the 19th century farmstead of a poor peasant from Dzūkija, which lies in a scenic valley. From here proceed to its neighbor, the farm of a moderately-prosperous peasant from Aukštaitija, followed by buildings of the Sūduva region. Further on stand farmhouses of poor, average and rich farmers of the Žemaitija region. In this section there is a numas, a dwelling structure of the type which was used as early as the Bronze Age. When Lithuanians advanced to log houses, the numas survived only in Žemaitija as an auxiliary building.

During the summer a folk song and theater troupe gives performances which often involve audience participation. Afterwards, you may wish to sample Lithuanian fare in the old-fashioned inn.

Rumšiškės' farm tools, furniture, the colors and patterns of woven fabrics and folk dress, the folk songs of Lithuania and much, much more recreate the country's rural life the way it was lived many generations ago.

A forester's cabin

Windmill

KERNAVĖ

For those with an archeological bent, a brief visit to Kernavė (40 miles north of Vilnius) would be recommended. A few years ago locals working in the fields near the town of Kernavė quite unexpectedly came upon fragments of a long-forgotten medieval town. Historians were aware of the existence of the Kernavė castle ruins on the nearby castle hill, but little suspected that a town had flourished a short distance away.

Archeological work began in 1987 and to date has uncovered a surprisingly rich cache of medieval weaponry, coins and household items. A general outline of a fair-sized town of perhaps over 10,000 inhabitants is emerging. Portions of wooden houses have been brought to light as well as much of the foundations of the structures.

Archeologists estimate that decades of digging remain to uncover the entire town. But, in the meantime, plans are afoot to restore the former buildings to their original state and recreate Kernavė as a national monument.

THE BALTIC COAST

Klaipėda

The third largest city in Lithuania, Klaipėda (Memel in German) is an important port on the Baltic Sea. The Klaipėda region, long inhabited by Baltic-speaking people, was seized by the Livonian Order in 1252. The invaders quickly built a fort near the Dane River, which runs through Klaipėda today, and successfully resisted all further Lithuanian attempts to regain the territory. From that time Klaipėda remained subject to various forms of German-speaking authority for almost 700 years. In the 19th century the town became an important timber port, receiving and processing timber products from as far away as Byelorussia and the Ukraine.

In 1923, Lithuania recaptured the city of Klaipėda and its hinterland in a bold coup. German claims to Klaipėda, however, resurfaced in a virulent form soon after Hitler's advent to power in 1933 and played a major role in keeping German-Lithuanian relations strained right up to the outbreak of World War II. Agitation by the local German-speaking population (generously supported by the Nazi regime) provided a useful pretext for Berlin's annexation of Klaipėda in 1939. It followed German occupation of Czechoslovakia, and hence was Hitler's last land-grab before the outbreak of World War II.

The Baltic coast

The city suffered tremendously during the war, for it served as a German submarine base and came under severe Soviet attack towards the end of the war. When Soviet troops finally seized Klaipėda, they reportedly found only 8 of the original inhabitants of the city still living, since most of the local population had been evacuated to Germany.

Since the war Lithuania's port city experienced dramatic growth, attracting tens of thousands of inhabitants from the surrounding rural communities of Žemaitija (Samogitia) and parts of the Soviet Union. Today Klaipėda has a population of over 200,000, of which 61% is ethnic Lithuanian. Half of the population is in some way dependent on the sea for its livelihood. The city is a busy merchant as well as fishing port with shipbuilding and repair facilities. There are fish processing plants, canning factories as well as 2 textile enterprises, a pulp and paper mill and a plant producing dry cells. Klaipėda's importance for the East bloc increased in the fall of 1986 with the opening of the Klaipėda-Mukran (East Germany) rail ferry. Once the ferry is fully operational, it will engage 5 ships, each carrying about 100 railroad cars, and provide a much cheaper and faster trade link with East Germany.

Despite its turbulent history, Klaipeda still retains considerable charm, with much of its old quarter (bearing distinct reminders of the city's German influences) carefully restored since the end of the War. The old town, with its narrow streets, merchant houses, and remnants of medieval fortifications, generally lies on the left bank of the Danės River nearest to the Kuršių Marios coast. A number of attractive shops, cafes and restaurants are housed in the old structures.

Dominating the old quarter is the Protestant Church of Saint George, which stands on Turgaus (Market) square. St. George's was built in 1696 and has a spire well over 200 feet high. A short distance away is the Klaipėda theater, which was built in 1819 in the neo-Classical style. In the 19th century the theater hosted a number of luminaries (including Wagner) who would stop by in Klaipėda on their way from Germany to Russia.

Klaipėda is also known for its venerable "Fachwerk" warehouses that date from centuries past, but now have been converted to other uses. In fact, in the 18th century Klaipėda was known as the city of warehouses. The largest of these, a fish warehouse over 60 feet high (located on Aukštosios Street), recently underwent restoration work and now serves as an exhibition hall. Restoration work is proceeding on several warehouses on Daržų Street which are interesting for their peculiarly indented roofs.

In restoring the older structures efforts are being made to retain their original functions where possible. The neo-Gothic post office on Gorkio Street (completed in 1896) still serves as a post office. Its 40 musical chimes are being readied to play again just as they did at the turn of the century.

Klaipėda also has a number of museums worth a brief visit. The Art Museum (Gorkio Street 39) opened its doors to the public only in 1975, but it houses a respectable collection of East and West European artists dating back to the 16th century. Among the museum's better exhibits are those of Russian artists from the 19th and 20th centuries. After viewing the interior of the museum, step outside for a view of the sculpture garden.

The Sea Museum and Aquarium on Herkus Manto Street, which incorporates fragments of the town's old defensive works, includes displays of navigational equipment and a sizable collection of sea shells.

The Ethnographic Museum (Gorkio Street 7) accommodates over 17,000 exhibits, ranging from amber to 17th century coins to antique household items. There is also a Museum of Folk Art at Pakalnės Street #6.

After taking in a whole day of sightseeing, you may wish to try supper in the Meridian Restaurant, which is housed in an old sailing vessel permanently moored in the Danes River next to the main bridge.

Palanga

A vacation resort 18 miles north of Klaipėda, Palanga has excellent white sand beaches which had already gained popularity at the beginning of the 19th century. It receives plentiful sun and steady, cooling sea breezes. The air is fragrant with pine and salt from the sea. Unfortunately, these attributes are the cause of one of Palanga's chief drawbacks: the resort tends to be over-crowded in the peak season.

The old section of town is known for its charming wooden bungalows and tree-lined streets. Palanga is also renowned for its numerous sculptures. The Jūrate and Kastytis sculpture by N. Gaigalaitė is especially beloved. It is based on the tale about the sea goddess, Jūrate, and the fearless fisherman, Kastytis, whose love for each other invoked the wrath of the god of Thunder, Perkūnas.

Legend says that Birutės Kalnas (Birutes Hill), one of the area's higher sand dunes, was once a Lithuanian pagan shrine where vestal virgins tended the holy flame. Kęstutis, Grand Duke of Lithuania in the 14th century, fell in love with one of the vestal virgins,

Jūrate and Kastytis sculpture by N. Gaigalaité

A cottage in Palanga

Birutė, and had her kidnapped so he could marry her. Interestingly, historical records confirm that the wife of Kęstutis was indeed named Birutė. Atop Birutės Hill stands an octagonal red brick chapel designed by German architect K. Mayer and built in 1869.

Palanga was first mentioned in historical documents in 1161 and is thus one of the oldest towns in Lithuania. During the 13th century it was caught in the crossfire of the battles between the Knights of the Sword and the Teutonic Knights, both of which wanted to control the Baltic coast. The Swedes also attacked the coast many times in the late Middle Ages and Palanga suffered from various epidemics as well as other disasters.

When Klaipėda fell under German rule in 1939, Palanga substituted for Lithuania's chief port, hosting ships from England, Holland, Denmark and Sweden.

But over the years, trade gave way to recreation. The only reminder of the busy port is the long wooden pier extending out to sea from the beach. It is one of Palanga's best-known landmarks. Walking along the pier in the evening, one has an unforgettable view of the sun setting into the sea, casting a golden glow on the white beaches, dunes and pine forests of the coastland.

Also worth a visit is the artistically landscaped Botanical Park, which was established in the 19th century and numbers among its exhibits over 200 types of plants. It is one of the most beautiful parks in Lithuania. Nestled inside the park is the Museum of Amber, which is located in a neo-Renaissance palace, the former residence of the noble Tyszkiewicz family. The museum exhibits a complete history of this "Lithuanian gold", including extraordinarily large pieces of amber and some containing fossilized insects from millions of years ago. Ancient amber jewelry and modern-day decorations are also on display. The sculpture, "Eglė, Queen of the Serpents", by R. Antinis stands outside on the park grounds.

In addition to sun, sand and surf, Palanga also features amusement parks, concerts, festivals, and art shows.

NERINGA

Lofty sandy dunes stretching along the Baltic coast, quaint fishing villages, and verdant pine forests characterize Neringa, a narrow sandy peninsula separating the Kuršiu Marios from the Baltic Sea. Neringa was formed over the last 5,000 years, as sand grains slowly accumulated in the shallower waters along the coast.

Three sisters - a sculpture in Šventoji on the Baltic coast

In the 16th-17th centuries large portions of Neringa's forests were felled by the axe, thereby severely disrupting the delicate ecosystem. Severe sand shifting resulted, as the surrounding dunes were deprived of natural protection against the harsh Baltic winds.

The remaining woods were buried and fourteen entire villages were swallowed up by the relentlessly moving sands. In the 18th century a reforestation project was launched to help save life on the spit.

Neringa is between 400 and 4000 yards in width along its nearly 60 mile-length. There is a 30 mile road linking the northern tip of the spit nearest Klaipėda to the Nida settlement in the southern end. Access to the peninsula, however, is restricted because of ecological concerns. Visitors must obtain an entry in Klaipėda and then take a ferry across to Smiltyne, the northernmost village of Neringa. Here you can view ruins of an 18th century fortress which once protected the approaches to Klaipėda.

The next village on the main road is Juodkrantė, one of the oldest settlements in Neringa, first mentioned in early 16th century. Juodkrantė boasts of the most beautiful forest on the spit. Moose, wild boar, deer and many types of birds make this forest their home. The Raganų (Witches') Hill in the vicinity of Juodkrantė is famous for its unusual exhibit of wood sculpture.

Just before reaching Neringa itself you will pass the fishing village of Preila, which comprises a whole of 30 houses. The settlement of Nida is the center of Neringa's tourist area. As one of the most popular resort areas in Lithuania, it is understandably crowded with visitors from early Spring to late Fall. Thomas Mann, the eminent German writer, made Nida his summer home in the 30's. A modest museum has been established in his house.

A half-mile to the South lies the Tylos (Serenity) valley. This is one of the most charming spots on the entire peninsula.

KAUNAS

Kaunas, the second largest city in Lithuania, is an important industrial and educational center. It is located 60 miles west of Vilnius at the confluence of Lithuania's two largest rivers, the Nemunas and the Neris. Part of the city lies in the valley formed by these rivers, and the rest of it spreads up onto a hilly terrace about 200 ft. in height.

The population of Kaunas is 425,000, the majority of which (89%) is Lithuanian. Thus, unlike Vilnius, Russian is seldom heard and the city has a definite Lithuanian ambience. Kaunas also has a country-wide reputation (especially in Vilnius, its chief rival) as a city of "kombinatoriai", i.e., of individuals adept at obtaining scarce material goods through sale, barter or even occasionally dubious means. Its residents enjoy a relatively high standard of living and like to point out that Kaunas has one of the highest rates of car ownership in the Soviet Union.

Understandably, perestroika, particularly its free enterprise aspects, found a ready response among area residents. As of late March, 1989, Kaunas had 635 registered cooperatives with a membership of over 10,000 local inhabitants. Many of the members have joined the "Kaunas" cooperative association, whose newspaper "Bendrija" (The Association) has become the national publication for all of Lithuania's cooperative groupings.

Kaunas also prides itself as the home of the renowned basketball team Žalgiris, winner of the 1986 European Championship and several times champion of the Soviet Union. Four of the team's players (along with an Estonian) made up the core of the gold medalist Soviet basketball team in the 1988 Olympic games in Seoul.

History

Although Kaunas first appears in written history in 1361, when the castle on the confluence of Nemunas and Neris is mentioned in the chronicles of the Crusaders, some archeological findings date inhabitation of the territory as early as several centuries B.C.

The town grew around the castle and in 1408 acquired the Magdeburg charter, which guaranteed the townspeople's self-rule. Kaunas expanded especially quickly in the 15-16th centuries and, because it was an important river port (the largest customs branch of Lithuania was located here), trade blossomed and the city became a commercial link between Poland, Lithuania and Russia. Also, the Hanseatic League established an office in Kaunas.

During the 17th century the city's importance drastically declined. Wars and the plague depleted the population, fires destroyed the buildings and enemies plundered the city. Kaunas passed to the Russians in 1795. The Tsarist government tried to turn the city into a stronghold on the western frontier of the empire, but that proved ineffective against the German invasion during World War I.

When Poland occupied Vilnius, the traditional capital of Lithuania in 1920, Kaunas became the seat of government of the independent republic (the "provisional capital", as Lithuanians insisted on calling it). Despite its provisional character, it remained Lithuania's defacto capital until 1940 and advanced rapidly.

Today Kaunas is the chief industrial city of Lithuania, specializing in machinery, textiles, furniture and food products. It is also important as a center of applied research in technical sciences. The largest institution of higher education is the Kaunas Polytechnical Institute. Although Lithuania's second city lags behind the capital in its cultural and educational infrastructure, Kaunas has recently been working towards re-establishing its own full-fledged university.

The Old Town - Points of Interest

Right at the conflux of the Nemunas and Neris are the ruins of Kaunas Castle. The castle was built in the 11th century, much earlier than the 1361 date it was first mentioned in historical documents. Its walls were once 27 ft. high and 10-1/2 ft. thick, with four defense towers at the corners. After the Battle of Žalgiris (Gruenwald) in 1410, the castle lost its strategic importance. Nonetheless, the ruins remind one of a stormy past. There is a small branch of the History Museum in the restored tower. Nearby is the sculpture "Kanklininkas" (The Psalter Player) by R. Antinis, Sr. The view overlooking the rivers is pretty.

The large Church of St. George and adjacent former Bernadine monastery stand next to the castle ruins. The Gothic building with tall, narrow, arched windows was first built between 1471 and 1500, and then rebuilt in the 17th century after several fires severely damaged it. During the years of independence, it functioned as a seminary church. The interior is Baroque.

Ruins of Kaunas Castle

106

After the Soviet occupation, the church fell into disrepair and was used as a repository for the library and various archives of the seminary. Later the building underwent partial repairs, but the books and archives were taken to a paper mill and consumed as waste. Still later, St. George's was turned into a warehouse for medical supplies. The white monastery buildings next to the church are today used as a medical school.

Proceeding on Trakų street, the next architectural complex to come into view is the Church of the Holy Trinity (Rotušės Square 22) and the former Bernadine monastery (Trakų St. 1a). Surrounded by a stone wall, the ensemble was built in the 17th century and today houses the only functioning seminary in Lithuania.

The church is late Renaissance with strong Gothic attributes, although the interior was once richly decorated in the Rococo style. This church also testifies to the brutal treatment the Church was subjected to under the Soviet occupation. In 1963, the church was closed and converted into a dance studio, while the building markedly deteriorated. During the 80's the church was returned to the seminary and restoration work commenced.

The former monastery was built in 1634, also in the Renaissance style with arched windows and niches. Construction was financed by A. Masalskis, a Kaunas marshal.

The next stop is Rotušės (town hall) Square, whose dominating feature is the 18th century Town Hall. It has an elegant tower made up of five levels, with each segment progressively smaller and more ornate than the one below it. Owing to its bright white color, it is sometimes referred to as the White Swan.

In 1838 the interior was remodeled and the building became a temporary residence for the tsars, serving as a stopping place for their travels abroad. During the late 1960's, the Town Hall was restored and today houses the Wedding Palace and Ceramics Museum.

The following buildings are found on Rotušės square:

No. 1 - House of Photography. Home of the Kaunas branch of the Lithuanian Photographic Society.

No. 2-3 - Gildija restaurant and cafe.

No. 7-9 - The Adam Mickiewicz Middle School, formerly a Jesuit monastery and college. Between 1819 and 1823 the poet Mickiewicz lived and taught here. There is a small memorial museum inside. A professional technical school is also housed in this ensemble.

Rotušes - Town Hall in Kaunas

No. 8 - Church of St. Francis. Formerly a Jesuit church built in the Baroque style, the church is now closed and the building is used by the technical school.

No. 10 - Medžiotojų užeiga (Hunters Inn). Formerly the home of the aristocratic Zabiello family and a favorite haunt of Adam Mickiewicz.

No.13 - The Maironis Museum of Lithuanian Literature. The building was constructed in the 17th century by the chancellor of Lithuania, Kristupas Žygimantas Pacas (1621-1684). In the 18th century Count Chrapovick added the neo-Classical, four column portal. From 1910 to 1932 the great Lithuanian poet, J. Mačiulis-Maironis, lived in this house. A memorial statue to Maironis stands in front of the museum.

No. 27 - The Dailė souvenir shop, considered to be the best and largest retail outlet for folk handicrafts in Lithuania.

In the north-eastern corner of the square stands an enormous Gothic structure, the Basilica of Kaunas. It is believed that construction of the building started during the rule of Vytautas the Great, in approximately 1408-1413. Reconstruction took place many times over the 15th and 16th centuries and the 165 ft. tower was added in the 17th century. The basilica was last reconstructed in the early 1900's. It is the largest Gothic building in Lithuania.

The three-nave interior is characterized by the ornate and dynamic late Baroque style, especially evident in the nine altars, of which the most impressive is in the left nave. The vaults in the sacristy date from the late 16th century.

Outside, on the southern side of the church facing Vilniaus St., is the granite tomb of the poet Maironis. (Vilniaus St. leads to Laisvės Alėja, the main artery of the modern city center.)

A store sign in Kaunas

A street in Old Town Kaunas

To continue the Old Town tour, cross the square and take Aleksoto St. toward the river Nemunas. At No. 6 is a small Gothic structure of red brick, known as the House of Perkūnas. Legend has it that a pagan temple to Perkūnas (the god of thunder) existed on this site before Lithuania adopted Christianity. The building was constructed in the 15th century to house commercial administrative offices. Five graceful pinnacles, interwoven arches and a stylized flame composition make up the facade's focal center. The statue "Perkūnas" (sculptor R. Antinis, Jr.) looks down upon visitors from the yard. A museum of architectural restoration and archeology is found inside the house.

Directly on the shores of the Nemunas (Aleksoto St. 1) is one of the first brick buildings built in Kaunas. The Church of Vytautas was built in approximately 1399 by Vytautas the Great. Supposedly he built the church when King Jogaila, his cousin and political rival, finally recognized him as the ruler of Lithuania. Another version is that he commissioned its construction as thanksgiving for his successful escape during a battle against the Tartars. Since then, the building underwent reconstruction many times.

Narrow arched windows, an octagonal tower and red brick walls supported by buttresses form a harmonious Gothic facade. The interior is split into three naves by four pillars on which the vaults rest. Among the artistic details inside is a 17th century painting "Christ Crucified", by Pranciskus Smuglevucius, a famous contemporary Lithuanian painter, and a large bronze medal of Vytautas by the sculptor Petras Rimša (1930). The Church of Vytautas is used for worship, and many newlyweds come here to receive the sacrament of matrimony after the civil ceremony at the Wedding Palace.

The Modern Center

Early in the 1800's Kaunas began to expand and the administrative center moved to the area south-east of the old town, where it is today. The main street of the district is Laisvės Alėja (Freedom Boulevard) - a pedestrian mall and shopping area. (Laisvės Alėja connects with Vilniaus St., which leads to the Old Town.) Other main thoroughfares are Lenin Prospect, K. Donelaičio St. and Kęstučio St.

At one end of Laisvės Alėja is the former Russian Orthodox Church of the military garrison built in 1895. The grandiose style of the building was supposed to show the power of the Tsarist regime. Today the Museum of Sculpture and Stained Glass is housed in here. (See Museum section.)

Along Laisvės Alėja there are many stores, restaurants and cafes. At no. 71 is the Drama Theater of Kaunas, and at No. 91 is the Music Theater in front of which is a small park. The remnants of the city's defense wall and tower can also be seen here.

In 1972, Romas Kalanta, a young student, set himself aflame in this park to protest the Soviet occupation of his country. Several days of rioting followed this event, underscoring the discontent over the repression of Lithuanian national aspirations.

From here take L. Tolstojaus St. (across Laisvės Alėja) to No. 5., the Kaunas branch of the Lithuanian Philharmonic. This building was the home of the Seimas (parliament) of independent Lithuania.

Walk down Donelaitis St. to Vienybės Square (Unity Square), around which are clustered a host of significant cultural and political institutions (including party headquarters). To the left of the square near the bell tower is the sculpture "Knygnešys", a memorial to the men who smuggled Lithuanian books from East Prussia into Lithuania in the latter half of the last century when the Tsarist government severely restricted the press and prohibited the use of the Latin alphabet.

The museum complex houses the Kaunas Historical Museum and the Čiurlionis Museum. The entrance is from S. Neries St. on the far side of the building. This year, during the commemoration festivities of Independence Day, February 16th, the Freedom Statue was unveiled in the garden in front of the Historical Museum. The statue had been taken off its pedestal and put in storage after the Soviets occupied Lithuania.

At S. Neries St. 45 is the Čiurlionis Museum, which houses the works of the best-known Lithuanian artist, M. K. Čiurlionis, who painted and composed music at the turn of the century. In front of the building is the sculpture Karaliai (The Kings) by V. Vidžiūnas.

Across the street is a small sculpture garden with works by R. Antinis (father and son). Next to the garden at S. Neries St. 64, is the A. Žmuidzinavičius' Museum (sometimes called the Devils' Museum because of the large collection of folk art depicting man's nemesis.) It is one of the most popular museums in Lithuania. (See Museum section.)

Walk back across Vienybės Square to Donelaičio St. and continue back in the direction of the Russian Orthodox Church. At No. 16 is the Painting Gallery which houses a large selection of Western European art.

Around Town

The Pažaislis Monastery and Church

This striking Baroque ensemble stands in splendid isolation among the fields and woodlands of the right bank of the Nemunas river. Pažaislis acquired its name from the Žaisa stream which flows into the Nemunas on the opposite bank. Today it is surrounded on three sides by the Kaunas Sea, which was created when the local hydro-electric power plant was built across the Nemunas.

Beyond the central gates, lies an impressive driveway lined with linden trees leading into the ensemble proper. At the end of the lane is another entrance, The Holy Gate, through which the visitor enters a yard which is dominated by the church's towers and beautiful Baroque cupola. The cupola rises to over 150 ft. and is topped by a superstructure forming a light beacon similar to the ones on the towers. Behind the church are extensive orchards and gardens.

The interior of the church is reminiscent of St. Maria della Salute in Venice, which had been built twenty five years earlier. Arches connect six black marble pillars, against which stand six pink marble columns with Corinthian capitals. An entablature rests on the columns and the cupola rises to 150 ft. from the floor. Four chapels surround the central area. The families of the founders of the church and monastery heard mass from the balconies in the presbitary.

The decoration is very rich: marble and oak trimmings, bas-relief and paintings are found throughout the ensemble. Frescos depicting the coronation of the Virgin Mary adorn the cupola. The frescos on the walls and vaults were executed in the "al fresco" technique, which employs water colors on wet plaster. The frescos have all been recently restored.

This ensemble was built in the 1600's under the patronage of the Chancellor of the Grand Duchy of Lithuania, Kristupas Pacas. Construction took about 60 years and cost the considerable sum of approximately 2 million ducats. Marble of various colors was transported from Cracow down the Vistula River, over the Baltic and up the Nemunas. The whole process (from preparing the marble in Cracow to the final installation of it at Pažaislis) took over 20 years.

In 1832 the Russian government confiscated the church and monastery and turned it over to Orthodox monks. During this period up to the end of World War I, the structures suffered extensive damage and the treasures of Pažaislis were plundered by the Russians as well as the Germans.

During the years of independence the ensemble was restored and given to the nuns of St. Casimir, who had settled here from Chicago, Illinois. After the Soviet occupation, the nuns were expelled and a psychiatric-neurological hospital was established in the monastery from 1951 to 1964. Once again the buildings and artistic treasures suffered severe damage.

The Pažaislis ensemble was entrusted to the Čiurlionis Art Museum in 1966, and major restoration efforts have been underway ever since. It is definitely one of the architectural jewels of Lithuania as well as of Eastern Europe.

The Ninth Fort

A fortress dating from 1882, this structure currently houses a branch of the Museum of History. During World War I it served as a defensive stronghold of the Tsarist army against German forces. During the Nazi occupation, the Germans used the fortress as a concentration camp (Enterprise No. 1005-B), and approximately 80,000 people from Lithuania and other European countries, many of them Jews, were brought here and massacred. The museum exhibition testifies to these horrendous crimes against humanity. There is a large monument to the memory of those killed in the Ninth Fort on the

Žemaičiu Highway. (Address: Žemaičiu Highway 73, tel. 26-05-74.)

<u>Burial Place of Darius and Girenas</u>

In the district of Aukštieji (Upper) Šančiai there is a small military cemetery where the Lithuanian-American aviators, Steponas Darius and Stasys Girėnas lie buried. They both died when the small and ill-equipped airplane they had successfully guided across the Atlantic crashed on German territory on July 17, 1933, only several hundred miles from their goal. Profoundly grieved by the tragedy, the Lithuanian people gave the aviators a heroes' funeral and continue to pay homage to their courage to this day. The wreckage of their "Lituanika" is on display in the Museum of History.

The Kings - sculpture in Čiurlionis Museum

Museums

When visiting museums it is important to keep in mind that the Soviet version of history shows the Soviet Union as the savior of a backward Lithuania, not as an occupying force of a once free and independent nation. Nevertheless, with the advent of "openness", local historians have gone amazingly far in revising earlier Soviet misrepresentations of Lithuanian history.

Čiurlionis Museum (S. Neries St. 45, tel. 22-14-17).

The museum houses an impressive collection of works by Mikalojus Konstantinas Čiurlionis, as well as a very extensive collection of folk art. It is clearly the pre-eminent art museum of Kaunas.

The Picture Gallery (K. Donelaičio St. 16, tel. 22-05-29).

The permanent exhibition includes works by Reubens, Rafael and Chagall as well as paintings by emigre Lithuanian painters P. Domšaitis, V. Kasiulis and A. Veščiūnas.

Velnių Muziejus (S. Neries St. 64, tel. 20-84-72).

The private collection of artist A. Žmuidzinavičius includes over 500 devil images. They have been brought here from Europe, Africa, America and Australia. New additions to the collection are always welcome.

Museum of History (K. Donelaičio St. 64, tel. 22-27-56).

An extensive exposition covers Lithuania's history from its beginnings to today. A substantial exhibit is dedicated to the aviators Steponas Darius and Stasys Girėnas. The Ninth Fort (See Around Town section) and the ruins of Kaunas Castle (See Old Town section) are branches of this museum.

Stained Glass and Sculpture Gallery (Laisvės Alėja, tel. 22-66-76).

Housed in the former Russian Orthodox Church is a fine collection of works by the best Lithuanian sculptors and stained glass masters.

Music and Theater

The second largest city in Lithuania does not rank second in theater. The Kaunas Drama Theater (Laisvės Alėja 71, tel. 22-31-85 or 22-40-64), founded in 1920, ranks along with the Vilnius Youth Theater as one of the country's best, but with a distinctive style. It has a history of controversial directors who have left their mark on the company. The company is housed in a second-rate building, but the high quality of performances usually make up for that.

The Kaunas Musical Theater (Laisvės Alėja 91, tel.22-87-84 or 20-09-33) is noted for its second-rate musicals and mediocre opera and operetta performances with few appearances by the bigger names from Vilnius. There are some exceptions, but they are few and far between. One reason for going to this theater might be to recapture the atmosphere of pre-war musical life. The newly renovated, architecturally eclectic building (originally built in 1891) is quaint. Kaunas residents and visitors often pass silently through the square in front of the theater in remembrance of the self-immolation of Romas Kalanta in 1972.

Recreation

Recreation areas abound in Kaunas and its environs. The Vytautas Park is found in the Žaliakalnis district above the center of the city. One of the main entrances to the park is at the beginning of Laisvės Alėja near the Russian Orthodox Church. Climbing the steep steps up the hill, you will find an amusement area and assorted pavilions.

Next to Vytautas Park is Ąžuolynas, an extensive oak forest with plenty of trails for leisurely hiking. Dainų slėnis (Valley of Songs), where Song festivals regularly take place lies at the edge of the park. A large sports center, consisting of a stadium, sports hall and the Institute of Physical Fitness is also located in Ąžuolynas.

Lithuania's only Zoological Garden is in the Girstupio Slėnis (valley) and is home to over 2500 animals brought from the Arctic, Africa and Asia. You can get to the zoo on foot by walking across Ąžuolynas or by taking busses No. 10, 20, 21, 29.

A section of the Girstupio Valley is named after Polish poet Adam Mickiewicz, who used to come to these woods to rest and seek artistic inspiration.

Panemunės šilas (pine forests) and Kauno marios (sea) are also picturesque sites along the Nemunas where locals come to relax and enjoy nature. From the center of town take trolley No. 5 or 7 to Panemunės šilas, trolleys No. 4, 5 or 12 to reach Kauno marios.

USEFUL WORDS AND EXPRESSIONS

Hello	Labas
Good morning	Labas rytas
Good evening	Labas vakaras
Good night	Labanakt
Goodbye	Viso gero
Yesterday	Vakar
Today	Šiandien
Tomorrow	Rytoj
Please	Prašau
Thank you	Ačiū
Yes	Taip
No	Ne
You're welcome	Prašau
Excuse me	Atsiprašau
I'm sorry	Atsiprašau
My name is...	Mano vardas...
Do you speak English?	Ar kalbate angliškai?
I don't speak Lithuanian	Aš nekalbu lietuviškai
I don't understand	Aš nesuprantu
I would like to go to...	Norėčiau nueiti į...
Where is...?	Kur yra...?
I would like...	Aš norėčiau...
How much does it cost?	Kiek tai kainuoja?

At a restaurant

I would like to order	Norėčiau užsisa kyti
Some more, please	Dar prašau
That's enough, thank you	Užteks, ačiū
coffee (with milk)	kava (su pienu)
sugar	cukrus
tea	arbata
juice	sultys
mineral water	mineralinis vanduo
beer	alus
wine (red, white)	vynas (raudonas, baltas)
bread	duona
butter	sviestas

Locations

street	gatve
square	aikšte
hotel	viešbutis
castle	pilis
church	bažnyčia
restaurant	restoranas
hospital	ligonine
drug store	vaistine
movie theater	kino teatras
theater	teatras
museum	muziejus
post office	paštas

Days of the week

Monday	Pirmadienis
Tuesday	Antradienis
Wednesday	Trečiadienis
Thursday	Ketvirtadienis
Friday	Penktadienis
Saturday	Šeštadienis
Sunday	Sekmadienis

Cardinal numbers

1	vienas	16	šešiolika
2	du	17	septyniolika
3	trys	18	aštuoniolika
4	keturi	19	devyniolika
5	penki	20	dvidešimt
6	šeši	25	dvidešimt penki
7	septyni	30	trisdešimt
8	aštuoni	40	keturiasdešimt
9	devyni	50	penkiasdešimt
10	dešimt	60	šešiasdešimt
11	vienuolika	70	septyniasdešimt
12	dvylika	80	astuoniasdešimt
13	trylika	90	devyniasdešimt
14	keturiolika	100	šimtas
15	penkiolika		

Ordinal numbers

1st	pirmas	8th	aštuntas
2nd	antras	9th	devintas
3rd	trečias	10th	dešimtas
4th	ketvirtas	11th	vienuoliktas
5th	penktas	20th	dvidešimtas
6th	šeštas	100th	šimtasis
7th	septintas		

PRONUNCIATION GUIDE

The Lithuanian language belongs to the Baltic branch of the Indo-European family. Latvian and the now extinct Old Prussian are also in this branch.

The Lithuanian alphabet is as follows:
a/ą, b, c, č, d, e/ę/ė, f, g, h, i/į, y, j, k, l, m, n, o, p, r, s, š, t, u/ų/ū, v, z, ž.

Vowels are either short or long: a as in hot; ą as in father; e as in bet; ę as in bad; ė as the a in made; i as in sit; į and y as ee in keel; o as the o in boat; u as in put; ų and ū as in truth.

Common dipthongs are: ai as in aisle; au as in out; ei as in hey; ie as in the r-less beer with y-sound predeeding it; ui is unique to Lithuanian but can be pronounced very quickly as the vowels in phooey; uo as in the Italian buono.

The consonants b, d, f, g, h, k, l, m, n, p, t and v are almost as in English; j as the y in yet; r is always trilled; c is pronounced as ts in pants; č is ch as in change; s as in sit; š is sh as in shop; z as in zoo; ž as s in measure.

LATVIA

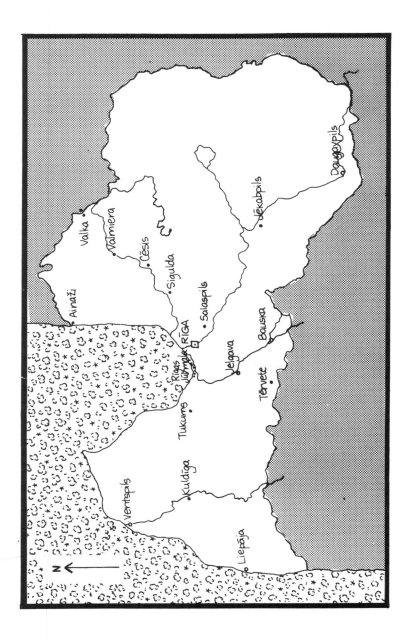

Daugavpils
Jēkabpils
Valka
Valmiera
Cēsis
Sigulda
Ainaži
Salaspils
RĪGA
Rīgas Jūrmala
Jelgava
Bauska
Tērvete
Tukums
Kuldīga
Ventspils
Liepāja

Z

LATVIA

As you cross Lithuania's northern border and enter Latvia, you enter a country that geographically differs little from its southern neighbor. The Lithuanian hills, forests and waterways flow unimpeded and largely unchanged into those of Latvia.

Culturally the flow seems gradual as well. The Latvian and Lithuanian languages are related, and both represent the only living examples of the Baltic branch of the Indo-European family of language. And yet despite their cultural closeness, fate and outside political forces shaped distinctly different histories for these neighboring peoples and nations. It could be said that as you cross the border from Lithuania to Latvia, you are leaving largely Catholic Eastern Europe and entering Protestant Northern Europe.

Although home to native Latvian inhabitants for thousands of years, beginning with the 13th century A.D., Latvia was overrun, ruled and partially shaped by succeeding German, Swedish and Russian conquerors for the next 700 years. Its largest city, Rīga, gained international renown as a bustling and prosperous member of the Hanseatic League. Its strategic ports and beautiful beaches drew the attention and frequent presence of German barons, Swedish kings and Russian Czars.

Through it all, the native Latvians maintained and strengthened their love for their land, culture and language. By 1918 they reassumed control of their ancestral homeland and forged the independent state they had long sought. Even Stalin's takeover of Latvia in 1940, and subsequent four decades of Soviet rule, have failed to dampen the Latvian sense of national identity and pride. With the advent of Gorbachev and glasnost, the people of Latvia have begun yet another difficult yet exhilarating climb toward national independence.

Latvia today is a nation rediscovering its history, reshaping its present and redirecting its future. For the tourist, Latvia offers a unique opportunity to be an eyewitness to all three.

LATVIAN HISTORY

As far as can be determined, the first human inhabitants of what today is known as Latvia, were nomadic tribes of reindeer hunters. They migrated to the forests along the Baltic Sea from the west and southeast following the last Ice Age, around 10,000 years ago.

By 2000 B.C. these nomadic hunters, fishers and gatherers were replaced by a distinctly new group of Indo-European settlers from the south. The Proto-Balts literally set down roots in Latvia, Lithuania and East Prussia, introducing both agriculture and permanent settlements. These evolved into various Baltic tribes, the major ones being the Cours, Semigallians, Livs, Sels and Letgallians.

Over the ensuing centuries these tribes, and the amber that proliferated on the shores of the Baltic, became well known to traders as far south as the Mediterranean. Between the 2nd and 5th centuries A.D., the Baltic tribes prospered from trade with the Roman Empire, increasing both their populations and territory as far eastward as Moscow. Pressure from Slavs in the east and Vikings in the west eventually forced the Balts to retreat, consolidate and reinforce their settlements. By the 10th century, the seafaring Cours emerged as the dominant force on Latvia's Baltic Sea coast, while the Livs commanded the lucrative trade that passed along the Daugava River.

In the 13th century heavily armed German crusaders swarmed up from the south and conquered not only the Livs and Cours, but the remaining Latvian and Estonian nations, establishing a rule that would last for 270 years. Under the Germans, the native Latvians and Estonians were united into a vassal state known as the Confederation of Livonia. German control came to end in 1558, when an unsuccessful Russian invasion, led by Ivan the Terrible, led to the breakup of the Livonian nation. Parts of Latvia came under Swedish and Danish rule, while the land mass jutting into the Baltic Sea west of Riga organized into the Duchy of Courland and became a semi-independent vassal of the King of Poland.

The Duchy of Courland survived for over two centuries and emerged as one of the great naval and commercial powers of Northern Europe. In the mid-17th century, the port city of Ventspils had established itself as a major shipbuilding center, supplying the fleets of England, France and Venice. Led by the enterprising Duke Jacob, the Latvian Courlanders briefly colonized the Caribbean island of Tobago, and a second island at the mouth of the Gambia River in Africa. Great Courland Bay in modern-day Tobago is named after this period of "benevolent" Latvian rule.

The Russians first began conquering parts of Latvia in 1710 and suceeded in subduing the remainder, including the Duchy of Courland, by 1795. The fate of the native Latvians throughout this period was bleak. When the German knights first invaded Latvia in the 13th century, they annihilated the leadership of native tribes and reduced the Latvians to the state of serfdom. Under succeeding Swedish and Polish rule, the Germans remained as landed gentry, while the plight of the Latvians worsened. When the Russians conquered Latvia in the 18th century, the Baltic German gentry took on prestigious positions in the Russian army and government. Latvian serfdom was transformed into pure slavery, and the Latvian people reached one of the lowest points in their long history.

With the coming of the 19th century European Enlightenment, and the advent of peasant land ownership, the Latvian people began to reassert their national identity. Through the efforts of Latvian writers, a National Awakening Movement was begun in 1856. Latvians rediscovered their national history and culture and took pride in the richness of their language. Despite a devastating Russification campaign in the 1880's, the Latvian people entered the 20th century with a new sense of national identity.

The first expression of Latvian political power occured in 1905, as the long-suffering Latvian peasants took up arms against their German landlords and Russian rulers. Although the revolt was mercilessly put down by Czarist troops, it set the stage for Latvia's successful war of independence thirteen years later.

Latvia's first truly national "army" came into being during World War I when Latvia was still part of the Czarist Russian empire. Eight regiments of Latvian Rifelemen were formed in 1915 to help in the Russian war effort against Germany. The Riflemen developed into one of the premiere military units in the Russian army, and remained intact throughout the war to eventually play a pivotal role in the Russian revolution of 1917. After the fall of the Czar, and with their eye on national independence, the Latvians sided with Lenin and the Bolsheviks against the new Russian government headed by Aleksandr Kerensky. Kerensky wanted to keep the old Russian empire intact, while Lenin had promised the Latvians and other national groups independence. After helping to ensure the success of the Bolshevik coup in Russia, the Riflemen split into factions, some assuming roles in the new Russian Bolshevik government, while others returned to Latvia to carry on the fight for independence.

On November 18, 1918 the Latvian people declared national independence and formed a provisional government. For the next two years they fought against the Bolsheviks, who despite Lenin's promises, wanted to incorporate Latvia into the new Soviet Russia, and the Germans, who had similar designs on Latvia. By 1920 the

Latvians had defeated both the Germans and the Bolsheviks, and in August of 1920 Latvia signed a peace treaty with the Soviet Union, wherein it recognized "unconditionally the independence and sovereignty of Latvia and declines, voluntarily and for all times, all claims on the Latvian people and territory which formerly belonged to Russia."

Thus began Latvia's modern era of political independence.   Its democratic, parliamentarian government was recognized by all world powers and Latvia was accepted into the League of Nations in 1922. Despite the ravages of war and revolution, Latvia successfully began to rebuild its economy, focusing its resources on agrarian reform, industrialization and education.   Its economy soon became self-sufficient and even began to export grain and dairy products to Europe.

The worldwide depression after 1931 had a devastating impact on Latvia's promising but fragile economy. This, combined with growing internal political problems, eventually led to a collapse of Latvia's parliamentary government. In 1934, Latvia's elected Prime Minister, Kārlis Ulmanis, declared a state of emergency, suspended the parliament, and assumed the presidency of a newly formed Government of National Unity in 1936.   Despite its authoritarian nature, Ulmanis' government retained popular support and introduced successful economic reforms. By 1938 the state of emergency came to an end and there was hope that a new, democratic constitution and government would be formed.

This hope was dashed with the outbreak of World War II. In 1939 the Soviet Union and Nazi Germany signed the Molotov-Ribbentrop Pact, which included secret protocols that consigned independent Latvia to the Soviet sphere of influence.

On June 16, 1940 Latvia received an ultimatum from Moscow, demanding the immediate free entry of Soviet troops into Latvia's territory. On the following day, the Red Army occupied Latvia. Within two months the Latvian government was dismantled and replaced by a Soviet-installed puppet government which called for Latvia's annexation to the USSR. The brutal Soviet takeover of Latvia was accompanied by massive terror against the Latvian population. During a 12-month period over 32,000 people were deported or executed - 16,000 alone on the night of June 14, 1941. Although the terror focused primarily on Latvia's political, military and social leadership, entire familes, including women and children were deported to slave labor camps in Siberia.

The Soviet terror was replaced by Nazi terror in July of 1941, when German troops occupied Latvia.   Still recoiling from Soviet atrocities in their country, the Latvians initially welcomed the

Germans as liberators, believing that the Germans would reinstate Latvian independence. Instead, the Gestapo launched its own terror campaign against the Latvian people. As they had done elsewhere in Europe, the Nazis built concentration camps and virtually exterminated Latvia's Jewish population.

Latvia was reoccupied by the Soviet Union in 1944. Soviet rule, begun in 1940, now came into full force. Although Latvia's incorporation into the Soviet Union was not recognized by the governments of the United States and most other Western nations, in Moscow's eyes the formerly independent Latvian Republic became the Soviet Socialist Republic of Latvia.

The reinstatement of Soviet rule in Latvia was accompanied by new waves of deportations and terror. Armed resistance against Soviet rule, which lasted for eight years, was effectively crushed by 1952. All symbols of Latvia's independence - its national flag, anthem, monuments and history - were either outlawed or altered to fit the new Soviet Communist ideology. Russian was imposed as the official language of the republic and hundreds of thousands of Russians and other Soviet nationals were flooded into the country to dilute the local Latvian population. Farms were collectivized and industry nationalized. While some Latvians Communists did take positions in the local government, real power was in the hands of Russians and the central Soviet government in Moscow. Once again, Latvia had been reduced to a colony in the Russian empire, this time under the title of the Union of Soviet Socialist Republics.

Until the late 1980's, the popular desire for a return to Latvian independence had been successfully silenced by the police state rule of the Communist Party and its security arm, the Soviet KGB. Religious and human rights activists were routinely arrested and consigned to prison camps in the Soviet Gulag. Outside of Latvia, an international campaign for independence was carried on by over 100,000 Latvian exiles in the West who had fled the country after the second Soviet takeover. While the well organized exile community was unable to alter Latvia's political status, it did keep the hope and spirit of independence alive through contacts with the homeland.

Recent History - Latvia's Peaceful Revolution

A dramatic new chapter in Latvia's history began on June 14, 1987 and continues to unfold at this very moment. As in the neighboring Estonia and Lithuania, and throughout the Soviet Union, Mikhail Gorbachev's policies of glasnost and perestroika have created a political and social upheaval in Latvia. While the average tourist may not necessarily be interested in local politics, the political changes that have taken place in Latvia in the last few years have begun to alter the very nature of the country. The proliferation of long forbidden national symbols, the frequency of political rallies and the accessibility of areas previously closed to tourists, is all a product of these changes.

What Latvians themselves describe as their third National Awakening, began on June 14, 1987, when 5,000 people defied local authorities and held a public rally at the Freedom Monument in Rīga. The peaceful gathering, organized to commemorate the victims of the 1941 Soviet deportations, set the stage for successively larger and politically bolder public demonstrations and events.

With each rally, old taboos established by the Soviet regime, began to fall. The Latvian people began to assert themselves, reclaiming their national symbols and history after five decades of Soviet denial. Under Soviet rule, Latvia's 20-year period of independence had been a blank page in official history books. Beginning in 1987, Latvia's independence was not only discussed publicly as a historical fact, but was soon viewed as a real possibility in the near future.

During 1988, peaceful public demonstrations became commonplace. Massive rallies were held to honor the victims of Stalinist deportations, and to protest the building of a subway in Rīga. In June the long forbidden maroon-white-maroon flag of independent Latvia began to appear at public events. In July, the flag itself became the focus of a rally as 30,000 people gathered in an outdoor amphitheater in Rīga to demand its rehabilitation. By November the flag had found a permanent place atop the Rīga Castle.

The summer of 1988 also saw the emergence of new grass roots political organizations. In July the National Independence movement of Latvia (LNNK) set forth 20 demands, including the end to Russification in Latvia, a free press, independent political parties and the reestablishment of an independent Latvian republic. In September, the Environmental Protection Club of Latvia (VAK) organized an anti-pollution rally, where over 45,000 people joined hands along a 36 kilometer stretch along the Baltic Sea coast.

In October, in response to the growing popular movement, and in support of Gorbachev's own restructuring policies, Latvia's Communist Party leaders were replaced with new, pro-reform politicians with closer ties to the populace. The new leaders immediately "legalized" the maroon-white-maroon flag and made Latvian the official language of the republic. That same month, over 150,000 people rallied to celebrate the founding of the Popular Front of Latvia (LTF), a massive new grass roots political movement which united all of Latvia's emerging social and political groups, including Communist Party members. One month later, for the first time since the Soviet occupation of Latvia, hundreds of thousands of Latvians publicly celebrated the anniversary of its November 18, 1918 declaration of independence from Russia.

By 1989, the Popular Front of Latvia (LTF) became a formidable force in Latvia's social and political life. It had a 100-member council, 18-member executive board, 19 different committees that operated from a bustling headquarters in Rīga, its own weekly newspaper Atmoda (Awakening), and over 200,000 dues-paying members. By contrast, there were only 180,000 Soviet Communist Party members in Latvia; most of the Latvians in the Communist Party also joined the LTF.

The LTF, working with other informal groups and sympathetic Communist Party leaders, began lobbying for changes in Latvian laws which would give the local residents greater say in their own affairs. The LTF, whose members included professionals, journalists, artists, academicians, tradesmen and working people, established a network that penetrated all aspects of Latvian society, up to and including government agencies. In a very real sense, the LTF became a "shadow government", with the power to influence not only local government leaders, but even the central Soviet government in Moscow.

August, 1989 saw the largest Baltic demonstration to date - perhaps the largest political demonstration ever held in Soviet controlled territory. The LTF, together with popular fronts in Estonia and Lithuania organized the "Baltic Way", a 400-mile human chain that stretched from Tallinn, through Rīga, all the way to Vilnius. An estimated 2 million people participated in the peaceful demonstration, marking the 50th anniversary of the 1939 Stalin-Hitler Pact which had led to the Soviet invasion of the Baltic States.

Although the LTF had initially called for Latvia's state sovereignty within the USSR, by its second congress in October of 1989, its program had changed to a call for total political and economic independence outside the USSR. Despite Moscow's objection to Latvia's secession from the USSR, the LTF's program of peaceful change through public pressure and parliamentary procedure has widespread public support, not only among Latvians, but more notably, a growing portion of Latvia's ethnic Russian population. The LTF expects to assume even greater political power in republic-level elections scheduled for March of 1990.

Two important points should be noted about the political upheaval which has taken place in Latvia since 1987. First, despite the inroads made by grass roots organizations such as the LTF, Latvia remains - as this book goes to print - a Soviet-ruled republic. The Soviet military and political bureaucracy remains in place and still holds ultimate power in the country. A tourist wishing to go to Latvia still has to get a Soviet visa and still must contend with a

Soviet-installed infrastructure.

Second, the political and national resurgence which has taken place in Latvia has been characterized by a remarkable degree of discipline, order and peacefulness. Despite the high degree of emotion and large numbers of people present at the recent political rallies, there have been no incidents of violence or civic unrest. Unless you are present on the day of one of these rallies, or were to attend one of the many political meetings, conferences and debates that take place in public buildings, you may not even notice that anything out of the ordinary was happening in the country.

If, however, you understand Latvian (or Russian), and can follow local events in the media, you can get a sense of the remarkable change that is sweeping the country. Latvia, like its neighbors Estonia and Lithuania, has had a history filled with dramatic change and almost cyclical political upheaval. From its tribal beginnings, through centuries of foreign rule, up to the 20th century when it has experienced both independence and occupation, Latvia has managed to retain a unique national and cultural identity. It is the strength of this national pride that now takes the Latvian people into the uncertainties and hopes of the 1990's.

Vidzeme region countryside

GEOGRAPHY

Latvia comprises an area of 25,400 sq. mi. (66,000 sq. km.). This makes it roughly equivalent in size to West Virginia. Hardly a huge country, it nonetheless is larger than Switzerland, Denmark and Israel. For those of you who enjoy pinpointing co-ordinates, Latvia is located between 55° 40'23" and 58° 05'12" latitudes north and 20° 58'07" and 28° 14'30" longitudes east. What that means is that only three European countries - Iceland, Estonia and Finland - are further north in their entirety. Those famous white nights of Northern Europe can also be experienced in Latvia: the longest day in summer lasts a full 17 1/2 hours! It also means that the 25° longitude of Greenwich, the approximate east-west center line of Europe, runs right through the heart of Latvia.

The Baltic Sea and the Gulf of Rīga mark the western boundary of Latvia. To the north is Estonia, to the east is Russia and to the south is Lithuania. Previous to World War II Latvia shared a 66 mile (105 km.) southwestern border with Poland, but that ceased to exist when Russia occupied the adjacent territory.

Latvia's landscape consists primarily of rolling plains and gentle hills and has an average elevation of 292 ft. (89 m.) above sea level. The western-most region - Kurzeme - consists of the Coastal Plain. At one time a sea bottom, this generally flat area has its share of coastal and dune ridges reaching a height of 125 ft. (38 m.) above sea level south of Liepāja near Nīca, as well as steep banks created by sea erosion. At the southern tip of the Gulf of Rīga is the famous Jūrmala (seashore) with its beautiful powder-like sand beaches, majestic pines and sulphur springs. It has long been regarded as the Baltic Riviera - one of northern Europe's finest resort areas and you can read all about it in the section marked "Jūrmala".

The Zemgale Plain merges with the Coastal Plain in the area of Jelgava and extends south toward Lithuania. This Zemgale region is considered the breadbasket of Latvia as it contains the richest soil in the country. The overall flatness of this bountiful area is broken up by the ancient riverbed of the Lielupe near Bauska, as well as by its many tributaries.

Moving eastward toward the Vidzeme region the Maliena Plain takes over. The country's largest plain, it covers an area 200 km. long by 80 km. wide. Its most distinguishing features are vast forests and a full one third of Latvia's marshlands.

To the north are the Sandstone Plateau as well as the Plain of Northern Vidzeme. This area features smooth glacial rifts, moraine hills and ridges rising from the plain. Numerous rivers and long, narrow lakes are deeply etched into the sandstone bedrock and are surrounded by birch, pine and spruce forests which give way to fields and meadows. All in all, this area is a delight to nature lovers.

The Uplands, which account for almost 40% of Latvia's territory, are found in the Vidzeme region as well as in the western part of the country. The highest point in Latvia, the 1,017 ft. (310 m.) Gaiziņš, is found in the Uplands of Central Vidzeme.

Birch trees on Gaiziņš in winter

The Uplands of Eastern Vidzeme extend north into Estonia, where they attain their highest elevation in the Suur Muna Mägi, which reaches 1,040 ft. (317 m.) above sea level. The diversity of the landscape in this area is breath-taking: steep hills, wildflower fields, misty lakes, dense pine forests, and lush meadows.

While the Uplands of Kursa in western Latvia are considerably lower than their counterparts in the east, they nonetheless offer a rich variety of scenery to the interested observer. Rapid rivers pounding their way through sandstone rocks, hills shrouded in mist, well defined glacial valleys, and the ever-present pine forests all contribute to the beauty of the area.

The last major landform is found in the southeastern part of Latvia, and it includes the most lake dense region of the country. The Plateau of Latgale in the Latgale region offers a beauty all its own. It is laced with a network of island-filled lakes which are interconnected by numerous streams. The largest lake in Latvia, the 21 sq. mi. (56 sq. km.) Rēzna, and the deepest lake, the 213 ft. (65 m.) Drīdzis are both found in this area.

Lakes

Scattered throughout Latvia are some 5,000 lakes which were formed during the last Ice Age. The Plateau of Latgale enjoys the highest concentration of lakes, while the Zemgale Plain has the lowest. Although large in number, the lakes themselves are generally small and shallow. They cover approximately 2% of Latvia's surface. In contrast, Baltic neighbors Finland and Sweden have enough lakes to make up 9% of their countries. Even so Latvia is considered a lake-rich country, which supplies outdoorsy types with ample opportunity for fishing, boating, swimming, etc.

Latvians have always taken great pride in their natural wonders. So much so that independent Latvia designated 17 lakes along with their 53 islands as natural monuments. Thus when the Soviets drained Latvia's largest lake, Lubāns, to half its original 35 sq.mi (90 sq. km.) size, it had a detrimental impact on the people as well as on the local ecological balance. What was once a major habitat for storks is no more. The necessary food supply for the birds was destroyed along with the marshlands that sustained it.

Rivers

Latvia's river network consists of close to 1,000 rivers and streams which total over 6,000 mi. (9,600 km.) in length. From the mighty Daugava to the smallest stream, these inland waterways are inextricably linked to the hearts of the Latvian nation, and figure prominently in Latvian folklore.

The Daugava - Latvia's largest river - begins 804 ft. above sea level in the central highlands of Russia. It enters Latvian territory at its southeastern tip and flows for 230 mi. (370 km.) past some 80 islands and the capital of the country, before emptying into the Gulf of Rīga. The Daugava is directly connected with the Volga and Dnieper Rivers and historically, the river was an important part of the trade route (known as the Amber Route) connecting the Baltic Sea with the Mediterranean. Today, the Daugava is the primary provider of hydro-electric energy in Latvia, the bulk of which comes from the Ķegums Works built during Latvia's independent period.

In the southern part of the Zemgale region, the confluence of the Lithuanian rivers Mūsa and Mēmele forms the Lielupe River. The two rivers merge at Bauska creating a lovely 66 ft. (20 m.) deep ravine. This 75 mi. (120 km.) long river both irrigates and drains the fertile breadbasket area of Latvia. Because the Lielupe is well suited for navigation, it is utilized as a commercial waterway.

The Venta River

The river Venta begins its journey to the Baltic Sea from Lake Vene in the Uplands of Žemaitija in Lithuania. Latvia's westernmost major river, the 111 m. (178 km.) long Venta flows northward through the Kurzeme region before emptying into the Baltic Sea at the ice-free port city of Ventspils. At the city of Kuldīga, the Venta forms a scenic 8 ft. (2.5 m.) high waterfall, the Kuldīgas Rumba. During the independence years, salmon swimming upstream were caught in baskets, providing a culinary feast for fish lovers. North of Kuldīga, the Venta is joined by a major tributary, the Abava, and then slows down considerably allowing small, ocean-going ships access.

The only major river in Latvia that runs its entire length within Latvian territory is the Gauja. This 274 mi. (440 km.) rapidly flowing river cuts its course through the exceptionally scenic countryside of northcentral Latvia, forming dramatic ravines and carving numerous caves into the sandstone bedrock. The beauty of this glacial river valley culminates near the town of Sigulda. The Gauja National Park offers the tourist grand vistas of the river valley, and is one of the most popular tourist attractions in Latvia - but more about that in the Cities section under Sigulda.

The Baltic Sea

In prehistoric times (about 5000 B.C.), the Baltic Sea was a freshwater lake. Around 2000 B.C., the Danish Straits opened up and the Baltic again became salty. Compared to the nearby North Sea, it is shallower and less saline - due in part to the numerous fresh water rivers which empty into it. The Baltic Sea can be considered a huge inland gulf of the Atlantic Ocean, as it is surrounded by European nations on all sides.

Latvia's Baltic coastline is 307 mi. (494 km.) long. Half of this seacost lies on the Gulf of Rīga. The remainder faces the open sea. Historically, this stretch of land - with its ice-free ports and precious amber along the shoreline - has been coveted by numerous nations. In turn it has served Latvia as a trade and cultural link with the Western World.

Throughout history, Latvian fisherman have thrived due to the bounty of the Baltic. Latvian merchants and shipbuilders have benefited from the ice-free ports and easy access to the rest of Europe and the world. And the Latvian people have been rested and restored on the pine-scented, powdery sand beaches of the Jūrmala resorts. The Latvian nation is inextricably linked to and defined by the Baltic Sea. After all, its shores have been home to the Latvians for over 4,000 years.

Climate

Although Latvia is rather far north (sharing a common latitude with northern Canada), its weather is actually quite mild. Thanks to the east/northeast path that the warm Gulf Stream takes over the North Atlantic, Latvia enjoys relatively mild winters and moderately warm summers. The same air mass also provides humid conditions, notable cloud cover, and significant rainfall - 20% of which takes the form of snow.

Moving further inland (east), the Gulf Stream influence decreases as the extreme weather patterns coming out of the Eurasian continent increase. This battle between opposing weather forces is evident in temperature readings and days of snow cover across Latvia. In western (coastal) Latvia, the coldest month is February, whereas in the east, the lowest temperatures of the year begin in early January. Snow cover lasts an average of 65 days in the west and 130 days in the east.

Springtime comes to Latvia in late March/early April. Flooding in low-lying areas is common due to melting snows and the break-up of river ice. Although daytime temperatures can be pleasantly warm, overnight frost is frequent.

Summer weather warms up Latvia from June til September. Temperatures attain their peak in July, when the average high in Rīga is 64.2^c F (17.9^c C). New York averages 75^c F (24^c C) and Stockholm 63^c F (17^c C). This is also the season of heaviest rainfall in the country. Thunderstorms, often accompanied by hail, are common throughout the summer months, with the heaviest concentration of storms being in late June. This natural phenomenon has given rise to a common saying among Latvians regarding heavy rains: "līst kā pa Jāniem" - raining like on Midsummer's Eve. This holiday is known as Jāni and falls on June 23rd.

As autumn approaches, daytime temperatures drop and overnight frost appears. The number of overcast, rainy days increases although actual rainfall is significantly less than in the summer months. Humidity is high and fog is prevalent, especially in coastal areas. Latvia's annual precipitation rate of 23.6 - 31.5 inches (600 - 800 mm.) is roughly equal to the amount which Stockholm and New York receive.

Winter usually sets in around November. When the cold weather settles in and snow begins to fall, children of all ages are out enjoying winter sports. The frozen lakes and snow covered hillsides are a delight to skiers, skaters and tobogganers alike. The average of seven snowstorms a year guarantees ample snow cover for these favorite winter pastimes.

Flora

Latvia's location within the continental and maritime time zones, and the climactic changes which occurred since the last ice age are two of the major contributing factors in the evolution of Latvia's distinctive plant life.

Retreating glaciers created a warmer, drier climate ideally suited to birch, aspen, spruce and common pine. Further warming and increased humidity allowed for the development of broadleaf forests consisting of oak, elm and alder. Around 900 B.C. the abrupt change to cold and rainy weather allowed for the creation of marshlands and dense pine and spruce forests.

Before the advent of farming, forests covered approximately 85% of Latvian territory. Today the figure is about 26%. More than half of all the trees in Latvia are pines. They attain heights of 35 m. and can be as old as 500 years. The sandy coastal belt is home to some of the tallest and straightest of Latvian pine trees. For Baltic shipbuilders, they were the trees of choice for use as masts on sailing ships.

Inland forests consist of spruce and mixed-woods. Broadleaf forests are less common because of the cool climate. But the oak and the birch are nonetheless favorites among Latvians. Both trees are common motifs in Latvian art and folklore. The mountain ash, willow, alder, ash, aspen, common linden, maple, yew, juniper and hornbeam fill out the forest floor, while the undergrowth consists of raspberry, hazel, heather, whortleberry and red huckleberry.

A vast variety of mushrooms can be found throughout Latvia's forests as well. Just walk through any open-air market and you will see an abundant display. The dark-capped boleti are the most popular. But the chanterella, cep, russulas, saffron milk cap and other edible varieties are also plentiful.

Grassland meadows cover about 25% of the country. The dry soil on slopes is home to clover, caraway, lady's mantle, milfoil, red fescue, vernal grass, lady's hair and bent. Fertile river valley grasslands are made up of meadow fescue, timothy, meadow foxtail, meadow poa and red fescue. Latvia's dairy herds have thrived on this type of meadow as it produces a high yielding quality hay. Over 50% of Latvia's grasslands consist of peat bog meadows and they contain cotton grass, poa and bend. Marshy meadows near rivers and lakes contain common reed, water poa and sedge poa, although this type of

Bebra purvs - Beaver marsh

meadow has been greatly reduced due to cultivation and drainage.

Moss and grass covered marshlands constitute 10% of Latvia's territory. They vary in size from one, to over 39,500 acres, and are home to birds, reptiles, insects and other animals. Brown leaf moss and greenish-brown sage varieties dominate, but the marshes are enlivened by numerous flowering species: wild rosemary, heather, cotton grass, cloudberry and sundew.

Latvians have always had a powerful bond with nature, and the richness and variety of native flora certainly contributes to it. Typical of Northern Europe, the growing season is a short one in Latvia. Perhaps that is the reason why Latvians have assigned an almost magical quality to plant life. That Latvians see themselves as inextricably tied to the natural world around them is evidenced by the extensive use of nature in Latvian folklore, literature and art.

Fauna

The diverse animal kingdom (13,000 registered species) in present-day Latvia can be attributed to four factors: 1) the retreat of the glacier cover 12,000 years ago, 2) farming practices, including deforestation, pasture formation and land cultivation, 3) the proximity of Latvian territory to seven different zoogeographic zones, and 4) the accidental and deliberate importation of animals by man.

The sub-arctic, tundra covered Latvia of 10,000 years ago was inhabitated by reindeer, white hare, willow grouse, and others. The broadleaf forests which followed were home to elk, red deer, wild boar and aurochs. As the climate became more humid, roe deer and swamp turtles appeared. The advent of pine and spruce forests gave rise to the squirrel, wood marten, brown bear and wolverine. Around 900 B.C. the climate stabilized to its present cool and humid state. As the land was deforested and cultivated, steppe animals such as the gray hare and gray partridge found conditions hospitable.

Currently, Latvia shares common animal species with seven zoogeographic zones. Included among these are: common water fowl, turtle dove, wild boar, bunting, lesser early bat, tree frog, hoopoe, elk, several species of grouse, red deer, barn owl, swamp turtle, penduline tit, lesser gray shrike, swift, rock dove, black redstart, house swallow, greenish warbler, Arctic loon, whimbrel and the willow ptarmigan.

The American mink and the Norwegian rat have been accidentally brought into Latvia where they have proliferated. Beavers and red deer were near extinction, but have been intentionally reintroduced, while fallow deer, raccoon dogs, and wild rabbit are among several new species introduced to Latvia.

All told, Latvia has approximately 60 species of mammals, including rodents (squirrels, beavers, mice, rats, rabbits), carnivores (wolves, fox, racoon, lynx, brown bear - which only occasionally ventures into Latvia from Russia and Estonia, marten, otter, badger, ermine, weasel, skunk, mink), bats, insectivores (mole, hedgehog, shrew), hoofed animals (wild boar, red deer, elk, roe deer), and pinnipeds (seals).

Latvia also has over 300 species of birds, although only 50 of those inhabit the country year around. The majority - over 225 species - are migratory birds with predictable patterns of arrival and departure. A small group - about 10 species - spend their winters in Latvia before departing for traditional nesting areas elsewhere, and the remainder - some 40 species - only occasionally drop in for a visit.

The animal kingdom of Latvia is rounded out by 7 species of reptiles, 12 amphibian species and 72 species of fresh and saltwater fish.

With such a wealth of animal life, its no wonder that independent Latvia passed detailed laws regulating fishing and hunting and forest usage. Wild life sanctuaries were also protected by law. After the Soviet occupation, USSR nature protection laws were instituted. As they were generally unsuited for conditions in Latvia, serious ecological damage resulted. With the rise of nationalism, Latvians are striving to reverse this negative trend.

RELIGION

Before the introduction of Christianity in the early 1200's, Latvia had a highly developed indigenous folk religion. The foundation of this ancient nature-centered religion was based on such virtues as justice, wisdom, truth, beauty, joy, sacredness, and love. All of creation was viewed as a harmonious entity, to be respected and honored.

Of some 5000 deities, three were worshipped as divine beings: Dievs, Māra, and Laima. Dievs was the supreme God, in charge of all that is sacred and profound in the universe. But rather than taking the role of a masterly sovereign, he was envisioned as a wise council who participated in human endeavors. Māra was the Mother Earth Goddess, who gave life and also claimed it. She was responsible for the earth, the waters, and every living thing therein. By determining the destiny of all newborns, Laima, the Goddess of Fate, was responsible for the realms not specifically covered by Dievs and Māra. Prominent supporting roles were played by Saule (Sun), Pērkons (Thunder), and Jumis, eternal life. The worship of these deities goes far back in time, as evidenced by the extensive use of their symbols as design elements in textiles, metals, pottery, wood, etc. as long ago as the Bronze Age (1500 B.C.).

DIEVS

MĀRA

LAIMA

During Latvia's independence, this traditional belief system experienced a revival and gained a considerable following under the name of Dievturība. There are numerous adherents to this uniquely Latvian religion, or way of life, to this day. Even among the Christians, elements of Dievturība are an integral part of Latvian tradition and culture.

Christianity was brought to Latvia by German Crusaders in the beginning of the 13th century. Initially, it was quite unsuccessful as services were held in Latin, and therefore not understood by the Latvians. The Catholic Church was forced out of the western half of Latvia after the Reformation, but still retained its influence in the Latgale region. The Aglona Catholic Church, built in 1699, became an important Catholic center in Latvia, and remains so today. During Latvia's independence, approximately 25% of believers were Catholic, practicing their faith in almost 200 parishes. In 1983, Pope John Paul elevated the Bishop of Rīga, Jūlijāns Vaivods, to the position of Cardinal.

By 1521, the Reformation reached Latvia. At this time, services were held in Latvian, and this accounted for a growth in membership in the Lutheran Church. With the abolition of serfdom in the 19th century came access to education for the masses, which in turn allowed Latvians to shape their own spiritual lives. The position of the Lutheran Church became much more prominent in Latvian society. By the independence years, 55% of all believers were Lutheran, and parishes totaled 325.

Independent Latvia had sizable Orthodox (9%), and Jewish (5%) communities as well as Baptists, Adventists, and other sects. The nation observed the separation of Church and State, and had laws guaranteeing the freedom of worship. Subsidies from the State Treasury allowed for groups of 10 or more believers of any faith to hold special classes in any public school.

This environment of religious freedom for all and any faith was squelched by the Soviet invasion. Large scale deportations and executions of clergy ensued. Church property was seized by the State. Churches were turned into concert halls, museums, warehouses, cinemas, and meeting halls. Some were burned down, and others were left to fall into ruin.

In recent years, the Latvian nation has reclaimed its spiritual life, and taken back many of its houses of worship from the grip of scientific atheism. Religious belief has flowered in this era of perestroika and glasnost. Although the Latvian Lutheran Church has experienced the strongest rebirth, the renewed opportunity for religious expression has led to interest in a wide variety of faiths. And the long held Latvian belief in religious freedom has taken a prominent role in the current political reforms. The Popular Front of Latvia has, as part of its platform for a free and independent Latvia, again called for complete religious freedom for all citizens of Latvia.

LITERATURE

Although Latvian civilization is quite ancient, its literature is relatively new, having come into its own in the mid 19th century. This late development can be attributed to the fact that for centuries, Latvians have been dominated by foreigners - Germans, Russians and Swedes. Throughout these periods of subjugation, Latvians nonetheless retained their ancient customs and language thereby developing a unique oral literature - poetical folksongs called "dainas". These dainas capture the cycle of Latvian life from cradle to grave on the farmstead - the center of the Latvian's world for hundreds of years.

The dainas are very musical, but the fine nuances of their poetical expression are lost in translation, which is one reason few other cultures are aware of them. Krišjānis Barons (1835-1923) spent over 40 years tracking down dainas from all over Latvia. He published 35,789 dainas along with 182,00 variations. By the mid 1960's the Institute of Latvian Folklore in Rīga had recorded over 900,000 dainas.

Until the 1800's any writing in Latvian was done by foreigners, mostly Germans. Alexander Stender (1744-1819) wrote "Lustesspēle", the first play in the Latvian language. Karl Gotthard Everfeld (1756-1819) wrote the first original Latvian play, "The Birthday", a play about smallpox inoculation. An Englishman, Karl Watson (1777-1826) published the first Latvian newspaper "Latviešu Avīzes" in 1822. It ran until 1915.

Latvian literature blossomed during the National Awakening (1850-1880). The new wave of nationalism sweeping through the country was brightly reflected in Latvian literature. Just before Barons published his first set of dainas, Andrējs Pumpurs, an army man who spent a great deal of time in Czarist Russia, wrote Latvia's great epic poem, "Lāčplēsis" (The Bear Slayer). It is a superhero tale in the style of the German "The Ring of the Nibelung" and the Finnish "Kalevala". Lāčplēsis, based on ancient Latvian folktales, overcomes his enemy, the black German knight of feudal ages, but in so doing, falls into the Daugava River. Legend has it that Latvia will suffer foreign oppression until Lāčplēsis returns. The tale has become a motif for generations of writers and poets, and today the hero Lāčplēsis remains a symbol of Latvia's political dissidents and their struggle for independence.

The first great Latvian novel, "Mērnieku Laiki" (The Time of the Land-Surveyors) was written during the period of the National Awakening. Its authors were two brothers - Reinis and Matiss Kaudzīte - who spent 20 years writing the novel which was completed in 1879. The story contains dazzling portrayals of Latvian characters, many so distinctive that they have become Latvian classics and have been incorporated into the Latvian vocabulary much like Scrooge or Pollyanna have in English.

The 1890's ushered in a new literary era, the New Current, in which Latvian writing rose to join the ranks of worldclass literature. The author who spearheaded Latvia's literary rise was Jānis Rainis (1865-1929). Born into a well-to-do family of an estate overseer, he received a law degree from the University of St. Petersburg - there was no Latvian university at the time. After denouncing the Baltic German barons' exploitation of the Latvian peasants, he was imprisoned and then banished for 6 years. In the Ural Mountains of Siberia he translated Goethe's "Faust" into Latvian. Rainis escaped to Switzerland after the unsuccessful 1905 uprising in the territory of Latvia. He lived there for 14 years as a political exile. It was during this period that he wrote his major works. "Fire and Night" (1907), a drama based on Lāčplēsis, is an artistic tribute to Latvia's continual fight for freedom. Well before the Soviet occupation during World War II, his 1928 play "The Witch of Rīga" symbolically warns of Russian aggression.

Equally colorful, and a very talented literary figure in her own right, was Rainis' wife. The poet Aspazija, a feminist, playwright and first class lyricist, shared her husband's Swiss exile. Known for her stormy temperament, Aspazija's many works are filled with fiery emotions.

Another great woman in Latvian literature is Anna Brigadere (1861-1933). Born to peasants, she only began writing in her thirties. A poet, novelist and dramatist, she also used Latvian folk motifs in her works. Brigadere is best known for her fairytale plays and vivid writings of Latvian life on the farm. Her highly descriptive works often evoke colorful, soothing images of a life lived close to nature.

Many Latvian writers joined the romantic literary movement that spread throughout the rest of Europe. The author Jānis Poruks (1871-1911) was fascinated by Wagner's music and drew inspiration from Goethe, Nietzsche, and Byron. After studying music in Dresden, Poruks lived in poverty in Rīga and wrote penetrating essays and masterful short stories. Suffering from depression, he died in a sanitarium.

Another neo-romantic was the lyrical poet Fricis Bārda (1880-1919) whose works are rich in visual imagery and musical rhythms. His was a platonic world where life exists ephemerally before returning to the ideal realm of perfect ideas, and also a pantheistic world where nature is a kind, loving earthmother whose touch can bring ecstasy and beauty to life. Bārda's works, while light and effortless to read, express profound ideas and often face eternal restlessness and poignant quiet despair.

One of Latvia's greatest playwrights and short story writers, Rūdolfs Blaumanis (1863-1908) was the son of a cook and a maid. Although at times he earned his living running the comic section of a newspaper, Blaumanis is best known for his tragedies, even though he did write comedies and poetry as well. The daily lives of his characters are a pale backdrop to the relentless turmoil they face within themselves. Blaumanis has a talent for penetrating into the core of his protagonists and powerfully and succinctly summing up their souls.

In addition to the new talent arising among the Latvian literati of realism, great works were also being produced in the realms of fantasy and folklore. Known as the Latvian Hans Christian Andersen, Kārlis Skalbe (1879-1945) wrote both verse and fairy tales. The youngest of a blacksmith's ten children, Skalbe grew up in poverty, and as an adult was forced to live in exile for his anti-czarist activities. He was one of the first intellectuals to openly discuss the idea of full independence for Latvia. When that idea became a reality, he was at the forefront of establishing a free Latvia. Two decades later, when the Russians invaded Latvia for the last time, Skalbe escaped by boat to Sweden where he died shortly thereafter. His poetic descriptions and allegorical representations of Latvia and the Latvian people give Skalbe's fairytales their power and beauty.

With Latvia's independence (1918-1939) came a new generation of writers who were very much open to foreign influence. The greatest modern poet of the time was Aleksandrs Čaks, the son of a tailor. He successfully ushered in a new genre of poetry. Čaks shocked his literary audience with his total disregard for rhyme in favor of rhythm as well as his choice of completely unexpected topics. Unlike the romantics who paid tribute to nature's beauty, Čaks extolled rain gutters and bars. A city boy, he wrote in great detail about Rīga, especially the Old Town.

Other writers of this era glorified the past. Novels set in the 18th and 19th centuries appeared, as well as ancient histories of the Latvian tribes. Towards the end of the 1930's, writers began to focus on urban society and love themes.

During the years of independence, Latvia's writers and poets produced quality works of literature. The literary climate was stimulating, intellectual and creative. But this open atmosphere changed virtually overnight with the invasion of the Soviet army. As soon as Soviet tanks rolled over Latvia's borders in June of 1940, the entire local press was commandeered and turned into a mouth piece for communist propaganda. Writers were tortured and banished to Siberian concentration camps.

Under the Soviets, the sole aim of literature was to praise Stalinism, and thus works produced in Latvia during the 1940's and early 1950's were dull industrial and agricultural narratives to this end. With Stalin's death in 1953, Latvian literature was given some breathing space. Soviet authorities tolerated some rehabilitation of pre-Soviet Latvian culture and Latvian folk songs, folk tales and riddles reappeared. By 1957 some works of past Latvian writers were legalized and this in turn stimulated the next generation. Soviet authorities tried to turn many well known Latvian writers such as Fricis Bārda and Jānis Rainis into communists by publishing excerpts of their works in tandem with the party-line interpretation.

Some of "The Siberians" - deported writers - were given permission to write again, but by this time they had become weak and aged. One such writer was Jānis Medenis (1903-1961). In his prime he had written fiery patriotic poetry. When the Soviets occupied Latvia he fled to Sweden in a fishing boat. Before reaching freedom, Medenis was captured by the Soviets, jailed and finally deported to a forced labor camp in northern Siberia. When he was finally allowed to return to Latvia in 1955, he had to be taken from the train in a stretcher and hospitalized. Of lost freedom he has written:

> *To reach you there is but the Milky Way*
> *Across the tundra cut by icy rivers,*
> *Where every leaf in cold and turmoil shivers,*
> *And to the ceaseless angry wind falls prey...*
> *But shimmering across the heavy sky*
> *Wild geese are leaving tracks for mind and eye,*
> *And sweet lost freedom with their voice recall.*
> *Already snow and dusk and darkness fall,*
> *Only these wings will fly amid the storm,*
> *And as I dream of you, your breath will keep me warm.*

The Soviet era did, however, produce a number of world class writers. The works of many of them have come to light only in the current age of glasnost. Writers such as Vizma Belševica suffered through political trials and long periods of exile from Latvia. Others never saw their own works in print. Currently one of the more famous Latvian names in literature is the poet Imants Ziedonis, who managed in his poetry and prose to keep alive the spirit of the Latvian nation in spite of heavy-handed censorship. Ziedonis has of late devoted his energies to the rebirth of Latvian culture, by taking a breather from strictly literary pursuits to head the Latvian Culture Fund - an organization promoting the independent development of all Latvian art forms.

A new generation of writers has taken advantage of the current thaw in censorship to publish heretofore unthinkable works, and also to raise a number of classics up from the dust heap of history. The playwright Māra Zālīte, for example, adapted the classic Latvian epic "Lāčplēsis" into a rock opera. It received rave reviews from critics of all ages.

With the Soviet takeover of Latvia, hundreds of thousands of Latvians fled their homeland and settled in the West. As a result, a new type of Latvian literature arose - of Latvian life in exile. Two big names from this period are Anšlāvs Eglītis (1906-) and Mārtiņš Zīverts (1903-). During Latvia's independence Eglitis was a popular playwrite as well as an author of numerous novels depicting Latvian society with all its foibles. He is best known for his piercingly accurate portrayals of personalities and for his ever present sense of humor. Currently living in California, Eglītis continues to produce plays and novels in exile.

His contemporary, Mārtiņš Zīverts, is considered Latvia's best modern dramatist, and has authored over 40 plays. An experimentalist, he evolved a long one act play whose finale is a dramatic monologue. His works often contain touches of existentialism. With the Soviet occupation, Zīverts fled to Sweden, where he currently resides.

A passionate nationalist whose fire for Latvian independence burns strongly to this day is the poet Andrejs Eglītis (1912-). His classic poem "O God, Thy Land is Aflame" has been set to elegiac music and continues to be a monument to Latvia's struggle for survival. Suppressed for decades, this poem is again surfacing in Latvia in light of Gorbachev's glasnost policies.

A new literary era is dawning in Latvia as a result of glasnost. Not only have the works of the aforementioned Latvian writers in exile been rehabilitated, works of once banned native writers and poets are being openly read. Nationalism has re-emerged and emotions stifled for decades are pouring forth. Latvia's long pent-up literary talent has for now found an outlet. Numerous new writings have appeared and many more are in the works. After years of intense suppression, Latvia is a nation with many stories to tell. And Latvian writers are ready and able to do so...again.

MUSIC

Music has always been a way of life for the Latvian people. Their culture is founded on folksongs which they sang and played to mark all of life's major events. The concept of Latvian music as an art form, however, did not evolve until the second half of the 19th century. Until then, the only music Latvians had to call their own were folksongs.

In 1869 Jānis Cimze began collecting folk song melodies, some of which were over 1,000 years old. Approximately 20,000 such melodies have been found.

Cimze's cycle of songs found their way into school choirs and became popular. His collected works formed the basis of Latvia's first Song Festival where thousands of singers gathered in huge choirs to sing before a large enthusiastic audience. This Song Festival, the first of many, played a major role in forging strong feelings of national identity which eventually led to Latvia's independence.

One of Latvia's greatest composers was Jāzeps Vītols, known throughout the world as Joseph Wihtol. Composer of numerous choir songs, Vītols replaced Nikolai Rimsky-Korsakov as a composition teacher at the St. Petersburg Conservatory. Some of his students included Sergei Prokofiev and Nikolai Myaskovski. Upon returning to Rīga after the Bolshevik Revolution, Vītols founded the Latvian National Opera and the State Conservatory of Music.

One of the masters of solo composition was Alfrēds Kalniņš. He wrote several hundred solo and choir songs and created many outstanding ballads. He also wrote the first Latvian opera "Baņuta", based on an old Latvian myth. It was first performed in 1920. A musical giant, Kalniņš advanced Latvian music into the European mainstream.

The three Mediņš brothers were all noted musicians. Jāzeps, the eldest, co-founded the first Latvian opera ensemble. He wrote a lyrical opera "Vaidelote" and two symphonies. Jēkabs was a music teacher who wrote piano pieces. Jānis was the youngest brother, and the most famous of the three. He wrote the music for Rainis' epic "Uguns un Nakts" (Fire and Night), created and conducted his own operas, taught composition at the State Conservatory of Music, and directed the Latvian Radio Symphony Orchestra.

Latvian music basically came to a standstill when the Soviets occupied Latvia. Numerous composers fled to the west. Those who remained in Latvia had to toe the party line if they wished to compose. Any criticism of the new regime resulted in deportation to Siberia. Creative individualism was prohibited. Music which underscored Soviet ideology was the only game in town.

Under Soviet occupation, Latvian music, Song Festivals, and music projects in general have been Russified. Yet Latvia has retained some world class choirs which travel regularly throughout Europe and Asia - always as Soviet citizens. Ave Sol, a Latvian choir that is internationally known for its musical excellence, toured the United States in 1987 where they were enthusiastically praised by American, as well as exiled Latvian audiences.

Other Latvian musicians have found conditions to be so intolerable that they have left their homelands in order to pursue their musical careers. Violinists Rasma Lielmane, Ieva Graubiņa and Ruta Krumoviča all married American music students in Moscow and thereby emigrated to the west.

Attendance at Rīga's concert halls showed a marked decrease by the early 1980's. It was evident that the Latvian people - who are passionate music lovers - were growing intolerant of music which served as a bland backdrop for communist ideology. The rise of nationalistic sentiment and Gorbachev's glasnost policies could well result in a new wave of high-quality Latvian music compositions.

The Song Festival tradition has been kept alive in spite of the attempts at Russification and Soviet domination. Due to the advent of glasnost, the next Song Festival in Rīga, in 1990, will once again be controlled by Latvians alone. Latvians from around the world are expected to attend.

Opera

Opera has always been popular in Latvia. In the 1600's Italian operas were shown in Rīga. In 1782, the ruling German gentry founded a German opera and drama theater in Rīga which staged performances in Russian, German, Italian and Polish. Richard Wagner was the director of this theater from 1837-38. Here he showed Mozart and Bellini operas and composed his first opera "Rienci". During a trip from Riga to Norway, he wrote his opera "The Flying Dutchman".

In 1893 Jēkabs Ozols wrote the first opera in Latvian, "Spoku Stundā" (The Haunted Hour). Another Latvian opera "Gunda" by Adams Ore (1853-1927) was shown in Berlin, Stuttgart, Leipzig, Tallinn and Odessa, but never in Latvia. Eižens Buke's (1877-1919) work "Liktenis" (Fate) was shown in Moscow. But the Czar did not allow him to perform his other two operas which were based on Aleksey Tolstoy's plays.

In 1913 Latvian Opera was permanently established. The first company had 12 soloists, 32 musicians, and 36 choir members. In 1919, a new opera organization was created, the Latvian National Opera. Its first production was Wagner's "Tannhauzer". There were 122 performances during the first season.

In the beginning, the Latvian National Opera had no ballet. This soon changed when the prima ballerina of Petersburg's Mariinsky Theatre, Aleksandra Feodorova, began to work with the Latvian ballet. The company soon metamorphised into a high quality dance troupe which travelled throughout Europe. In over ten years, Feodorova staged 18 classical ballets. During Latvia's 20 years of independence, the Latvian National Opera performed over 160 operas (11 originals, 5 of them Latvian), ballets and operettas.

Latvia has produced several great opera singers. During Latvia's independence the stars of Latvian opera were Adolfs Kaktiņš - baritone, Mariss Vētra - tenor, and Artūrs Priednieks-Cavara - tenor. Later Jānis Zābers (1935-1973), a tenor of international stature died of cancer before reaching the summit of a potentially world famous career. Today, Pauls Berkolds is an emerging baritone in the west, while Ingus Pētersons, Latvia's top rock star ten years ago, is today Latvia's top tenor.

Since the Soviet occupation, new Latvian operas have been written, but most are politically correct and therefore are considered weak works of art. One of the best operas to come out of this bland era was the comic opera "Minhauzena Precības" (The Wedding of Minhauzen). It is based, ironically, on a play by Mārtiņš Zīverts, (see Literature section) who fled to Sweden when Latvia lost its independence.

Rock

Rock music came to Latvia in the late 1950's. Though frowned upon by Soviet authorities, rock nonetheless filtered into Latvia via radio, relatives from the West, and sailors returning from foreign ports. Elvis Presley was very popular among Latvian youth in the 50's, and in the 60's The Beatles and Rolling Stones predominated. Young Latvian musicians imitated American and English rock bands and performed in English.

Rock music was not supported by the Soviet regime. All groups had to register with the official Soviet Orchestra Bureau. In order to gain the Bureau's approval, a group's music had to include Soviet songs. Officials regularly appeared at concerts to check up on the content of songs. If they lacked sufficient Sovietisms, the musicians were slapped with high penalty fees, their instruments were confiscated, and they were prohibited from giving public concerts. Officially outlawed groups were the norm rather than the exception.

By the 1970's, the Latvian rock community was divided into two spheres. Those who followed the party line could pursue a public career. But those groups who maintained their creative integrity were forced underground. This in turn created a musical subculture in which Latvian hard rock developed.

When French, German and Italian rock groups began singing in their own languages, the dominance of English in Latvian Rock was broken. More and more groups began writing and performing in Latvian. However, western rock music is still a major source of inspiration and fascination. Rock albums and tapes from the free world continue to fetch extremely high prices on the black market.

The early 1980's saw the emergence of several new Latvian Rock groups. Those deemed too radical by Soviet authorities were banned despite their popularity among Latvian youth. For a long time officials outlawed all rock festivals in Latvia even though they were allowed in other Soviet republics.

Rock concerts in Latvia provide yet another arena for expression of long suppressed nationalistic pride. The group "Modo" was extremely popular as their lyrics contained many patriotic references. The group did not last long under Soviet scrutiny. "Opus" which was formed after "Modo" broke up, was a big hit in the Caucasus, Middle Asian republics, Moscow and Leningrad. "Credo" has a loyal following not only in Latvia, but in other republics as well. When "Zodiaks" began playing their new jazz music, no one in the band was older than 22. Their first album, "Disco Alliance" the first of its kind in the USSR, was a hot sellout the moment it came off the presses.

"Pērkons" refuses to follow the party line. Any references to acceptable Soviet ideas are sung with noticeable irony. The group's lyrics deal with the daily problems of life in the Soviet system such as alcoholism, the abominable state of the environment and the privileged life of party members. These are all musical expressions of the frustrations felt by Latvian youth. Pērkons was often in trouble with the authorities and they were forbidden to perform to large audiences. The group's lead singer, Ieva Akurātere, has been described as having a voice somewhere between that of Joan Baez and Janis Joplin. Her popularity in Latvia transcends beyond rock enthusiasts. On October 7, 1988, she sang before an audience of 150,000 people at rally celebrating the founding of the Popular Front of Latvia.

Today, the line between "official" and "underground" rock groups has become somewhat blurred. Rock groups either have official sponsors who pay their bills, or they operate as independent agents. Some "official" groups you may come across in and around Rīga: Opus, Remix, Jumprava, Līvi, Neptūns, Zodiaks, Turaidas Roze, Sīpoli, Elpa and Tip-Top. Among the independent groups: Dzeltenie Pastnieki, Nebijušo Sajūtu Restaurēšanas Darbnīca, Dzelzceļš, Jaunais Sektors, Bastardi, Melnā Kafija, Arhīvs, Asociācijas Sektors, Linga and Jaunais Mēness.

Folklore Music

Over the past several years Latvia has experienced a revival of folk music. Many groups, of which "Skandinieki" is one of the most popular, formed to recreate Latvia's rich musical past. There is great variety within this genre. Some groups are made up of only female singers. Others feature various traditional instruments, such as the "kokle" (a small board zither), "koku zvani" (wooden bells), "klabatas" (wooden boards set into a frame) and "stabules" (endblown fipple flutes with fingerholes). Still others specialize in regional music or include folk dancing in their repertoire.

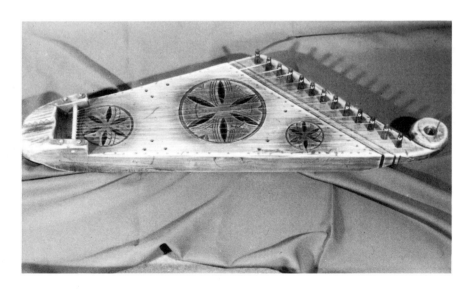

Kokle - a board zither

Students make up the majority of these groups. Their music ranges from "pure" folksongs - those that are a direct recreation of music from the past - to folk music which includes elements of country and rock. Folklore music is not considered a cultivated art form, but rather a spontaneous outlet for a daily life no longer allowed to exist.

Folklore concerts are very well attended. The audience is drawn to the concerts, as the folklore movement helps maintain nationalism, allows Latvians to hold on to their cultural and traditional roots, and gives them a deeper sense of national identity as their daily lives are increasingly worn down by Russification and Sovietization. Although the movement as a whole has not been suppressed by the authorities, individuals have been harassed. But the concerts continue to flourish nonetheless.

FINE ART

When the first Latvian painters brushed color onto a canvas, they were expanding upon a cultural heritage that dates back 4,000 years. The ceramics, textiles, metal work, and woodcrafts of Latvian folk art indicate the extent to which visual aesthetics appeal to the Latvian people. Although Latvia has suffered through slavery to foreign rulers, endured famine, plague, and countless wars, striving for beauty and harmony has prevailed and flourished.

The mid-19th century marked the beginning of Latvian fine art. Several artists from this period were educated at the St. Petersburg Academy of Arts, and they traveled and worked in West European art centers. Coupled with the National Awakening sweeping the nation, Latvian artists began to assert their national identity. Portrait painter Jānis S. Roze (1823-97) worked in Paris and Munich before returning to Rīga. Kārlis Hūns (1830-77) shared exhibitions in Paris with such greats as Cezanne, Monet, and Renoir. His subject matter focused on Latvian life from an historical perspective.

This period also saw the emergence of three artists who would have a profound influence on Latvian art through the ages: Jānis Rozentāls (1866-1916), Vilhelms Purvītis (1872-1945), and Jānis Valters (1869-1932). Although they were contemporaries, their works are as diverse as the personalities that created them.

Considered the founder of Latvian national painting, Jānis Rozentāls depicted the essence of peasant life in Latvia. "From the Cemetery" and "Leaving the Church" exemplify the rural lifestyle which

A landscape by Jānis Valters

Rozentāls captured so accurately. Travels abroad resulted in the influence of Symbolism, Art Nouveau, and Impressionism on his works, which focused on national themes. He was also a superb portrait painter, especially adept at capturing the softness, composure, and character of female subjects.

Vilhelms Purvītis is, without a doubt, the most outstanding Latvian painter of landscapes. His favorite subject was early springtime in Latvia, with melting snow, swelling rivers, budding trees played upon by an ever changing parade of light and shadow. A renowned Impressionist, Purvītis was awarded the bronze medal in the 1900 World Exhibition in Paris and the gold medal in Munich in 1901. His works can be seen in major museums, as well as in private collections, throughout Europe. Purvītis was the founder of the Latvian Academy of Art, the director of the Art Museum, and teacher to many of Latvia's finest landscape painters.

A brilliant colorist, Jānis Valters created lyrical landscapes. Although strongly influenced by Impressionism, much of his work was done in plein-air. In his later years, Valters lived in Dresden, Germany, where he is known as Johann Walter-Kurau, and his works began reflecting the influences of German Expressionism and Fauvism. The intense contrast of light and shade, and the use of pure, brilliant color set Valters apart from his contemporaries.

There are several other noteworthy painters from this period, among them Voldemārs Zeltiņš (1879-1909), whose deeply textured works projected a mood of deep emotionality, and Voldemārs Matvejs (1877-1914), a powerful experimenter who utilized various trends and styles to create his paintings. Rūdolfs Pērle (1875-1917) worked in water-colors and created dream-like, mystical paintings.

Around the time of the First World War, Latvian art reflected the mood worldwide. The old, established styles were discarded, while artists searched for new means of expression. While Latvia was struggling for independence as a nation, Latvian artists struggled for freedom of expression. This trend is best exemplified by Jāzeps Grosvalds (1891-1920), and Jēkabs Kazāks (1895-1920). Grosvalds' studies abroad strengthened his artistic idiom, which was a realistic representation of his people's lives. Spatial depth, static figures, and integrated composition all contributed to his creation of the Latvian experience during this turbulent time. Kazāks, greatly influenced by Grosvalds, used broken lines, haunting color relations, and plasticity of form to create descriptive legends of the Latvian people.

The independence years (the 1920's and 30's) saw the emergence of experimental, progressive artists - the Rīga Group. Niklāvs Strunke (1894-1966), and Romans Suta (1896-1944) favored Constructivism with its solid and simple composition, definite rhythms, and relation of color areas. Oto Skulme (1889-1967), and Uga Skulme (1895-1963) were both drawn to Cubism, with the later also incorporating Primitivism.

Voldemārs Tone (1892-1958), while displaying elements of Constructivism and Cubism, favored soft tonal effects. Leo Svemps (1897-1975), on the other hand, used intense color schemes with receding contours. In this sense, he was greatly influenced by Jānis Tīdemanis (1897-1964), who created beautiful orchestrations of color.

Augusts Annuss (1893-1984) was a master of figure compositions full of vitality and dramatic intensity, while Konrāds Ubāns (1893-1981) had a lyrical, yet exuberant, richly expressive style full of sensuous warmth.

A representative collection of the classic Latvian painters can be seen at the National Fine Arts Museum (see Museum section). The National Museum also hosts a variety of temporary exhibits of contemporary artists.

The Soviet occupation of Latvia in the Second World War halted the freedom of artistic expression, and many of the best artists fled the country. Social Realism became the dominant style. Creative expression was allowed - but only within the confines of government dictates.

Some prominent names of the early post-war era include Jūlijs Viļumainis, Ārijs Skride, Eduards Kalniņš, Valdis Kalnroze, Jānis Pauļuks, Leonīds Āriņš, and Rūdolfs Pinnis. The next generation includes Edgars Iltners, Boriss Bērziņš, Džemma Skulme, Ojārs Ābols, Indulis Zariņš, Biruta Baumane, Imants Vecozols, Edvards Grūbe, and Maija Tabaka. The most current group includes Lija Būmane, Leonīds Mauriņš, Helēna Heinrihsone, Ivars Heinrihsons, Inta Celmiņa, Anita Meldere, Laima Eglīte, Vija Maldupe, Līga Purmale, Miervaldis Polis, Juris Dimiters, Ieva Iltnere, Ģirts Muižnieks, Dace Lielā, Aija Zariņa, and Sandra Krastiņa.

Within the atmosphere of glasnost and perestroika, perhaps Latvian art will again reclaim the freedom of expression upon which it was originally built.

Doma Church in Old Town Rıga

RĪGA

As is the case with most European capitals, Rīga is the cultural and historical heart and soul of Latvia. Rīga is often referred to as "the Paris of the North", and the comparison is indeed justified. The broad, tree-lined boulevards, and numerous parks and gardens are very reminiscent of the grace and splendor of Paris. Yet Rīga has a charm and flavor all its own.

But do keep in mind the fact that Rīga's evolution as a Latvian city was arrested with the Soviet occupation. Signs of Soviet decay are visible. Restoration and upkeep of national treasures has been lax, and historical accuracy often takes a back seat to Soviet propaganda. But perestroika has created an atmosphere which allows nationalistic feelings to be openly expressed. And Latvians have always been extremely proud of their homeland and their accomplishments. Various Latvian groups are already working on restoring Riga, as well as the rest of Latvia, to its pre-Soviet state. If the current political climate continues, Rīga may soon reclaim its status as a first-class European capital.

So put on a pair of comfortable shoes and walk around Rīga as much as possible. This is an exciting time to be visiting the amber land. It is at yet another cross-road in its development. As you wander through this city, you are sure to stumble upon a sight or sound of particular interest. From the medieval Old Town to the museums, monuments, the river front, lakes and the Central Market - there is truly something for everyone.

HISTORY OF RĪGA

When the ancient tribes of Scandinavia sought access to the wealth of the lands across the Baltic Sea, they chose the Daugava River as their entry point. When early traders from the Russian heartland looked to the West, the same Daugava River offered them their needed outlet into the Baltic Sea. Whether viewed as an entry point or an outlet, the land along the banks of the Daugava River just before it empties into the Baltic Sea has been treated as a choice location for settlement, trade and military strategy for over 3,000 years. This is where the city of Rīga was born.

In the first written record of the settlement twelve miles from the mouth of the Daugava River, second century chroniclers called it "Duna urbs" (city on the Duna River). In the early Middle Ages marauding Vikings built a factory complex of barns and storehouses within the settlement and used the site as a staging area for attacks into the mainland.

The Teutonic Knights invaded Latvia in the 13th century and the ancient settlement was formally founded as the city of Rīga in 1201 by German Bishop Albert of Bremen. Some historians believe the city's name was taken from a Germanized version of 'rija', the Latvian word for barn. Along with the arrival of German settlers and rulers came city walls and fortifications. By 1207 Rīga had become the capital of the Livonian principality and the seat of the Archbishopric under direct Papal rule. While surrounded by native Latvians, the walled city became a military stronghold for the Teutonic Knights, who used it - just as the Vikings had centuries earlier - as a base of operations for launching attacks into the Latvian and Lithuanian heartland. During the ensuing centuries, these two powers - the Papacy and the German Crusaders - would vie for control of the city.

In 1272 the walls enclosing the city were completed. (Although these walls were completely torn down in the late 19th century, the moat that surrounded them still exists as a city canal and marks the boundary of modern Rīga's Old Town section). Within these walls, customs, social life, religion and architecture were dominated by German influence, following established patterns in other German-ruled cities. In 1282 Rīga officially joined the Hanseatic League and began its rapid development into one of the major trading and commercial centers on the Baltic Sea, doing a brisk trade in the export of amber, grain, wax, honey, hides, furs, smoked fish and meats.

During the 14th through 16th centuries, Rīga developed into an increasingly independent political and commercial power. Despite their German origins, Rīga's rulers looked upon themselves as indigenous natives and sought to loosen their ties to the Papacy and the Teutonic Knights. The Livonian Order, which had been formed out of the original invading force of the Teutonic Knights, sought to cut ties with Germany and assert its independence. The power of the Papacy also waned. By 1524 all the churches of Rīga had been taken over by Lutherans, who extended their influence among the peasants throughout the surrounding Latvian countryside. Major fortifications were completed in the 16th century, enabling the city to withstand raids by Ivan the Terrible of Muscovy.

In the latter part of the 16th century Rīga became, for all intents and purposes, an independent city loosely tied to the German empire. It had its own court, control over the Daugava River and the right to issue passports and coin money. It was a city divided into three classes, the first two made up of German aristocracy and merchants, while the third was composed almost exclusively of Latvians. The

Latvians had neither electoral nor administrative rights and mostly engaged in humbler occupations. Architecturally, Rīga had been shaped for the most part by its German rulers. Despite its size and importance as a Hanseatic commercial center, however, Rīga's German landlords invested little in the city, viewing it simply as a trading center.

Rīga came under Swedish influence in 1621, and quickly grew to become the largest city in the Swedish realm, surpassing even Stockholm in population. By 1648, Rīga had a thousand merchants importing goods from Russia, and forty devoted to Lithuanian imports. Swedish rule also had one other major consequence: for the first time, local Latvians were allowed to participate in the cultural life of the city. The first Latvian language bible was printed in 1638, as well as several other books and a newspaper. Latvians were also allowed into the city's Cathedral School. After four centuries of exclusion by the Germans, native Latvians began asserting their national identity and assuming a larger social role in Rīga. It was during this period that the city itself expanded beyond its original walled boundaries into the area known as Outer Rīga.

In the early 18th century, Peter the Great defeated the Swedes and established Russian rule over the Baltic region. Rīga, which fell to the Russians in 1710, nevertheless retained its German-Baltic nobility. Although a Russian Governor-General was appointed to rule the city, real control remained in the hands of the landed German gentry.

During the Napoleonic campaigns of the next century, Rīga became a center for English runners of the French continental blockade. Although Napoleon never reached the city, he had threatened to destroy this "suburb of London." In fear of a French invasion, the Russian governor of Rīga burned the city suburbs on July 12, 1812, leaving over 7,000 Latvian citizens homeless.

In the mid 19th century, Rīga's growth was spurred, oddly enough, by two major developments in the Latvian countryside. In the 1830's farmers gained permission to live in cities and in 1840 a rural education law was passed. Subsequently, educated farmers began to stream into Latvia's cities to take up trades. In Rīga, a new middle class of Latvian artisans, merchants and intellectuals was formed.

The influx of skilled workers was followed by major industrial development in the city. In 1862 a Polytechnical Institute was founded, in 1868 the Rīga-Jelgava railway was opened and in 1872 an iron railway bridge over the Daugava River was completed. To further its modernization and open transport to other cities, electricity was introduced in 1887 and the Rīga-St. Petersburg railway was opened in 1889. As a result, Rīga surpassed most Russian cities in its industrial and technical development.

Rīga's rapid modernization, combined with the emergence of a solid Latvian middle class, was accompanied by the awakening of a national consciousness and increased cultural activity. The first Rīga newspaper in the Latvian language appeared in 1824 and a Latvian Literary Society was formed the same year. The society, ironically, was formed by German pastors with the purpose of providing Latvian language courses to Germans preaching to Latvians in rural parishes. By the 1860's a growing Latvian intelligentsia emerged, determined to revive and strengthen the long supressed German and Russian-dominated Latvian culture. In 1868, the first truly Latvian cultural society - the Rīga Latvian Association - was formed. This group served as the nucleus of a national movement that became known as the Latvian National Awakening, and initiated projects such as the publication of the Latvian encyclopedia, the founding of the national theater and opera, and encouraged literary and musical projects. In 1873 the Society organized the first National Latvian Song Festival, which among other things, served as a forum for the initial performance of the Latvian National Anthem, 'God Bless Latvia'. Shortly thereafter similar societies were formed throughout Latvia, based on the Rīga model.

Until the beginning of the National Awakening, the city's most prominent structures were German-built churches and the formidable Rīga Castle. The Doma Church, one of the oldest places of worship in Latvia, was begun under Bishop Albert in the 13th century. St. Jacob's was built in 1226. The Cathedral of St. Peter was built in 1491 and featured the highest wooden steeple in the world. The Rīga Castle, first built by the Teutonic Knights in 1330, was rebuilt and expanded by the Swedes. Under the influence of National Awakening, and through efforts of the Rīga Latvian Association, distinguished new structures such as the Latvian University, Court of Appeals and Conservatory came into being in the late 19th century.

The growth of Latvian national consciousness came into full maturity during the cataclysmic events of World War I. At the outbreak of the war, Latvians did not hesitate to join forces with their Russian rulers against their age old foe, Germany. Since Russia was allied with the West, there was even hope that victory would bring democratization to Russia, and greater autonomy for Latvia.

Always an object of conquest throughout its history, Rīga was devastated once again during the war. In 1914 it had a population of over 500,000. As the Germans invaded Latvia, Russian authorities ordered the evacuation of local industries and their workers. This, combined with other war-related factors, reduced Rīga's population to 181,000 after the war. Of these, only 54.9% were Latvians.

The Latvian military regiments, known as the Latvian Riflemen, experienced some of the greatest successes - and highest casualties - of any troops in the Russian army. Their valiant defense of Latvia, combined with lack of support from, and in some cases betrayal by, the Russian High Command, led to increasing resentment against the Czar. After the war, many Latvians welcomed the Russian Revolution and began making their own revolutionary plans for Latvia. On July 30, 1917 a Latvian National Political Conference was held in Rīga, in which a far-reaching program for Latvian self-determination and autonomy was laid out.

The program, however, was threatened by both the Germans, who sought to annex Latvia to their empire, and the Bolsheviks, who had seized power in Russia and now wanted to retain control over former Czarist territories. Faced by these two threats to self-determination, a Latvian National Council of leading political and military leaders was formed. They gathered in the National Theater in Rīga on November 18, 1918 and solemnly declared Latvia's independence.

Two weeks later the Bolshevik Red Army crossed the Latvian border, intent on toppling the newly formed government in Rīga. On January 2, 1919, one day prior to the Red Army's entry into Rīga, the Latvian Government, supported by the Western allies and headed by Kārlis Ulmanis, left Rīga and established headquarters in Liepāja.

While Ulmanis and his cabinet were under British protection in Liepāja, the Germans launched a campaign to liberate Rīga from the Bolsheviks and seize Latvia for themselves. In May 1919 they succeeded, replacing the Bolshevik terror in the city with an equally bloody German terror campaign. Thousands of real or alleged Bolsheviks were left dead in the streets. When the Germans attempted to extend their conquest into Estonia, they were defeated by combined Estonian and Latvian forces. In July the Germans were forced to sign a peace treaty, and the Ulmanis government returned to power in Rīga. Despite the treaty, the Germans made one last attempt to seize the city in October. They were repulsed by Latvian forces with the help of French and British gunships positioned in the mouth of the Daugava River.

It took several months for the Latvians to defeat the remaining Bolsheviks, and on August 11, 1920, the Soviet government signed the Treaty of Rīga, renouncing forever all claims to Latvian territory. With the end of Latvia's war of independence, the task of rebuilding the war torn land began.

During Latvia's ensuing two decades of independence, Rīga once again began to flourish as a major political, cultural and commercial metropolis. As the seat of the Latvian government, Rīga finally had a chance to grow and develop as a truly Latvian city, ruled for the first time in over 700 years by its native Latvians. It nevertheless retained its international character and because of its strategic location, quickly attracted both diplomatic and commercial interest from around the world. Many Western business interests established branches in Rīga, in hopes of extending their business ties into the neighboring Soviet Russia. Foreign diplomats and intelligence agents also flocked to Rīga, using it as an observation post for monitoring developments in the Soviet Union.

In June of 1940, despite the Treaty of Rīga signed twenty years earlier, 200,000 Red Army troops entered Latvia, effectively ending Latvia's independence. On June 17 the Ulmanis government was forced to resign, and on June 18 the Russian cruiser 'Marat' arrived in Rīga, bringing with it Soviet Communist agitators and a new puppet government. Within a month, Latvia was 'annexed' to the Soviet Union and a new reign of terror was unleashed on the population.

When Nazi Germany began its invasion of the Soviet Union in 1941, Latvian nationalists initiated an insurrection against the Soviet occupiers. By June 28, Latvians in Rīga had seized the radio station and key buildings and announced the successful overthrow of the Soviet regime. Soviet forces fleeing the Germans in Lithuania, however, reentered the capital city in their retreat to Russia. They executed hundreds of Latvian partisans and in a last act of vengeance left many of Rīga's historical buildings in flames.

German troops entered Rīga on July 1, 1941. Despite initial Latvian hopes of a return to independence, the Nazis promptly proved that they were no less ruthless than the Soviet occupiers they had replaced. Latvian partisans and Jews were singled out for persecution and extermination. Rīga's large Jewish population was decimated, as tens of thousands were executed in nearby forests or sent to Nazi concentration camps. In 1943, the Germans began their retreat from Russia, and on October 13, 1944, Rīga was once again taken by Soviet forces. In the months prior to the arrival of the Soviets, hundreds of thousands of Latvians fled to the West to escape the Soviet terror. In Rīga, as elsewhere in Latvia, the fleeing Latvian refugees were soon to be replaced by an even larger number of Russians and other Soviet citizens.

Under Soviet rule, Rīga again assumed a key role in Moscow's military and political plans for the Baltic region. Soviet Russification and industrialization of Latvia was concentrated in and around the capital city. Rīga became the headquarters of the Soviet Baltic Military District, and was flooded with Soviet military personnel, bureaucrats and workers.

Today, Rīga is a city of over 900,000 inhabitants, approximately 37% of which are Latvians. The dramatic growth of Rīga's non-Latvian population under Soviet rule can be attributed to several factors. Under Communist rule, Rīga retained much of its Western attitude and character. In relative terms, Rīga had a higher standard of living than other Soviet-ruled cities and a more open cultural life. The Rīga Ballet produced, among others, such international stars as Mikhail Baryshnikov and Boris Godunov, both of whom were born and raised in the city. Rīga filmmakers also gained international renown. One Russian youth told a Baltimore Sun correspondent in 1989 that it was his life's goal to move to Rīga, because it was almost "like being in Western Europe."

Moscow has also been accused of encouraging immigration into Latvia in order to dilute nationalism in the country. For example, retired Soviet military officers are traditionally given a choice of where they can live in the Soviet Union upon leaving active duty. For many years, Moscow, Leningrad and Kiev were listed as off-limits, thus making Rīga the first major city open to the retired Soviet military. It is estimated that over 40,000 Soviet military pensioners now live in the Rīga metropolitan area.

Nevertheless, in the Gorbachev era Rīga has again assumed a central role in the national awakening of the Latvian people. Although Latvians make up a minority in the city, they have begun to predominate the city's political and cultural life. The Latvian language, once almost absent on the streets of Rīga, is now the official state language and is reassuming its leading role in civic life. All major Latvian political organizations are based in the city, and the country's largest political rallies have taken place there. On November 18, 1989, over 500,000 people - nearly 1/5th of Latvia's entire population - gathered on the banks of the Daugava River in the heart of Rīga to peacefully commemorate the 71st anniversary of Latvia's independence.

As political reform continues, and immigration of non-Latvians into the country is reduced, Rīga's Latvian character is expected to emerge and flourish once again. While Latvia's political independence has not yet been achieved, the independent spirit of this great city on the Baltic Sea has never been stronger.

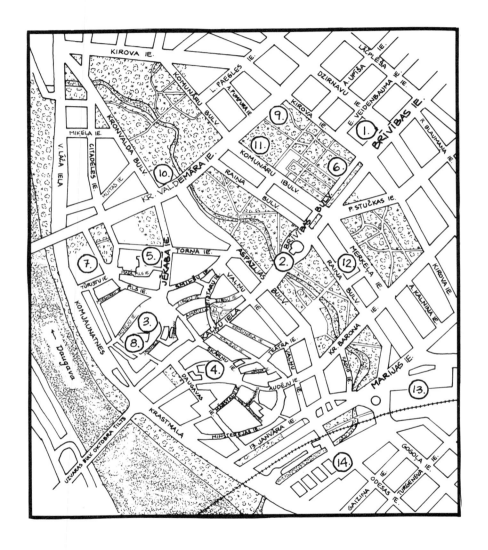

OLD TOWN RĪGA

1. Hotel Latvija
2. Freedom Monument
3. The Doma Church
4. St. Peter's Church
5. St. Jacob's Church
6. Planetarium (formerly the Orthodox Cathedral)
7. Rīga Castle
8. Doma Museum (Museum of History and Navigation)
9. National Fine Arts Museum
10. National Theater
11. Academy of Art
12. Latvian State University
13. Railway Station
14. Central Market

Rīga Castle viewed from across the Daugava River

THE OLD TOWN

The city of Rīga - as so many of its European counterparts - is blessed with a wide variety of architectural styles. Austere Romanesque, upward soaring, pointed Gothic, voluted pediments of the Renaissance, Baroque sculpted facades and portals, and the restrained forms of Classical architecture are all represented. Always a point of national pride to the Latvian people, the Old Town had fallen into a state of disrepair since the Soviet occupation. A major effort is currently underway to restore and clean up this historic part of Rīga. Although there is much work to be done before the area is returned to its pre-Soviet state, a walking tour of the Old Town will nonetheless give you a sense of returning to another century. As you enter the narrow cobblestone streets, you will see Hanseatic style warehouses, intricately decorated portals and tile roofs. Suddenly, you will find yourself stepping back to a time when high speed transportation and mass-communications were merely flights of fancy in fertile imaginations. Shrug off your twentieth century cloak and allow the sights and sounds of eras past to envelop your senses.

The walking tour starts from the Rīga Castle which stands on Pils Square, located at the corner of Kr. Valdemāra (Gorkija) iela and 18. Novembra boulevard (Komjaunatnes Krastmala) on the Daugava River. The present Castle was built by 'the Livonian Order in 1330, and served as residence for the Livonian Governors. During the years of Latvia's independence, 1918-1940, the Castle was used as the President's residence. Today, the Castle complex houses the Pionieru Pils (Pioneer Palace) and three museums: the Museum of Latvian History; the Museum of Foreign Art, which displays works by German and Dutch masters, as well as French graphics and sculpture; and the Rainis Museum of the History of Literature and Art. Jānis Rainis is considered Latvia's greatest poet. Although the museum bears his name, other writers are also represented, and there is a section of the museum dedicated to the history of the Latvian theater. The adjoining gardens display sculptures by Latvian masters.

From Pils Square turn right into Torņa iela. On the right you will see a long, low building - the Rīga Arsenal. It was built between 1828-1832, and used to be part of the city wall.

Walking past the Arsenal, turn right on Jēkaba (Komjaunatnes) iela. The Supreme Soviet House at number 11 was built in the style of Florence's Renaissance palaces. From 1919-1934 it was the seat of the Latvian national parliament. To your right is Jēkaba baznīca (St. Jacob's Church). The church was originally built outside the city walls in the beginning of the 13th century. Although Jēkaba baznīca has gone through several reconstructions, the sanctuary and three-naved basilica remain in their original form. The 240 ft. (73 m.) high steeple shows traces of 16th and 18th century restoration work in the Gothic style. The first Lutheran service in Latvia was held in this church in 1522. It is the seat of the Roman Catholic archbishopric, and an active Catholic church.

Continuing past the church, turn right on Mazā Pils iela. Numbers 17, 19 and 21/23 are known collectively as Trīs Brāļi (Three Brothers). These three buildings are outstanding examples of Rīga's medieval architecture. Number 17 was built in the 15th century and is the oldest surviving residential building in Latvia. In 1687 it was used as a bakery. The building has been very carefully restored. Number 19 was built by a merchant in 1646, who used the ground and first floors as living areas and the upper floor for storage purposes. Although the front of Number 21/23 remains intact in its original form, the interior has been modernized.

Back-track along Mazā Pils iela to Jēkaba (Komjaunatnes) iela and continue on to Smilšu iela where you will turn left. Turn left into Aldaru (Brewer) iela. At the end of the street you will find Zviedru Vārti (the Swedish Gate) at Number 11 Torna iela. This is the only surviving city gate of Rīga. It was built into the city wall in 1698 during the Swedish occupation. The gate, along with the adjoining bastion and the neighboring houses are known collectively as the Zviedru Vārti. The Soviet Latvian Architects Union is headquartered here. Walking through the Zviedru Vārti, turn right on Torņa iela,

Zviedru vārti - The Swedish Gate, dating back to 1698

at the end of which you will see the Pulvertornis (Gunpowder Tower).

Walk back to Smilšu iela and proceed to Pulvertornis. This is one of Rīga's oldest buildings, mentioned by the chroniclers as early as 1330. Of the original 18 fortification towers built into the city walls, Pulvertornis is the only surviving one. Glimpses of Rīga's turbulent history can be seen in the 9.5 ft. (2.5 m.) thick walls.

Pulvertornis - Gunpowder Tower, 1330

Nine cannonballs, dating back to Russian invasions in 1656 and 1710, are embedded in the wall. Ironically, the very walls which were built to keep foreigners out of the city today house the Soviet Latvian Revolutionary Museum.

From Pulvertornis, turn right into Meistaru iela. Walking toward the Daugava River proceed down Meistaru iela til you reach Amatu iela.

Numbers 5 and 6 at one time housed the Guild Halls, which were prominent business and social centers for the city's merchants during the Middle Ages.

Lielā Ģilde or the Great Guild Hall at Number 6 took its present form in 1859, when it was reconstructed in English Gothic style. The original structure was erected in 1330. It contains a well preserved meeting hall - Minsteres istaba (Münster room) - built in the 14th century. In the center of this original hall is a display of gifts received by the Philharmonic Society, which currently uses the hall for concerts. A second, smaller structure was added in 1521 - the Bridal Chamber. Today it contains a collection of national instruments.

Mazā Ģilde or the Small Guild Hall (Number 5) currently houses the Soviet Latvian Trade Union Council. It was built in the mid-1800's in Gothic style to match the Great Guild Hall.

Continue along Amatu iela, turn right into Doma laukums (square) and you will see the magnificent Doma baznīca - the largest church in the Baltic States. Construction of the building was begun in 1211, and it was consecrated in 1226. The remains of the first Bishop of Rīga, Meinhards, and of Archbishop Alberts are contained in the crypts. The building has seen several reconstructions and it bears evidence of the Romanesque, Gothic, Renaissance and Baroque styles of architecture. Built by German craftsmen in 1884, the pipe organ in the Doma baznīca is one of the largest, and among the most well known in the world. The organ has 6,768 pipes ranging in size from 8 mm. to 10 m. in length. Because of the superb acoustics, famous organists from around the world have traveled to Rīga in order to perform at this world-class organ, as well as to record. The latest restoration of the organ was done by Holland's Flentrop Company between 1981-1984.

Be sure to step into the inner court of the church so as to enjoy the beauty and serenity of the Doma dārzs (garden). Another point of interest is the Museum of History and Navigation of the City of Rīga. Located in the abbey building, it is situated in the longest crosspassage (containing 29 vaults) in Northern Europe.

Since the Soviet occupation, Doma baznīca has been converted into a museum and concert hall. However, on October 9, 1988 the first church service in over 30 years was held in the Doma in connection with the founding of the Tautas Fronte - the Popular Front of Latvia. There are now regularly scheduled services. (For more details on political developments, see the Recent History section.)

Leaving Doma baznīca, turn right on Palasta iela and head toward the river. Take a left turn at Komjaunatnes krastmala and watch for a

Church service in Doma Church, March, 1989.
Note the pipe organ on rear balcony.

residential building just before you reach Kaļķu iela (Lenin Street). This was the residence of Peter the Great when he lived in Rīga in 1711. It is said that he was especially fond of this house, as he could indulge his green thumb in the garden terrace as well as the hanging garden on the roof.

Continue along the riverfront crossing Strēlnieku laukums (Riflemen's

Square) until you reach Mārstaļu iela where you'll turn left. At number 21 you will find an excellent example of a Baroque mansion. This one was built in 1696 by a rich burger - Dannenstern. Further up the street at number 2/4, is the home of Johann von Reitern, a rich merchant who built this house in 1685. The mansion retains its original 17th century facade including an exquisitely ornamental portico.

Returning along Mārstaļu iela, turn left into Alksnāja iela and left again at Kalēju iela. Numbers 5-11 are typical examples of 17th century warehouses. Their narrow frontages belie the depth of these buildings. The one at number 11 still has an intact hoisting mechanism, and each main entrance is graced with the relief of a camel, elephant, etc., which served as an identifying sign. Numbers 10 and 11/17 Vecpilsētas iela are other examples of the twenty-odd medieval warehouses which are in evidence in the Old Town.

From Kalēju iela, turn left into Vecpilsētas iela. The headquarters of the Popular Front of Latvia are located at number 13/15. Walk along Vecpilsētas iela to Audēju iela. Turn left and then go right into Skārņu iela. Immediately on your right at number 24, you will see Jāņa baznīca - St. John's Church, which is first mentioned in the chronicles as a chapel of the Dominican's abbey (built in 1234). By the time the church was enlarged in 1330, the area had been developed and thus the buttresses were placed inside the church. These formed four alcoves which accomodate the side altars. During the 15th and 16th centuries, the church was heightened by a 100 ft. (30.5 m.) graduated tympanum, and lengthened by the addition of three naves - the Renaissance features of which were added to the orignal Gothic nave. The richly ornamented Baroque altar was added in the 18th century. The church vestry houses a painting by famous Latvian artist, Jānis Rozentāls.

Right next door to the church is Ekes konvents at 22 Skārņu iela. It was built in 1435 as a guest house for out of town visitors. In 1592 Rīga's Mayor N. Eke had it converted into a home for widows. The original structure with its wooden staircase and medieval heating system is still intact. Further on at number 16 is Jura baznīca (St. George's Church). It is one of the oldest churches in Rīga, having been erected in 1208 as a chapel for the first Rīga castle. Today it houses the Museum of Applied Arts.

Turning back along Skārņu iela, look to your right and you will see the most definitive landmark in all of Rīga - Pētera baznīca (St. Peter's Church). The entrance to this historic and beloved church is on Vecrīgas Square. It was originally built of wood in 1209. In 1408 it was replaced by a stone structure. In 1721 the wooden steeple was struck by lightning and consequently suffered severe damage. By special order of Peter the Great, who himself helped to

Pētera baznīca - St. Peter's Church

fight the fire, the steeple was rebuilt in 1746. The golden rooster perched atop this 380 ft. (121.7 m.) spire for close to 200 years, only to be destroyed by the retreating Red Army on June 29, 1941. A steel replica of the steeple was erected by the Soviets after World War II. At one time, Pētera baznīca was the tallest structure in Rīga. But Intourist usurped this status by building the Hotel Latvija which tops the steeple by three feet. Nonetheless, the viewing platform at the top of the steeple will give you a lovely panorama of the entire city as well as glimpses of the Baltic Sea. Don't miss it!

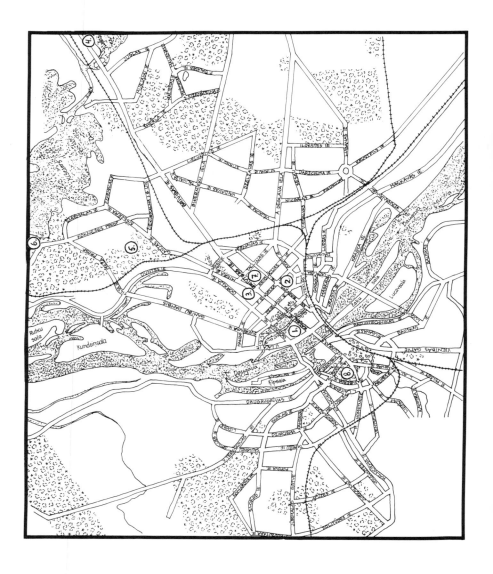

RIGA

1. Doma Church in Old Town Rīga
2. Young People's Theater
3. Dailes Theater
4. Open-air Ethnographic Museum
5. Brāļu kapi - The Cemetery of Heroes
6. Song Festival Stage
7. Rīga Sports Palace
8. Theater Museum across the Daugava River

The way in which a country depicts its attitude toward freedom, and consequently, the way in which it honors its fallen sons, is very telling of the nation's soul. The United States has the Statue of Liberty in New York harbor, and Arlington National Cemetery outside of Washington, DC. Latvia, too, has such powerful symbols. The Freedom Monument in Rīga represents the high esteem which Latvia has for the sweet, yet short lived freedom the country experienced for 22 years. The skeptic may sneer and say that's its only a piece of rock and metal. But in Latvia's case, this piece of rock and metal embodies all that is dear to the nation. And it has served as a constant reminder of what once was, and will be again. The yearning for freedom runs deep, and even an occupation force can't wipe it out from the collective mind and soul of an entire nation.

Brīvības Piemineklis

At the intersection of Brīvības (Lenina) and Raina blvds.

The Latvian Freedom Monument, located in the center of Rīga, has always been one of the most recognizable architectural landmarks of the capital. As a symbol of Latvia's independence, the monument has also been a highly volatile focal point of national pride and political yearning.

The monument was built with money donated by the Latvian people and dedicated, while Latvia was an independent republic in 1935. Between 1935 and 1940, an honor guard stood watch by the monument around the clock. Engraved on the base, are the words TĒVZEMEI UN BRIVĪBAI (For the Fatherland and Freedom). The monument features a bronze female figure symbolizing liberty, atop a travertine obelisk. In her outstretched arms are three stars, representing the major geographic territories of Latvia: Kurzeme, Vidzeme, and Latgale. Around the base of the obelisk are sculpture groups symbolizing events from Latvian history and mythology.

The history of the monument itself, however, is as dramatic as the epic liberation struggles it depicts. When the Soviets invaded Latvia in 1940, the monument was inexplicably left standing - a bold reminder of the independence the Latvian people had lost. Rather than tamper with this sacred symbol, the Soviets declared the monument off limits to locals and built a statue of Lenin 2 blocks down the street. While Lady Liberty atop the obelisk faces the West, Lenin faces East toward Moscow.

Up until the late 1980's the area around the monument was a no man's

Brīvības piemineklis - the Freedom Monument

land, carefully guarded by KGB agents in the nearby parks. These agents quickly apprehended anyone who dared approach the monument. Any attempt to place flowers at its base, or to undertake any other "political" act, resulted in arrest and charges of anti-Soviet activity. Soviet tourist books about Rīga pretended that the monument didn't exist. Intourist guides, if asked, would state that the monument was built to welcome Soviet rule in Latvia. What they neglected to mention was that Soviet rule came to Latvia 5 years after the monument was dedicated.

All of that changed in the summer of 1987, when a fledgling Latvian human rights group called Helsinki 86 decided to test Gorbachev's policy of glasnost. The group called for an illegal demonstration at the monument on June 14, 1987, in order to honor the victims of the Stalinist deportations which began on that day in 1941. Five thousand people defied the authorities and held the first public rally at the monument in over 4 decades.

Within days, local authorities were forced to politically "rehabilitate" the monument and articles began appearing in the Soviet Latvian press, praising its historic value to the Latvian people. As glasnost-inspired political activity in Latvia grew

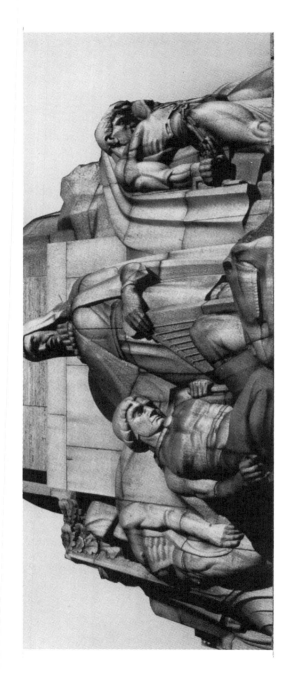

Detail of sculptural groups on the Freedom Monument. On the right are the "chain breakers", representing liberation from foreign oppressors.

bolder, the monument became the focal point for every succeeding demonstration or rally.   One year later, on June 14, 1988, over 30,000 people attended a memorial service at the monument, this time with the blessing of local authorities.   In a very real sense, the Latvian people had retaken possession of a sacred shrine which had, in effect, been locked up by the Soviets for 47 years.

Today, the monument serves as the political and social heart of the Latvian independence movement.   Its base is constantly carpeted with flowers, flags, and other national symbols.   Arrangements are lovingly cared for and rotated on a daily basis.   The steps along one side of the monument have become a political bulletin board, and are covered with announcements, flyers and other messages.   During the day, the small square around the base has become a Hyde Park-style debating center, as groups of people gather daily to engage anyone within earshot in political discussions.   The monument has also become a mecca for newlyweds, who come to the site after wedding ceremonies to be photographed with friends and family.

The monument sits on an island in one of the busiest intersections of Rīga and there is growing concern that the steady flow of traffic around the monument is causing structural damage.   Since the monument's rehabilitation, a campaign has begun to close off the area to traffic and convert it to a pedestrian mall.   Although several sit-ins have been held in the street to block traffic, local authorities have resisted this change.   Nevertheless, traffic around the monument has diminished considerably in the last year, largely because Latvian drivers, including cabbies, make a point of avoiding the area.

Cemeteries are usually not considered as places of interest for tourists.   But if you want to take a stroll through Latvia's history, and see diverse examples of Latvian sculpture and architecture in a serene, natural setting, then the 3 cemeteries listed below are definitely worth a visit.   They adjoin one another in an area directly south of Meža Parks, and are easy to reach via public transportation.

Brāļu Kapi

Bērzu av. 1b.
Public transportation: take bus #9 east on Brīvības (Ļeņina) blvd. (in front of the Hotel Latvija), or tram #4 or #11 from the National Opera.

The Cemetery of Heroes is a striking ensemble of architecture, sculpture, and nature.   The cemetery was planned in 1915, and that

Mother Latvia sculpture in the Cemetery of Heroes

same year the first group of soldiers were buried. Construction of the cemetery took 12 years (1924-1936) to complete. There are approximately 2000 graves in Brāļu Kapi. 300 of them are marked only by the word nezināms (unknown). On March 25, 1988, a memorial service for the 49,000 victims of Stalin's terrorism was held in Brāļu Kapi. 10,000 people attended the ceremony organized by the Latvian Writer's Association.

In Latvian folklore the oak stands for masculine strength, while the linden symbolizes feminine love. These powerful symbols are used extensively in the design of the cemetery. The Latvian coat of arms decorates the entrance gate. On both sides of the gate are sculptural groupings of cavalrymen. A linden-lined avenue leads to the main terrace. In the center is the eternal flame flanked by oak trees. Beyond is the cemetery itself. It is bordered by trees, shrubbery and walls, which are decorated with the coat of arms of every Latvian city and region, as well as numerous sculptures. Especially moving are the Ievainotais jātnieks (The Wounded Horseman), and Divi brāļi (The Two Brothers). All of the sculptures, so eloquent in their silence, are the work of Kārlis Zāle, who is buried here. At the far end, looking down in sorrow, is the statue Māte Latvija (Mother Latvia). In her hand she holds a wreath to honor her fallen sons.

Raiņa Kapi

Bērzu av. 1a.
Public transportation: take bus #9 east on Brīvības (Ļeņina) blvd. (in front of the Hotel Latvija), or tram #4 or #11 from the National Opera.

Latvia's beloved poet and playwright, Jānis Rainis died on September 12, 1929. After his burial 3 days later in this cemetery, it was officially renamed in his honor. A birch-lined avenue leads to his grave, which is marked by a red granite sculpture. Surrounding the monument in a semi-circle, is a travertine colonnade entwined with ivy.

Raiņa Kapi is the final resting place for many of Latvia's writers, artists, musicians, etc. The sculptures marking their graves are as creative as the people whom they honor.

Meža Kapi

Bērzu av. 2.
Public transportation: take bus #9 east on Brīvības (Ļeņina) blvd. (in front of the Hotel Latvija), or tram #4 or #11 from the National Opera.

Meža (Forest) Kapi was designed by architect G. Kūfelts (Director of Rīga's Parks) in 1913. Numerous government officials from Latvia's independent period are buried here: President Jānis Čakste, Secretary of State Zigfrīds Meierovics, and Foreign Minister Vilhelms Munters. Many of Latvia's artists, writers and poets, as well as scientists are laid to rest in this cemetery, among them

Jānis Rozentāls, Anna Brigadere, and Paulis Stradiņš.

In April, 1988, Latvia's foremost human rights activist, Gunārs Astra, was buried in Meža Kapi. In December of 1983, the Soviet authorities sentenced Astra to 7 years in strict regime incarceration, followed by 5 additional years in internal exile for the following "crimes": possession of radio program recordings, photo negatives, and books, showing a book to another person, and authoring a manuscript of a purely personal nature. The following quote is an excerpt from Astra's final statement delivered in court. "I fervently believe that these nightmarish times will end some day. This belief gives me the strength to stand before you. Our people have suffered a great deal and have learned how to survive. They will outlive this dark period of their history."

MUSEUMS AND ART EXHIBITIONS

Rīga offers the museum buff a wide variety from which to choose. Although you will note a decidedly Soviet influence in many of them - often at the expense of historical accuracy - don't let it deter you from wandering through the various museums. Much of Latvia's rich and varied past can be glimpsed and savored. This is especially true of Brīvdabas muzejs. Even if you hate museums, this one is an absolute must! The beautiful open-air setting of this ethnographic museum alone makes a visit worthwhile.

Doma Muzejs

Doma Square in Old Town, tel. 213461.
Hours: Monday, Tuesday, Thursday and Friday from 14:00-18:00, and Sunday from 10:00-14:00. Closed Wednesday & Saturday.

Founded in 1764, the Museum of History and Navigation is Rīga's oldest museum. It offers a broad overview of Rīga's historical development, as well as the evolution of navigation within Latvian territory.

Latvijas PSR Vēstures Muzejs

3 Pils Square in the Rīga Castle, tel. 223004.
Hours: Wednesday and Friday from 13:00-19:00, and Thursday, Saturday and Sunday from 11:00-17:00. Closed Monday & Tuesday.

Founded in 1869, this museum houses a wealth of material show-casing the social and cultural development of the Latvian people. Everything from coins and weapons to work tools, textiles and ceramics are on display. There is also a collection of books, maps, documents, newspapers, etc. dating as far back as the 14th century.

Latvijas PSR Dabas Muzejs

4 K. Barona street, tel. 229843 or 213291.
Hours: Monday, Wednesday and Sunday from 10:00-17:00, and Tuesday and Thursday from 13:00-20:00. Closed Friday & Saturday.

This museum of natural history will give you a close-up look at Latvia's flora and fauna. There are also regularly scheduled special exhibits on Latvian mushrooms, fruits and berries, flowers, etc., as well as some unique displays such as the herbarium of Latvia's first botanist, J. Ilsters.

Latvijas PSR Revolūcijas Muzejs

20 Smilšu street, tel. 228147.
Hours: Monday, Wednesday and Sunday from 10:00-17:00, and Tuesday and Thursday from 12:00-19:00. Closed Friday & Saturday.

This museum was created in 1940, after the Soviet occupation. The exhibits are intended to show how the Latvian nation struggled to become a revolutionary Soviet state. Part of the museum occupies the pulvertornis (Gun Powder Tower).

Latvijas Sarkano Strēlnieku Muzejs

Latvijas sarkano strēlnieku square, tel. 211030.
Hours: Tuesday and Thursday from 12:00-19:00, and Wednesday, Friday, Saturday and Sunday from 10:00-17:00. Closed Monday.

The purpose of the museum (created in 1970), is to recount the legendary accomplishments of the Latvian Riflemen. Numerous historical events have been covered up and falsified.

Paula Stradiņa Medicīnas Vēstures Muzejs

1 L. Paegles street, tel. 334228 or 220477.
Hours: Wednesday - Sunday from 12:00-18:00, closed Monday & Tuesday.

This medical museum was created by well-known Latvian surgeon Paulis Stradiņš. It primarily consists of material from his private collection. Pharmaceutical equipment, medical instruments and rare books and papers from the last century are all on display.

Farmācijas Muzejs

13/15 Riharda Vāgnera street, tel. 224221. For group tours call the director, Mr. Agris Briedis at 216903.
Hours: Wednesday - Sunday 10:00-16:00, closed Monday & Tuesday.

A branch of P. Stradiņa Medicīnas Vēstures Muzejs, showing the pharmaceutical history of Rīga. The museum is housed in a recently renovated building in the Old Town.

Latvijas PSR Valsts Mākslas Muzejs

10 Kr. Valdemāra (Gorkija) street, tel. 323204.
Hours: Wednesday and Friday from 13:00-19:00, and Thursday, Saturday and Sunday from 12:00-18:00. Closed Monday & Tuesday.

The national fine arts museum houses the treasures of Latvian artists. The first floor of this Baroque building displays mostly Russian works. The second floor is where you will find the Latvian masters. Oil paintings, watercolors, graphics, and sculpture from pre-19th century, through Latvia's independent years, to present day works are all show-cased. There are also special exhibits which you can find out about in the weekly newspaper Literatūra un Māksla (Literature and Art). The next to last page shows a listing of current exhibits. Be sure to pick up the paper early on Friday morning in the first floor lobby of the Hotel Latvija. This popular weekly tends to sell out very quickly.

Jāņa Rozentāla un Rūdolfa Blaumaņa Muzejs

12 F. Gaiļa street, apartment 9.
Hours: Call for appointment. Telephone # 331641.

Both artists lived and worked in this building. Rozentāls lived in the fifth floor apartment from 1904-1915, but Blaumanis for only two years. The garret served as a studio and displays work-related objects and personal memorabilia. The apartment on the fifth floor has changing exhibits.

Krišjāņa Barona Memoriālais Muzejs

3 K. Barona street, apartment 5, tel. 284265.

Hours: Tuesday, Thursday, Saturday & Sunday from 11:00-17:00 and Wednesday and Friday from 13:00-19:00. Closed Mondays.

The museum is housed in the apartment of Latvia's "Father of Oral Literature (dainas)" - Krišjānis Barons, (see section on Literature). The life and work of Barons are recreated within these walls.

Latvijas PSR Aizrobežas Mākslas Muzejs

3 Čakstes (Pionieru) square in the Rīga Castle, tel. 226467.
Hours: Monday and Thursday from 13:00-19:00, and Friday, Saturday and Sunday from 11:00-17:00. Closed Tuesday & Wednesday.

The museum of foreign art houses paintings, sculptures and drawings by artists from Germany, Holland, France and elsewhere. Also on display is a priceless porcelain collection.

Raiņa Literatūras un Mākslas Vēstures Muzejs

3 Čakstes (Pionieru) square in the Rīga Castle, tel. 225083.
Hours: Tuesday, Thursday, Friday and Saturday from 11:00-17:00 and Wednesday from 13:00-19:00. Closed Sunday & Monday.

This museum is a memorial to Latvia's greatest poet - Jānis Rainis, as well as it's other literary giants. If you want a history of Latvia's literature and theater - this is the place.

Jauno Mākslinieku Apvienības Nams Jāņsētā

Jāņa sēta 7 in the Old Town, tel. 210172.
Hours: Open daily from 10:00-20:00.

The new artists exhibition hall has changing displays. A recent exhibition showed the works of six of Latvia's most well-known avantgarde artists.

Ķīpsalas Izstāžu Zāle

34 Balastu dambis. Cross the Daugava River via the Vanšu bridge to Pārdaugava, and make an immediate right turn to Ķīpsala. The Balastu dambis runs parallel to the Daugava. Telephone 612467.
Hours: Wednesday-Sunday from 12:00-18:00. Closed Monday & Tuesday.

The exhibition hall has an ever-changing display of ceramics. There is also a ceramic work shop in the same building. This off of the main path exhibition hall is worth the trip as you can get a spectacular view of Rīga's skyline and harbor.

Gustava Šķiltera Piemiņas Muzejs

9 Daugavgrīvas street - across the river in Pārdaugava, tel. 625364.
Public transportation: take bus #3 or #20 from the main bus terminal to Daugavgrīvas street.
Hours: Wednesday-Sunday from 12:00-18:00. Closed Monday & Tuesday.

This memorial museum is dedicated to one of Latvia's master sculptors, Gustavs Šķilters. There is a permanent collection of his works, as well as changing displays.

Teātra Muzejs

37/39 Ed. Smiļģa street - across the river in Pārdaugava, tel. 611893.
Public transportation: tram #1 from the Strēlnieku laukums across the Daugava will deposit you at the intersection of E. Smiļģa and Slokas sts.
Hours: Wednesday from 12:00-19:00, Thursday-Sunday from 11:00-18:00. Closed Monday and Tuesday.

This museum serves as a memorial to Latvia's "Father of the Art Theater", Eduards Smiļģis. It also has a large exhibition hall where you will find changing displays as well as theater arts expositions.

Teodora Zaļkalna Memoriālais Muzejs

18 Biķernieku street, tel. 557681.
Public transportation: take trolley #14 northeast on Brīvības (Ļenina) street. It will turn off on Biķernieku street.
Hours: Call for times.

This museum is a memorial to Latvian sculptor T. Zaļkalns. He studied in Paris from 1899-1903. Also a portrait painter and art critic, Zaļkalns had a profound influence on the development of Latvian sculpture. The building served as his studio from 1936-1972.

Brīvdabas Muzejs

21 Brīvdabas street - on the eastern outskirts of Rīga by Lake Jugla, tel. 994106.

Windmill in Brīvdabas muzejs - the open-air ethnographic museum

Public transportation: take the #1 bus from the Hotel Latvija going northeast on Brīvibas (Ļeņina) blvd. The bus will drop you off near the Jugla lake, at the entrance of the open air museum.
Hours: Open daily (May 15-October 15) from 10:00-17:00.

This 200 acre, open-air, ethnographic museum in the style of Skansen in Stockholm is not to be missed! Plans for the museum, which recreates the daily life of the Latvian peasant and contains farmsteads, fragments of farming and fishing villages, housewares and work tools, were begun in 1924. When it opened to the public in 1932, it contained six structures: 5 from the Vidzeme region, and one from Latgale. By 1940, the other two regions of Latvia (Kurzeme and Zemgale) were also represented and there were a total of 48 buildings and 2000 artifacts. The museum is the first, and largest of its kind in the Soviet Union, and has been used as a model for similar museums in Lithuania, Estonia, Ukraine and Georgia.

Today, there are 98 authentic structures from various periods in Latvian history, recreating the lifestyles of poor, average and wealthy peasants and craftsmen. Although most of the exhibits are from the 18th-20th centuries, some date back even further. The oldest exhibit is Bornes baznīca (church) built in 1537, which was moved from the Zemgale region and set-up in the museum in 1937.

During the summer months, there are regularly scheduled ethnographic ensemble performances and various exhibits. Organ music concerts can be heard in the Usmas baznīca (built in 1704-5). An annual fair is held on the museum grounds during the first weeks of June. There are displays of folk crafts and art works - many of which are for sale.

Dekoratīvi Lietišķās Mākslas Muzejs

10/16 Skārņu st.
Hours: Tuesday-Sunday from 10:00-18:00.
Admission: 40 kopeks, 15 for students, 5 for trade school students.

The museum of applied arts opened in the summer of 1989 in the restored Jura baznīca (St. George church) in the Old Town. The lofty exhibition hall is housed in the former church, and has a distinct church-like feel. The architects have paid tribute to the church by excluding the former altar from the exhibition space. Opening exhibitions in the hall included tapestries, installations, pottery, glasswork and sculpture. The old churchyard has been transformed into a unique, if small, sculpture garden. The museum contains a modern cafe, which serves champagne and cognac as well as coffee, soft drinks, and other standard cafe fare.

Rīgas Motormuzejs

6 S. Eizenšteina st., tel. 552777
Public transportation: take bus #21 or #T-10 from the Hotel Latvija northeast on Brīvības (Lenina) blvd. to Mežciems.
Hours: Open daily from 10:00-20:00, closed Mondays.

The Rīga Automobile Museum opened in April, 1989. The facade of the building in which the museum is housed is reminiscent of a Rolls Royce radiator. On display you will see new and restored cars, motorcycles, bicycles, and other vehicles. From Stalin's limousine with its several centimeters thick windows, to a 16 cylinder German sports car valued at 2 million dollars, the auto buff as well as the historian is sure to spot something of interest in this unique museum.

Orthodox Cathedral - now the planetarium

Zinību Nams

23 Brīvības (Ļeņina) blvd.

Founded in 1964, the Hall of Knowledge (refered to locally as the planetarium) serves to educate the masses. Within the lecture hall, speakers discuss such topics as communism, economy, environmental issues, international relations, etc. The exhibition hall has ever changing displays. The planetarium has celestial shows, and lectures on topics related to the latest discoveries about the cosmos.

The Hall of Knowledge is housed in what used to be Rīga's Orthodox Cathedral. Built between 1876-1884, this beautiful, Byzantine style structure is topped by 5 domes, which originally were covered with gold leaf and topped by crosses. The dome-encased bell tower rises above the entrance. The interior, which once held ikons and paintings, was completely gutted and rebuilt.

THEATERS, CONCERT HALLS

In the mood for opera, ballet, the circus, a play or a concert? Rīga has it all! The theater and opera season runs from October to June, but concerts are held year round. The summer months abound with visiting theater groups and operas from Europe and regions of the Soviet Union. Check with the hotel service desk for a current listing.

Nacionālais Teātris

3 Kronvalda blvd., at the intersection of Kr. Valdemāra (Gorkija) st.

It was within these walls that Latvia declared independence on November 18, 1918. The main hall of the National Theater seats approximately 1000, while a smaller hall, Aktieru zāle (Actor's hall) in the basement accomodates 100 people. Built at the turn of the century, the National Theater is in the Baroque style with Classical elements. During the independent period (1918-1940) this Theater was THE showcase for new talent - authors, producers, actors. Included in the repertoire were native Latvian works, as well as translations of classics such as Shakespeare and Ibsen.

Jāņa Raiņa Dailes Teātris

75 Brīvības (Ļeņina) blvd.

Founded in 1920, the Dailes teātris noteworthy achievements are directly attributed to E. Smiļǧis who served as producer for 50 years. Under his leadership, numerous Latvian classics were staged, as well as just about every single play by the beloved Rainis (who was the producer in the first season of the theater's existence). Works by foreign playwrights, such as Max Frisch and Jean Annouilh, have also been performed in more recent times. As a result of the new openness, a Latvian epic about the legenedary riflemen, "Mūžības skartie" (Touched by Eternity), written by Aleksandrs Čaks was performed in 1988. Dailes teātris was moved to its present location in 1976. This modern, multi-leveled building has 2 theater halls: the large one holds over 1000 people, while the smaller can accomodate 400.

Operas un Baleta Teātris

3 Aspazijas (Padomju) blvd.

Sculpture by the National Opera. The Freedom Monument can be seen in the distance.

191

Founded in 1919, the Nacionālā opera (National Opera) was one of the highlights of Latvia's cultural life during the years of independence. The first Latvian operas were performed in this building which was completed in 1863. A fire in 1882 completely gutted the interior which was reconstructed in 1885. The building facade has a Classical style portico with 6 columns decorated with allegorical sculptures. The interior of the theater is done in luxurious Baroque. Today you can hear performances of the classics as well as Latvian works.

The Rīga Ballet has international stature. Many of the company's dancers have gone on to star in other companies, for instance Māris Liepa - a luminary in the Bolshoi Ballet. The tradition continues with his son, Andris Liepa. Because of glasnost, Andris is able to dance with the American Ballet Theatre (ABT) in the 1989/90 season without defecting. The ABT, by the way, has been under the exquisite leadership of Mikhail Baryshnikov who traces his ballet beginnings to the Riga Ballet, as does Aleksander Godunov.

Operetas Teātris

96 Brīvības (Ļeņina) blvd.

The Operetta theater was founded in 1945. Latvian, as well as Russian troupes perform classic works and also works by Latvian playwrights and composers.

Jaunatnes Teātris

The Latvian troupe works out of the old Dailes teātris at 25 Lāčplēša st.
The Russian troupe is at 37 Lāčplēša st.

The Young People's Theater was founded in 1940. Under the leadership of Ādolfs Šapiro, the group has frequently performed in other countries. In February, 1988 they were invited to perform in the Bertold Brecht Festival in West Berlin.

Leļļu Teātris

16/18 Kr. Barona st.

The Puppet Theater was founded in 1943. There is both a Latvian and a Russian troupe, both of which have international stature, having performed in such diverse places as France and Sri Lanka. Don't let the fact that this troupe performs children's plays put you off.

Adults have been known to get as enthralled as the little ones...

Rīgas Pantomīma

Connected with the VEF Cultural Palace located at 1 Ropažu (Gagarina) st.

Founded in 1956, the Rīga Pantomime is the only theater of its kind in all of Latvia. The ensemble is popular with Latvia's youth and many of the performers are themselves young people. They often perform at the above address, but periodically can be seen in other theaters. Check with the hotel service desk to find out where they are performing.

Kabata

4 Krāmu st.

This experimental theater group has put on several performances, but they are not regularly scheduled at this writing. Inquire at the hotel service desk for details.

Rīgas Cirks

4 Merķeļa st. at the intersection of A. Kalniņa st.

Housed in a building completed in 1889, the Rīga Circus is the only permanent circus in the Baltic States.

Philharmonic Society Concert Hall

6 Amatu st. in the Old Town.

Concerts are held in the Lielā Ģilde (the Great Guild Hall) whose original structure dates back to 1330. The hall holds over 800 people.

Philharmonic Society Chamber Music Hall

11a Brīvības (Ļeņina) blvd.

The 22-member orchestra plays classic and contemporary works covering a broad range of styles and periods. The hall seats 220.

Doma Koncertzāle

Doma square in Old Town

The supurb acoustics and world-class organ in this magnificent church make for incredible listening pleasure. The church seats 1436 people. For more details on the church itself, see Walking Tour of Old Town section.

UNIVERSITIES

Rīgas Politehniskais Institūts
1 Brīvības (Ļeņina) blvd. (Chancellory and Library). The school itself is in Ķīpsala, across the Daugava River.

Founded in 1862, the Rīga Polytechnical Institute is the oldest institute of higher learning in Latvia. Originally it was located in a building on Arhitektu st., which is now part of the Latvian State University. RPI was incorporated into the State University in 1919, but in 1958 it became a separate entity once again. The school's 13,000 students pursue studies in 15 different faculties.

Latvijas Valsts Universitāte
19a Raina blvd.

Built between 1866-1885, the Latvian State University's buildings incorporate Roman, Byzantine and Renaissance architectural elements. The school is easily recognized from a distance by its rotating rooftop observatory. Founded in 1919, the University has 12,400 students and 11 faculties.

Latvijas Valsts Konservatorija
1 Kr. Barona st.

The Latvian State Conservatory was founded in 1919, and today, the school is housed in an 1873 Classic style building. Over 700 students choose their study programs from 3 faculties with 11 areas of specialization.

Latvijas Mākslas Akadēmija
13 Kalpaka (Komunāru) blvd.

The Latvian Academy of Art was founded in 1919. The graceful, neo-Gothic style building which it occupies today was constructed in 1902. 350 students specialize in 9 areas within 2 faculties.

Zinātņu Akadēmija
19 Turgeņeva St.

Founded in 1946, the Academy of Sciences has 3 main branches: Social Sciences, Biology and Chemisty, and Physics. The main building was erected in 1958. This standard 1950's Soviet-style high rise building was supposed to be an architectural compliment to the towers of the Old Town buildings...judge for yourself!

PARKS

The Latvian people love nature. Just walk around Rīga and you will see how true this is. There are parks and gardens everywhere. To be specific, there are 11 parks, 17 gardens and 35 squares, which constitute the city's so-called "green zone" encompassing some 6000 hectares. Among the trees and flowers there are statues, monuments, sculptures and fountains. While most of the parks and gardens were created in the late 1800's, there are several which date back to the early 1700's. Whether you need a rest from sightseeing, want to take a leisurely stroll, or merely want to sit back and contemplate, there is a natural haven nearby.

Dziesmu Svētku Parks

Bounded by V. Lāča, Hanzas & Rūpniecības sts.

This park - the oldest in Rīga - was created in 1721 and named in honor of Peter I - Ķeizardārzs (the Czar's Garden). It encompasses 7.6. hectares and is made up of straight alleys, paths and canals. An elm tree planted by Peter himself still grows in the park, along with 15 native and 57 introduced tree species. In the 1920's, the park was renamed Viestura dārzs, and was extensively rearranged. Located at the main entrance on Hanzas st. is the Aleksandra Vārti (Alexander's Gate). The Roman-style structure has sandstone columns and cornices and is decorated with 4 bronze medallions. Built between 1815-17 to commemorate Napoleon's defeat, it was moved to its present location in 1936. This was also the site of the first Latvian Song Festival held in 1873. To mark the 100th anniversary, a memorial wall and rock sculpture was unveiled on July 21, 1973. The park was renamed Dziesmu Svētku Parks (Song Festival Park) in honor of the event.

Kirova Parks

Bounded by Elizabetes (Kirova), K. Barona, Merķeļa and Tērbates (P. Stučkas) sts.

The park opened in 1817 and was named Vērmanes Dārzs after the woman who donated the property to the city. Its original purpose was to serve as a place of rest and relaxation for those Rīga residents, who due to poor health, could not get to outlying areas. It soon became one of Rīga's most magnificent and popular parks - containing a restaurant, open-air concert platform, a bronze fountain cast in Berlin, playground, an ice skating rink in winter, a sun-dial, and the very first rose-garden in the city. This park was the sight of various activities ranging from hot-air balloon demonstrations to book fairs and photography exhibits. After the Soviet take-over, a bust of the Russian, Sergei Kirov was installed and the park was named after him.

Arkādijas Parks

Across the Daugava River, bounded by O. Vācieša and F. Brīvzemnieka sts.
Public transportation: take tram #5 or #10 from the Strēlnieku laukums in Old Town.

This park began as a private garden in the 1850's. Purchased by the city in 1896, the park was completed in 1911. Situated high on the ancient shores of the Daugava River, the multi-leveled natural beauty of the terrain lent itself to the creation of diverse landscapes and scenic overlooks. It was named after Arcadia - a mountainous region in ancient Greece, traditionally known for the pastoral innocence of its people. Within its boundaries are waterfalls, ponds, bridges, a restaurant (the original building now houses a movie theater), a view of the Rīga towers at one end, and of the Mārupīte River at the other end. Park expansion in the mid 1920's included an open-air concert platform, and playground. During the independence years, it was considered the second most beautiful park in Rīga, surpassed only by Vērmanes Dārzs (Kirova parks). Today, the open air concert platform and the only structure in the park are owned and operated by the Latvian Environmental Protection Club. The building houses temporary exhibits arranged by the environmentalists.

Ziedoņa Dārzs

Bounded by Marijas (Suvorova), Krāsotāju, Artilērijas and Matīsa (Revolūcijas) sts.

The park was created between 1937-39. It contains wide lawns, tree-lined alleys, a square with a fountain, rose garden, pavilion, wading pool, and playground. In recent years, various sculptures have been placed on the grounds. One of them, a statue of the poet Aleksandrs Čaks, was vandalized in 1987 but has since been restored.

Komunāru Parks

Bounded by Brīvības (Ļeņina) & Kalpaka (Komunāru) blvds., and Elizabetes (Kirova) & Kr. Valdemara (Gorkija) sts.

Formerly known as the Esplanade, the first plantings in this park are from 1884 when the Orthodox Cathedral (now the Hall of Knowledge) was built. The park evolved further in 1901 when the Rīga Stock Exchange (now the Art Academy) was built. During the years of independence, several song festivals were held in this park, as well as sport festivals, theatrical performances, and various fairs. The park was completed in 1952 and contains a rose garden, and a monument to J. Rainis - the great Latvian poet and playwright (see section on Literature). The opening day of the annual poetry festival is held in the park on September 11th, on Rainis' birthday.

Pilsētas Kanālis

A semi-circle beginning and ending at the Daugava River, basically separating the Old Town from modern Rīga.

The city canal, which was the castle moat in 1650, began evolving to its present state in 1856. In 1858-59 the first greenery was planted and the first bridges crossing the canal were built at Kr. Valdemāra (Gorkija), Brīvības (Ļeņina), K. Barona and Marijas (Suvorova) sts. In the 1880's-90's the greenery around the Opera and Ballet Theater was planted, and a sculptural fountain was erected in 1887 and reconstructed in 1986. The green belt on both sides of the canal is home to 19 native variety trees as well as 110 introduced species among those several rare varieties planted in 1900.

Bastejkalns

Bounded by the city canal and Aspazijas (Padomju) blvd.

The city canal near the National Opera

Bastion Hill was built on the site of ancient city fortifications. In 1887, greenery and paths were re-arranged and a pavilion (since torn down) was built. In 1898 a stream complete with cascades and waterfalls, and an alpine garden were created. In 1892 a foot bridge was built. Nearby you'll find a monument to Latvian writer R. Blaumanis erected in 1929. This was not only the first sculptural monument of a Latvian cultural figure, it was also the first to be erected in a park setting. In the late 1960's, various sculptures were added to the park's decor.

Botāniskais Dārzs

Across the Daugava River at 2 Kandavas st.
Public transportation: take tram #1 or #4 from Old Town across the Daugava to Kandavas st.

The Latvian State University Botanical Garden has everything from decorative flower gardens and arboretums devoted to particular types of trees and shrubs, to collections of tropical as well as medicinal plants.

View of Rīga from Bastejkalns - Bastion Hill

Mežaparks

On the shores of Ķīšezers between Meža and Viestura avenues.
Public transportation: take tram #1 or #4 from the Old Town going
northeast, or bus #9 east on Brīvības (Ļeņina) blvd.

Set in a pine forest on the western shore of Ķīšezers, Mežaparks

199

(Forest Park) is by far Rīga's largest. Within its boundaries you will find, among other things: an amusement park, movie theater, open-air concert platform, children's railway, dance pavilion, restaurants, boathouses, an exhibition hall, and a sports complex which includes a pavilion, ice-skating rink, skiing base and game fields. Also in the park is the Rīga Zoo, which was founded in 1912. It has 9 sections, including an aquarium and terrarium, and is home to over 3200 animals. Located in the northeastern part of town, Mežaparks was laid out in 1909, although the area, formerly called Ķeizarmežs (the Czar's Forest), was a popular rest and recreation area in the 1860's. It can be reached by bus, tram or boat from the center of Rīga.

MOVIE THEATERS

The advent of glasnost and perestroika has influenced the world of cinema in Latvia. The first of its kind International Film Forum "Arsenāls" was held in Rīga from September 23 - October 1, 1988. Over 200 experimental and avantgarde genre films were shown during the 9 day film festival. Entries came from 25 countries, including Sweden, Argentina, Great Britain, China, France, Portugal, USA, India, and West Germany among others. There was a daily festival newspaper, ARS, published by one of the organizers, The Rīga Video Centre. There are plans to hold this event on a more regular basis, although at this time there is no concrete date for the next festival. Call the Rīga Video Centre at 212131 to find out the latest status.

There are approximately 30 kīnoteātri (movie theaters) in Rīga. A large percentage of the movies are in Russian, although there are Latvian films, as well as foreign. The movies are not equal to those eminating from Hollywood, instead, they have their own unique charm. For a listing of what's currently showing at the movies, check page 8 in the newspaper RĪGAS BALSS (VOICE OF RIGA), page 3 of CĪŅA (STRUGGLE), or for information about movies, call 287472. Listed below are a sampling of movie theaters in Rīga, with addresses and telephone numbers. Some of the movie theaters have little cafes and bars. By all means go early enough to partake of some refreshment before the movie begins.

Aurora	1 Tilta st.	393956
Daile	31 K. Barona st.	283854
Daina	108/110 Maskavas st.	223904
Gaisma	54 Tallinas st.	295078

Ilga	27 Lidoņu st.	468318
Jugla	428a Brīvības (Ļeņina) blvd.	521280
Kosmoss	18a Pētersalas st.	329704
Lāčplēsis	52/54 Lāčplēsa st.	285884
Liesma	30 Vienības av.	612317
Maskava	2 E. Smiltēna st.	254118
Palladium	21 Marijas (Suvorova) st.	283353
Rīga	61 Elizabetes (Kirova) st.	289755
Teika	2 Zemitāna (21. julija) square	551110

Pils iela - Castle street in Old Town

SPORTS

Sports have always been an integral part of Latvian life. Latvian folklore gives evidence of the relation between mythological beliefs and physical activities. An annual contest was held between 2 teams who competed by rolling wooden discs to a finish line. It was always held in the springtime to assure that the sun, and therefore summer, would triumph over the darkness of winter. The skills necessary for sustenance as well as victory in wartime, such as archery, javelin throwing, horsemanship, sprinting, and wrestling, evolved into games and competitions.

And Latvians have proven their mettle in these areas in recent times as well. In Melbourne, Inese Jaunzeme set a new Olympic record in the javelin throw in 1956. In the same event, Jānis Lūsis took the gold in 1968 in Mexico City, and Dainis Kūla did likewise in the 1980 Moscow Games. In basketball, the women's team, Riga TTT, has won numerous European championships. Five Latvian men played on the silver medal winning Soviet basketball team in the 50's and 60's.

In recent years, Latvian athletes have also excelled in winter sports during World Championships as well as Olympic Games. Helmūts Balderis from the ice hockey team, Rīgas Dinamo, was a starter, and one of the highest scorers on the Soviet Olympic medal winning team in the late 70's. He is currently signed up to play with the Minneapolis North Stars. Vēra Zozuļa won the gold medal in luge at Lake Placid in 1980. And the Soviet bobsled team in recent Olympic Games has been dominated by Latvian men. In the 1984 Sarayevo Olympics, Zintis Ekmanis won the bronze, with Jānis Kipurs and Aivars Snepsts coming in 4th. In the 1988 Calgary Games, Kipurs won a gold medal in the 2-man bobsled, and a bronze medal in the 4-man bobsled.

There are numerous stadiums and arenas in Rīga. Listed below are some of the larger ones. Check out page 4 of the newspaper SPORTS for a listing of all upcoming sporting events along with times and locations.

Rīgas Sporta Pils	75 K. Barona st.	279669
Rīgas Sporta Maneža	160 Maskavas st.	241770
Daugava Stadions	1 Augšiela	274815
Dinamo Stadions	1a E. Melngaiļa st.	331211
Lokomotīves Sporta Nams	10 Uzvaras blvd.	236337

SAUNAS

The pirts (sauna) is a custom that Latvians share with their Scandinavian neighbors on the Baltic Sea. Traditionally, homesteads in the countryside had their own pirts. Often it would be dug into the earth. Inside the pirts, boulders were used as a stove. They were heated to a glowing red color, and then doused with water. Voila! A steam bath. Family members would sit or recline on benches to enjoy the steamy environment. Small brooms made of birch branches were used to encourage circulation and open up the pores. In winter, it was not unusual to rub down with snow after taking a sauna.

But the pirts was not limited to the countryside. Rīga had public saunas as far back as the end of the 13th century. By the 14th century, the city had 6 such public facilities. And the tradition continues to this day. There are numerous pirts in Rīga. Listed below is just a sampling.

1/3 Lubānas st.	242459
37 Tallinas st.	273367
38 Marijas (Suvorova) st.	276871
7 Dagmāras st.	458616
12 Mārtiņa st.	617989

MARKETS

Market places are a common sight in towns and cities world wide, and Rīga is no exception. In 13th century Rīga, the market place was set up right outside of the city walls. By the 14th century, it was moved closer to the Daugava River. One of the oldest, dating back to 1571, and longest standing market places was located outside the city walls right on the shores of the Daugava River. Merchants sold fish, fowl, game, fruits and vegetables, and eventually household items, tools, craft works, clothing, used furniture, etc. In 1928, it was the largest and busiest of Rīga's 13 market places. It was liquidated in 1930, when the massive Centrāltirgus (Central Market) was opened.

Before the Soviet takeover, Rīga's markets were overflowing with goods. Since the occupation, centralization, mismanagement, and outright ineptness created severe shortages of food, and other of life's necessities. Markets were as empty as store shelves. Because of Gorbachev's economic reforms, this is slowly changing - at least in the markets, where goods are again available. Unfortunately, the prices are so high that most locals cannot afford to shop there with any regularity. By Western standards, however, the prices are well within reach.

Centrālais Kolhozu Tirgus
7 Nēģu st., tel. 229981.

A prominent Rīga landmark near the Daugava River, the Central Market is housed in zeppelin hangars that were used by the Germans in World War I. The 5 huge buildings were rebuilt between 1924-1930 to accomodate the needs of a market place. It is one of the largest markets in all of Europe.

Āgenskalna Kolhozu Tirgus
64 L. Laicēna st., across the Daugava River, tel. 611564.
Public transportation: take tram #2 from the Strēlnieku laukums (square) in Old Town to the 4th stop after the Daugava river.

Čiekurkalna Kolhozu Tirgus
70 Ropažu (J. Gagarina) st., tel. 552541.
Public transportation: take tram #2 or #6 east boarding at the National Opera.

Torņakalna Kolhozu Tirgus
3 Telts st., across the Daugava River, tel. 612394.
Public transportation: take tram #5 from Strēlnieku laukums (square) in Old Town across the Daugava to the last stop.

Vidzemes Kolhozu Tirgus
90 Brīvības (Ļeņina) blvd., tel. 272263.

NEWSPAPERS AND MAGAZINES

You'll find several Latvian language newspapers and magazines at Rīga's kiosks. Newspapers are also displayed on boards at bus stops around Rīga. All of them have traditionally followed the government line until recently. With the advent of glasnost many have begun to write about previously taboo topics. Latvia's most popular newspaper is also its newest. ATMODA (AWAKENING) is the weekly information bulletin of the Popular Front of Latvia, and is the most independent publication in Latvia. A Russian-language edition is also gaining popularity throughout the Soviet Union. It is pro-independence (its motto is "For a free and independent Latvia"), lively and even-handedly critical - of the Soviet regime as well as of the Popular Front. This newspaper is not for sale at kiosks, but you will often find copies being sold near the Freedom Monument, and a copy of the current edition is posted on the boards at bus stops. It is also one of the few Latvian newspapers to offer a monthly English-language edition. If you can't readily find a copy, go to the Popular Front offices at 13/15 Vecpilsētas street in Rīga's Old Town. They may also have other English-language publications you might find of interest.

Without knowledge of the language, the newspapers and magazines listed below won't do Western tourists much good in so far as news of the day goes. However, some of them are worth picking up for purposes of entertainment information, i.e. concerts, movies, sports, theater, etc.

Rīgas Balss (Voice of Rīga)

An 8 page evening daily (no weekends), Fridays an expanded version. Costs 3 kopeks. Page 7 has a good sports section, and TV listing. Page 8 has entertainment information.

Cīņa (Struggle)

4-page daily published 300 times per year. The official newspaper of the Latvian Communist Party Central Committee. Costs 3 kopeks. Page 3 contains concert and movie programs.

Literatūra un Māksla (Literature and Art)

16-page weekly, every Friday, costs 10 kopeks. This publication sells out as soon as it hits the stands. It covers the entire spectrum of artistic and literary events: short stories, serialized fiction pieces, poetry, book and exhibit reviews, and information on upcoming cultural events, as well as articles on the preservation of historically and culturally significant buildings, artifacts, etc.

Sports (Sport)

4-page paper, 4 times a week on Tuesdays, Wednesdays, Saturdays and Sundays. Costs 3 kopeks. Page 4 is invaluable for the sports enthusiast who wants to know what games and competitions are scheduled, where they will be held, and at what time.

TELEVISION

Although most programming comes from Moscow, Rīga does have its own channel - 3. If you're into music, you might want to check out Videoritmi (Video rhythm) and Varavīksne (Rainbow). Labvakar (Good Evening) is Latvia's most popular news and information program in the very vanguard of glasnost. Its Western style investigative reporting takes on everything from formerly taboo Latvian history to bureaucratic incompetence in the government. A popular anecdote in Latvia concerned a former Latvian procurator who was often a target of the program's barbs: "Why doesn't Procurator Dzenītis go out at night? Because he's afraid someone will say 'labvakar' (good evening) to him." It airs every other Sunday evening and just about every Latvian family is glued to their TV set when this program comes on. Time and duration vary depending on material, although some programs have run as long as three hours.

A publication called RĪGAS VIĻŅI (RĪGA'S AIRWAVES) is available at kiosks, and gives air times and a rundown of all major musical, artistic and literary programs.

CHURCH SERVICES

Lutheran Churches:

<u>Doma Baznīca</u>
Doma Square in the Old Town.

Sunday at 10:00.

<u>Jaunā Ģertrūdes Baznīca</u>
119 Brīvības (Ļenina) blvd., at the intersection of Tallinas street.

Sunday at 10:00, Thursday at 19:00, Tuesday and Friday from 11:00-13:00.

<u>Vecā Ģertrūdes Baznīca</u>
8 Ģertrūdes (K. Marksa) street, at the intersection of Veidenbauma

street. Close to the Hotel Latvija.

Sunday and Monday 10:00, Wednesday and Saturday at 19:00.

Jāņa Baznīca
7 Jāņa street in the Old Town.

Sunday at 10:00 and 12:00, Thursday and Friday at 19:00.

Catholic Churches:

Sv. Jēkaba Katedrāle
2 Vēstures street in the Old Town.

Sundays and holidays at 08:00, 09:00, 11:00 and 18:30, workdays at 08:00.

Sāpju Dievmātes Baznīca
5 Pils street in the Old Town.

Sundays and holidays at 08:00, 09:00, 11:00, and 19:00, workdays at 07:00.

Sv. Franciska Baznīca
16 Kijevas street.

Sundays and holidays at 08:00, 09:00, 11:00, and 19:00, workdays at 07:00, 07:30 (mass is celebrated by the Bishop), and 19:00.

WHERE TO STAY

Western tourists traveling with group or individual tours, stay in the modern Hotel Latvija, at 55 Elizabetes (Kirov) st., tel. 212525, or in the older Hotel Rīga in the Old Town, at 22 Aspazijas (Padomju) blvd., tel. 224313, which was renovated in 1987. Both Intourist hotels provide visitors with a variety of services: arranging tours, exchanging money, making restaurant reservations, securing theater and concert tickets, ordering cabs, etc. Each has a bar, restaurants, kiosk, and foreign currency store. On an individual tour, a double costs about $100 per night, including breakfast.

Depending on length of stay (usually 7-15 days) and time of year, a group tour will cost between $1650 and $2800 and includes air fare, hotel, meals, etc.

There are numerous travel agencies which can arrange group or individual tours to Latvia. These are just a sampling:

New York -   Baltic American Holidays   Union Tours
              501 5th Av.   79 Madison Av.
              New York, NY 10017   New York, NY 10016
              1-800-835-6688   1-800-451-9511

Massachusetts - Baltic Tours
              77 Oak St. Suite 4
              Newton, MA 02164
              617-965-8080

California -   Biruta's Tours
              P.O. Box 5410
              San Mateo, CA 94402
              415-349-1622

Washington - Baltic Travel and Tours
              P.O. Box 98794
              Seattle, WA 98198
              206-824-6612

For the more independent, adventurous, or budget conscious traveler, it is possible to stay in a private home in Rīga for $175 per week (1989 rates). This is a wonderful way to meet a local family and to get a feel for every-day life in Rīga. For details on this unique plan, contact

                    Inroads, Inc.
                    P.O. Box 3197
                    Merrifield, VA 22116-3197
                    616-383-0178

EAT, DRINK AND BE MERRY

Latvian cuisine has evolved from peasant life. It is basic, hearty fare, created for the sustenance of hard working farmers and fishermen. Dairy products, whole grains, fish and meat, especially bacon, vegetables, and fruits and berries are the mainstay of the Latvian diet. Flavoring comes primarily from dill, caraway, onions, and cream. But more exotic spices are used for special occasions, and are an integral part of holiday fare.

A Bit of Background

During the independent years, Latvia's dairy industry expanded greatly, and soon the country ranked 4th among European countries in the export of butter. During these same years, Latvia went from a grain importing to an exporting country. The commercial fishing industry evolved from the 75 fishing hamlets which dotted the coast line. The fruits of the sea were delivered fresh to markets and processing plants in the cities. The 9 canneries in Rīga alone, exported their products to the rest of Europe, the United States, Australia, Africa and Asia. Rīgas Šprotes (Rīga's Sardines) were a well-known brand all over the world. Today, the Soviet method of collective farming and fishing, has changed the very essence of Latvia's traditional economy. It has created a situation, whereby the very products taken from Latvia's land and water, are often scarce or totally unavailable in the country. With major economic reforms looming on the horizon, this situation may soon be reversed.

About The Cuisine

Dairy products - in the form of biezpiens (cottage cheese), siers (cheese), and rūgušpiens (yogurt) - are used extensively in Latvian cooking. The same is true of putras (cooked whole grains), including griķi (buckwheat), grūbas (barley), and auzas (oats). You will always find rupmaize (rye bread) in a dark, dense manifestation, and saldskāba maize (sweet/sour rye bread). And no holiday or celebration would be complete without pīrāgi (yeast dough buns filled with bacon and onions).

Because of the proximity to the Baltic Sea, and the numerous inland rivers and lakes, zivis (fish) also rank high on the list. You will find them in the form of kotletes (cutlets), galerts (aspic), zupa (soup), tomātu mērce (tomato sauce), žāvēta (smoked), pildīta (stuffed), and salāti (salad). Siļķe (herring), līdaka (pike), lasis (salmon), and zutis (eel) are among the most common.

When it comes to gaļa (meat), you will encounter vērša (beef), teļa (veal), cūkas (pork), jēra (lamb), vista or cāļu (chicken), pīle (duck), and zoss (goose), or in the form of desa (sausage). Cūkas galerts (pork in aspic) is especially tasty and served with etiķis (vinegar) and sinepes (mustard) or mārrutki (horseradish). The meat may be prepared as a cepetis (roast), karbonāde (chops), frikadeles (meatballs), galerts (aspic), sautējums (stew) or salāti (salad).

The most commonly used vegetables include bietes (beets), kāposti (cabbage), kartupeļi (potatoes), skābi kāposti (sauerkraut), burkāni (carrots), redīsi (radishes), rutki (black radish), svaigi gurķi (cucumbers) and skābi gurķi (pickles), zirņi (peas), puķu kāposti (cauliflower), sēnes (mushrooms), sīpoli (onions), and tomāti (tomatoes). Among greens you will often find skābenes (sorrel), spināti (spinach), lociņi (green onions), and lapu salāti (lettuce). Vegetables and greens are combined in a myriad of ways. Salāti (salads) are most often dressed with skābais krējums (sour cream). Kartupeļu salāti (potato salad) is a delight, and when beets, herring, and apples are added it becomes rasols. Potatoes are often served as pankūkas (pancakes), and are a meal in themselves.

Zupas (soups) are very popular in Latvia, and appear in numerous variations. Buljons (bouillon) often accompanies the meat course, and pīrāgi with various fillings are served alongside. It becomes a full meal when frikadeles (meatballs) are added. Svaigu kāpostu zupa (cabbage soup) and zivju-piena zupa (fish soup with a milk base) make good use of local products. For a refreshing summertime soup, try skābeņu (sorrel), or biešu (beet). An ancient recipe handed down through the generations and still popular today is skābā putra (sour barley soup). It is made with cracked barley, buttermilk, milk and sour cream. It sounds more like a porridge, and indeed putra means just that. But it is actually in the form of a cold refreshing soup.

And finally, what would life be without dessert! Latvian desserts make extensive use of fresh berries and fruits. In summer, upenes (black currants), dzērvenes (cranberries), ērkšķogas (gooseberries), jāņogas (red currants), avenes (raspberries), and brūklenes (whortleberries) are often cooked into a ķīsels (thickened fruit soup) and served cold, either alone or over buberts (custard pudding). Fruit juices, usually cranberry or red currant, whipped up with mannā (cream of wheat) result in a divine, ancient dessert called debess mannā (heavenly manna), which is usually served with vaniļas mērce (vanilla sauce). In winter, dried apples, pears, and plums are cooked up as kompots (compote) and served with putu krējums (whipped cream).

A Latvian birthday, or other celebration, would not be complete without a klinģeris. This rich, yeast coffee bread is shaped in the form of a pretzel, studded with rozīnes (raisins) and mandeles (almonds), and flavored with safrāns (saffron), and/or kardamons (cardamom). And of course there are all manner of tortes (cakes), with fillings of jam and buttercreams, as well as countless variations of kucinas or cepumi (cookies).

Beverages

Besides fruit juices, you are likely to run across a concoction called kvass. This fermented, incredibly refreshing drink is made from either rye bread or fruit, water, yeast and sugar or honey. Another unique Latvian drink is bērzu sula (birch juice). Birch trees are tapped for their sap, which is then combined with rye bread crusts, and black currant bush twigs. The mixture is left in a cool place until it reaches the desired degree of tartness. Then it is bottled with some raisins and stored in a cool place for 6 weeks, when it is ready to enjoy. For a singular taste sensation, be sure you try some bērzu sula!

Alcoholic Beverages

For something that is uniquely Latvian, be sure to pick up a bottle of Rīgas Melnais Balzāms (Riga's Black Balsam). There is nothing like it anywhere. It is a thick, black liquid typed as a medicinal tonic. At best, the taste can be described as bitter. It calms the nerves, and also is great for an upset stomach. Production of Melnais Balzāms was begun in the 1700's in Rīga. The exact recipe is to this day a closely guarded secret. But some of the ingredients include: ginger, oak bark, bitter orange peels, linden blossoms, iris roots, nutmeg, peppermint, valerian, cognac, and sugar. This award winning (Paris, Naples), 45% alcohol drink is sometimes mixed with vodka before imbibing.

Allažu Ķimelis is a caraway flavored liqueur, while the dessert liqueur Kursa has a berry flavor. You will also come across Kristal Dzidrais - a locally made vodka. For the alus (beer) lover, there are several brands from which to choose: Aldara, Lāčplēša, Senču, Rīgas, Ilģuciema Tumšais (dark), and Bauskas Tumšais (dark) and Gaišais (pale).

Restaurants

Rīga has a multitude of restaurants. Most of the better ones are in hotels, and these also provide floor shows at dinner time. Its best to make reservations through Intourist. Below is a sampling.

Hotel Latvija, 55 Elizabetes (Kirova) st., has 3 restaurants, the largest, featuring a floor show is on the second floor. Pie kamīna (By the fireplace) is located on the 26th floor.

Hotel Rīga, 22 Aspazijas (Padomju) blvd. Restaurant, cafe and the more elegant restaurant, Vecrīga, where parties are served in individual rooms resembling farmhouses of the various regions of Latvia. A band is housed in a ship in the courtyard between the "farmhouses". The courtyard doubles as a dance floor. Rīga's most elegant parties are held in Vecrīga.

Hotel Rīdzene, 1 Kalpaka (Komunara) blvd. Restaurant and bar.

Hotel Daugava, 24 Kuǧu st. Restaurant and the Dzelme bar.

Hotel Metropole, 36/38 Aspazijas (Padomju) blvd. Restaurant.

Astorija, 16 Audēju st., tel. 213466, located on the 5th floor of the Centrālais Universālveikals (department store) building.

Pūt Vējiņi, 18/20 Jauniela (in the Old Town), tel. 228841

Pie Kristapa, 25/27 Jauniela (in the Old Town), tel. 227590.

Sculptural detail of building in Old Town which houses the restaurant Pie Kristapa

Cafes

Rīga is packed with cafes too numerous to mention. Here are a few of the more interesting ones.

Arhitekts	4 Amatu st.	225172
Baltā Roze	7/9 Brīvības (Ļeņina) blvd.	224424
Līgo	114 Brīvības (Ļeņina) blvd.	273821
Lira	45/47 Dzirnavu st.	334016
Možums	3 Skūņu st.	223943
Palete	12 Gļeznotāju st.	228057
Meža Pasaka	25 Juglas st.	531372
Pingvīns	47 Brīvības (Ļeņina) blvd.	227211
Polonēze	3 R. Vagnera st.	222759
Vidzeme	83 Brīvības (Ļeņina) blvd.	375707
Zelta Rudens	25 K. Valdemāra (Gorkija) st.	220751
Zem Ozola (a beer bar)	9 Blaumaņa st.	213983

WHERE TO SHOP

The best places for shopping in Rīga are souvenir shops for arts, crafts and jewelry, and book stores. Another option are the valūtas veikali (foreign currency stores). Purchases from the above mentioned stores can be taken out of the country without special permission. Be sure to keep your receipts, and don't remove tags from the items.

You will need permission to transport the following items out of the country: articles of cultural, historic, artistic or scientific significance, including, among others, antiques, works of art, rare books and manuscripts, semi-precious and precious stones and metals, porcelain, etchings, etc. IF IN DOUBT, CHECK WITH INTOURIST.

Permits for such items can be obtained from the Latvian SSR Ministry of Culture, located in the National Art Museum at 10a K. Valdemāra (Gorkija) st. You must bring in the item for documenting. A service fee will be charged and an export permit issued. The permit and all documentation must be presented at customs upon leaving the country, at which time the excise duty will be collected. This amount is equal to 100% of the value of the item as indicated on the permit.

Souvenir and Specialty Shops

Don't miss these shops if you're looking for souvenirs for friends and family, decorative pieces for your home or office, or if you simply want to have a keepsake by which to remember your trip. You are sure to find something appropriate and uniquely Latvian. When browsing through these stores, look for art, architecture, and photography books. You will also find all manner of folk crafts: beautiful straw, linen and wool weavings, traditional motif knitted goods, ceramics, and wood carvings, metal and leatherworks, jewelry, and of course, amber.

Bookstores

Mākslas grāmata	31 Kr. Barona st.	283810
Centrālā grāmatnīca	24 Aspazijas (Padomju) blvd.	226970
Gaisma	17 Brīvības (Ļeņina) blvd.	228929
Avots	32 Aspazijas (Padomju) blvd.	226466

Jewelry Stores

Pērle	3 Kr. Barona st.	284327
Rota	15 Brīvības (Ļeņina) blvd.	224124

Gift Shops

Sakta	32 Brīvības (Ļeņina) blvd.	211679
Daiļrāde	21 Valņu st.	

Children

Bērnu pasaule	25 Matīsa (Revolūcijas) st.	270442

Valūtas Veikali (Foreign Currency Stores)

- 2nd floor of Hotel Rīga, 22 Aspazijas (Padomju) blvd.
- 1st floor of Hotel Latvija, 55 Elizabetes (Kirova) st. The store can be reached through a separate entrance on Brīvības (Ļeņina) blvd.

These special stores are open only to foreigners, as they do not accept local currency, i.e. rubles. You can pay with foreign currency, traveler's checks, and major credit cards: American Express, Visa and Mastercard. When checking on the price of particular items, tell the clerk which currency you will be paying with so she can calculate the price. The daily exchange rate is posted above the entry.

The items you can purchase range from automobiles and electronic equipment to clothing, watches, jewelry, perfume and personal care items, records, books, folk crafts, cigarettes, food, beverages -

including alcoholic, and souvenirs. The goods are produced in the Soviet Union as well as Western countries. Not all items are available at all times.

GETTING AROUND TOWN

Rīga has a great public transportation network which makes it very easy to move around the city. There are busses, trams, trolleys and taxis - all relatively inexpensive by western standards.

By Bus, Tram, and Trolley

The main Bus Terminal is at 1 Prāgas street, telephone 213611. It is located between the Daugava River and the train station, kitty-corner across the city canal from the Central Market. Local as well as long distance routes originate from here.

There are numerous bus, tram, and trolley routes throughout the entire city. They run quite often (especially in the city center) and are cheap. Trolleys and busses run until midnight, and trams until 1 am. Tickets are available at kiosks (newspaper stands) or the bus depot. A single ride on the tram costs 3 kopeks, a trolley is 4 kopeks and the bus will run you 5 kopeks (unless it happens to be an ekspresis [express], which costs 10 kopeks). The honor system is at work here, as you must validate your own ticket upon entering the vehicle. The validating machine is usually located right next to the door. Just insert the ticket in the slot and push down the handle. If you should happen to have a lot of luggage with you, then you will need to purchase an additional ticket for it on busses, and two additional tickets for trams and trolleys. The penalty for riding without a ticket is 3-5 rubles. Monthly passes are available for 5.60 rubles. These will allow you unlimited travel on busses, trams, and trolleys for a month.

NOTE: If you are riding out to the airport (bus #22 across the Vanšu bridge), you have to validate two tickets for yourself and at least one for your luggage. The airport lies just outside the single ticket zone, and the zone crossing is a favorite point for a surprise check of valid tickets followed by the 3-5 ruble penalty.

By Taxi

The easiest way of getting around is by taksometrs (taxi). You can order a taxi by telephone - call 334041, 42, 43 or 44. Or you can go to the nearest taxi stand (see the listing below). If you're in the center of town, you can hail one on the street. Most state-operated taxis are light green colored Volgas. They are marked with a black "T" on the side and have a light on the roof. The fares on state taxis are 20 kopeks per kilometer plus a 20 kopek start up fee.

Another option is the set route taxi, which costs 30 kopeks. The vehicles are actually mini-busses, with room for 11 passengers. There are 13 routes, all originating in the center of town, at the train station. You can pick up maps of the 13 routes here as well. These taxis operate between 1 in the afternoon and 2 in the morning (13:00-02:00), except the route to Mežaparks which runs from 13:00-24:00. They will pick you up (room permitting) at any of the designated points along the set route. Waiting time is approximately 10-20 minutes, depending on the route and time of day.

And perestroika has created yet another option - private taxis. Fares in privately operated cabs are varied. They can be at the state price of 20 kopeks/km., or 30 kopeks/km., or at a price agreed upon by driver and passenger. If you don't want to be surprised at your destination, ask about the fare before you get in a private taxi.

TAXI STANDS

There are almost always taxis at the Hotel Latvija. Listed below are taxi stands that are centrally located, or near points of interest for tourists.

- The Bus Terminal square
- The Train Station square
- The Rīga Airport
- Brīvības (Ļeņina) blvd. at the Vidzemes marketplace (near the Dailes Theater)
- At the corner of Elizabetes (Kirova) and Plkv. Brieža (Sverdlova) sts. by Kronvalda parks
- Tērbatas (P. Stučkas) st. by Kirova park near Elizabetes (Kirova) st.
- At the corner of Veidenbauma and Ģertrūdes (K. Marksa) sts. at the Old St. Gertrude Church
- Aspazijas (Padomju) blvd. across from the Hotel Rīga
- At the corner of Meža and Kokneses avs. by Meža Parks
- At the corner of Brīvības (Ļeņina) blvd. and Juglas st. near Brīvdabas muzējs (the outdoor ethnographic museum)
- On Melnsila st. between Āgenskalna and Kristapa sts. (about 3 blocks from the Botanical Gardens, which are across the Daugava River
- At Bērzu av. and Gaujas st. at the entrance to Brāļu Kapi (Cemetery

of Heroes)

By Train

If you want to travel by train to Jūrmala, or elsewhere outside of Rīga, go to the Central Train Station located on Stacijas Laukums (Station Square). To order tickets by phone, call 226002. For train information call 007.

GAS STATIONS

- 386 Brīvības (Ļeņina) blvd.
- 349 Maskavas street
- 3 Miera street
- 32 M. Nometņu street
- 78 Pērnavas street
- 1 Skaistkalnes street
- 37 Vestienas street
- 9 Sporta street
- 142 Jūrmalas avenue
- 1 Krustpils street

AUTO REPAIR

- 116 Brīvības (Ļeņina) blvd.
- 35 Vagoņu street
- 97 Krasta street
- 1 Rencenu street
- 349 Maskavas street

TELEPHONES

Making a local call from a pay phone is quite easy in Rīga. There are free-standing phone booths, as well as newer models, which are built onto the sides of buildings. To execute your call, simply deposit a 2 kopek coin. When you hear the tone, dial the number. After your party answers, wait for the coin to drop and then proceed with your conversation. Information can be reached by dialing 09.

Long distance calls are another matter entirely. Direct dial does not exist. And long distance is expensive: a one-minute call to New York, for instance, will run you 6 rubles. The easiest way to place a long distance call is through your hotel service bureau. If you'd rather use a public phone, the long distance operator can be reached at 812. For long distance information, dial 818.

TELEGRAMS

To send a telegram from a public phone dial 06. You can also go through your hotel service bureau.

Note: Telegram and long distance phone services are also available at the main post office located at 21 Brīvības (Ļeņina) blvd. Call the post office at 224155 to confirm hours of operation.

POST OFFICES

When those post cards are ready to go, or the weight of souvenirs is too cumbersome - you can go to one of 60 post offices in Rīga to mail them back home. Listed below are those most centrally located.

Main Post Office	21 Brīvības (Ļeņina) blvd.	224155
# 1	13 Matīsa (Revolūcijas) st.	296778
# 8	In the Central Train Station	225342
#10	41/43 Elizabetes (Kirova) st.	333093
#22	2a K. Valdemāra (Gorkija) st.	227254
#36	110 Marijas (Suvorova) st.	274913
#50	On the Train Station Square	213197

PERSONAL SERVICES

If you need to have shoes or clothing repaired, your hair cut, or your clothes washed or drycleaned, check with the hotel service desk. They should be able to arrange for all these services. If you prefer to take care of it yourself, listed below are some of your options.

Self-service laundromats:

355 Brīvības (Ļeņina) blvd., tel. 521514
93 Murjāņu st., tel. 533992
15 Silciema st., tel. 523127

17 Kr. Barona st., tel. 284895 (clothes will be washed for you in 48 hrs.)

Drycleaner:

52 Kr. Barona st., tel. 271953.   One-day service available.   They will also clean stains, and iron your clothes on the spot.

Clothing repair:

49 Brīvības (Ļeņina) blvd., tel. 281459

Shoe repair:

Minor repairs done while you wait.
46 Maskavas st., tel. 280283.
29/31 Tērbatas (P. Stučkas) st., tel. 282912
29 Āgenskalna st., tel. 614002 (across the Daugava River).

Hairdressers for men and women:

69 Elizabetes (Kirova) st., tel. 224797

WHERE TO TURN FOR HELP

Medical Attention

If you take any prescription medication on a regular basis, <u>be sure to bring an ample supply with you</u>. Medicine IS NOT readily available in Latvia.   Even non-prescription items, such as aspirin, heartburn/acid indigestion remedies, eye drops, and cold relief medicines are the exception rather than the rule.

In a medical emergency, turn to your hotel service bureau for assistance. Listed below are some centrally located pharmacies and hospitals. But again, its much wiser to be prepared by taking medical supplies with you.

Pharmacies

# 4	4 Brīvības (Ļenina) blvd.	271619
# 7	21a Elizabetes (Kirova) st.	331809
#20	108/110 Maskavas st.	222558
#24	1 Patvērsmes st.	392589
#38	64 Matīsa (Revolūcijas) st.	272174

Hospitals

# 1	5 Aizsargu (Sarkanarmijas) st.	270136
# 3	122/128 Maskavas st.	241770
# 5	13 E. Veidenbauma st.	224864

Emergency Phone Numbers

Fire	01
Milicija (police)	02
Ambulance	03
Auto accidents	223074
Lost property	219635

Approaching the sandy beaches of Jūrmala from a pine forest

DAY TRIPS FROM RIGA

Jūrmala

Once you've taken in the sites of Rīga, or if you just want a change of pace from the hustle and bustle of the city, there is a haven nearby: Jūrmala. With its wide, sandy beaches and dunes topped by majestic pines, its picturesque cottages scattered in the woods, and its spas, which utilize the fresh sea air, and the curative qualities of the local mineral springs and mud, Jūrmala has been a favorite resort for the residents of Rīga as far back as the end of the 18th century. It will not take you long to understand why Jūrmala has been referred to as the Baltic Riviera.

Although technically a single administrative unit, Jūrmala is actually a series of coastal villages. This beautiful 10-mile stretch of land along the coast is bordered by the Lielupe River on the south, and the Gulf of Rīga on the north. Jūrmala is easily reached by land via train, bus or taxi from Rīga. Or if you prefer, take the scenic water route by catching a river bus in Rīga (embark at the foot of the Oktobra bridge), which will take you along the Daugava River to the Gulf of Rīga and into the Lielupe River.

A word of caution. For all its natural beauty, don't plan on swimming in any of the inviting beaches along Jūrmala. The Soviets have polluted the Baltic Sea to such a degree, that swimming now poses a health risk. By all means stroll along the powdery, white sand beaches and enjoy the view, and the sea air. It will relax, refresh and energize you. Keep your eyes open while on the beach, as you just might find a piece of dzintars (amber), especially if a storm has just passed. When you've had your fill, turn your back to the water and start exploring the quaint villages.

Traveling west from Rīga, the first stop is Lielupe, at the mouth of the Lielupe River. Be sure to climb up the sand dunes. Lielupe is the location of the highest dune along this section of coastline. You'll be rewarded by a glorious, wide ranging view of the sea. If you're so inclined, check out the Yacht Club on the river.

On to Bulduri. Check out the Horticultural College with its lime-tree studded grounds on Viestura st. Then head for the beach where you can stop for a bite to eat at the Jūras Pērle (Pearl of the Sea) restaurant. It's located at 2 Vienības av. The dining room juts out over the beach providing a lovely view and the sensation of being on a boat about to cast off.

Duly fortified, walk along the beach to Dzintari. You'll know you've reached it when you spot the Dzintaru Koncertzāle - a branch of the Latvian Philharmonic Society - alongside the shore on Turaidas st. The musical season in this open-air concert hall runs May - September. It is also the site of an historical non-musical event. In September, 1986, US government officials led a delegation of 270 Americans here to participate in the Chautauqua Conference, a week of uncensored debates with Soviet leaders. The US side pointed out that their government did not recognize the illegal incorporation of Latvia into the Soviet Union. Independent Latvia's flag pins, outlawed at that time in Latvia, were worn by US delegates. Hundreds of Latvians flocked to this site to express their dissatisfaction with Soviet rule. Some view this event as the first example of glasnost in Latvia, since there was open discussion of political topics without any repercussions to the local population.

As you leave the Dzintaru Koncertzāle, walk up Turaidas st., turn right on Jūras st. and you're in Majori. Take a left at the first street, J. Pliekšāna. On your left, at number 5/7 is the Raiņa Vasarnīca Muzejs. Its open every day from 10:00-17:00, but closed on Tuesdays. The beloved Latvian poet, Jānis Rainis, bought this house in the fall of 1926, and it is here that he died on September 12, 1929. Everything in his room has been left intact, including books, papers and the woven blanket on the bed, which his mother made for him. His dressing gown, in which he was photographed 2 days before his death, hangs between the windows. Another room contains numerous materials belonging to his wife, Aspazija, a poet in her own right. The third room belonged to the housekeeper. The ground floor is used for lectures and films about Rainis.

When you leave the museum, continue along Pliekšāna st. til you see the rail tracks. Near the train station is a statue of the legendary Lāčplēsis (The Bear Slayer), about whom Andrejs Pumpurs wrote in his epic poem of the same name. From here, head back towards the shore along Teatra st. Stop in at the Līgo beer bar at number 1, or keep walking to Jomas st., turn right, and you'll find a branch of the Jūrmala History and Art Museum. Further up Jomas st. is the Jūrmala restaurant at number 47/49.

The next, and oldest village along this stretch is Dubulti. At number 13 Muzeja st. you will find a Lutheran church which today houses the Jūrmala History and Art Museum. Open daily from 10:00-17:00, but closed on Tuesdays. Walk along the birch lined avenue to Jaundubulti, and then on to Pumpuri, Melluži and Asari. Along the way watch for market places which, depending on the season, can provide you with fruits, berries, vegetables, mushrooms and flowers.

Heading inland you will eventually reach Ķemeri, where you will find a spa complex. The health giving benefits of the sulphur springs, mineral water and peat and other types of mud found in the area, were first tapped into by a local forester named Ķemeris. His primitive baths and wooden huts built at the start of the 19th century, were a far cry from the resort complex, bearing his name, which exists today. Do stroll around the park grounds and enjoy the scenery. There is a little river which is spanned by several pretty footbridges. And don't miss the Orthodox church, built completely of wood in 1893, which is decorated with intricate wood carvings. Walk through the Cemetary of Heroes and then cross the bridge leading to the little house standing on an island in the middle of a man-made lake. Its a nice place to pause and reflect on your day at Jūrmala.

Salaspils

Salaspils, first mentioned as a settlement in 1186, has been the site of death and destruction throughout the ages. The battle of Salaspils, which took place in 1605 during the Swedish-Polish War, kept the Swedes from gaining a foothold in Latvia. Some 12,000 Swedes led by the King himself, Karl IX, attacked a Polish unit of approximately 4,000 men. During the day-long battle, the Poles killed 9,000 of the enemy. Only one-third of the Swedish army managed to retreat back to their ships docked in the Bay of Rīga.

In more recent times, Salaspils was the location of a Nazi concentration camp. Built by the Nazis during their occupation of Latvia in the 2nd World War, the camp was burned to the ground when the Germans retreated. By the time they left, 100,000 people had been put to death at Salaspils - among them Latvians, Jews, Czechs, Poles, French, Belgians, Austrians and Dutch.

The Salaspils Memorial was erected in 1967 to honor these victims. It is an eerie, solemn and moving sight. A huge concrete wall marking the entrance is engraved with the words, "Beyond these gates the earth moans". The seven sculptures located on the grounds evoke the suffering, as well as the spirit of those who died here.

Salaspils is also home to an atomic reactor located in the Physics Institute of the Academy of Sciences. The reactor was activated in 1961, and reconstructed in 1979 to provide more power.

Salaspils is 18 km. southeast of Rīga, and is easily reached by train. Exit at the Dārziņi station, and follow the footpath to the Memorial.

THE TOWNS AND CITIES OF LATVIA

Lovely as Rīga and its environs are, the rest of Latvia has its own unique charm, with much to offer the tourist. Traveling through the countryside to Latvia's other towns and cities will reveal sights and sounds unlike those you have experienced in the capital. From the Kurzeme coast, to the central breadbasket and out to the highlands and lake district in easternmost Latgale, you will find delights of all kinds. Many Latvian towns suffered considerable destruction during the second World War - yet others came through virtually unscathed. The picturesque setting of these towns is alone worth the trip.

Straupes pils - Straupe castle on the Brasla River in central Vidzeme near Cēsis

A number of Latvia's urban centers evolved from early tribal settlements near rivers. Towns grew up around wooden fortresses built for protection from enemies. Subsequent invasions by Poles, Swedes, Germans and Russians resulted in fortresses being replaced by stone castles. Remnants of these structures can still be seen today. These occupying powers also left their mark on local traditions, political systems and religious character of the towns.

Urban growth increased dramatically during Latvia's independent years. Since 1941, there has also been considerable growth in the larger towns and cities. Unfortunately, it is the result of Soviet industrialization and the consequent massive influx of a non-Latvian work force. The same phenomenon has also resulted in the creation of industrial settlements, such as Stučka. These are bland, characterless places implanted on Latvian soil. They reflect only sovietization - not the rich and varied culture, tradition, history and soul of the Latvian nation.

A word of caution. Despite glasnost and perestroika, free travel around all of Latvia is not yet a reality. Most regions outside of Rīga are closed to foreign tourists. In January of 1988, however, several regions were opened. The rules and regulations covering travel to these newly opened areas are still a bit complex.

The following regions of Vidzeme are open to travelers:

> Valka
> Valmiera
> Cēsis
> Limbaži
> Alūksne

These regions may be accessed by public transportation from Rīga. It is also possible to travel to Vidzeme by private car, but one must access the areas using the M-12 international motorist's route. Car travel is not permitted in transit through closed areas of Latvia. The open regions include some of the cities described in this section: Valmiera, Ainaži, and Cēsis.

The following cities are open to travelers, but may be accessed only via public transportation (with the exception of Saulkrasti, which may be accessed via M-12), given the fact that the regions surrounding them are still off limits:

> Jūrmala
> Ķemeri
> Saulkrasti
> Ogre
> Ikšķile

Salaspils
Sigulda
Ventspils

The following section contains information on Ventspils and Sigulda; Jūrmala and Salaspils are described in the section "Daytrips from Rīga".

Other cities contained in this section are not as yet officially open to foreigners. It is possible, however, to request permission from Intourist to travel to these cities.

The Baltic coastline in Vidzeme near Saulkrasti

AINAŽI

From Rīga, head north on M-12, the Rīga-Tallinn Highway. As you pass through Saulkrasti, past the gas station and the Saulkrasti road sign, on both sides of the road you will see a beautiful private summer resort district. After all, this part of the coastline is still protected by the Gulf of Rīga. Nearby is the Varava restaurant and beer tavern - a great place to quench your thirst.

As you travel further north, take the time to pull over to the seashore. There are some spectacular views of the Baltic, and the dune-grass covered, wind-swept beaches are dramatically different from those you saw at Jūrmala. You are definitely getting closer to the open waters of the Baltic Sea.

After you cross the little Salaca River, you will be in the town of Salacgrīva. This is a perfect place to stop for a bite to eat at the Pie Bocmaņa restaurant. Continuing north, just before reaching the Estonian border, you will enter Ainaži. This port city is the cradle of Latvia's maritime life. A ship building facility, which operated during the late 1800's, built over 50 ships. With the help of Krišjānis Valdemārs, the Ainažu Maritime School was founded here in 1864. Ainaži experienced dramatic economic growth in the late 19th century. But World War II inflicted heavy damage on the port town, and it never fully recovered. The Maritime School is now an interesting Maritime Museum, which is open daily from 10-16:00, tel. 43349. If you didn't get to Latvia by car, Intourist can arrange an excursion for you to Ainaži.

BAUSKA

The ancient town of Bauska (dating back to 1236) is located in the Zemgale region, due south of Rīga, near the Lithuanian border. It is easily accessed by highway M-12, which has recently been opened to tourist traffic. Bauska grew up around the area where the Mūsa and Mēmele Rivers meet, forming the Lielupe River. As a matter of fact, the area around Bauska boasts the densest river network in all of Latvia.

Bauska was a significant Semigallian center in 1236, but the first mention in historical documents comes much later in 1443. Bauska was officially registered as a town in 1609, and over time, it developed into a significant trade and commercial center. Today, Bauska is primarily known as a textile manufacturing center.

The ruins of the massive 15th century stone castle built by the Livonian Order offer an opportunity to walk back in time imagining the different historical rulers to which Latvians were subjected. The castle was used by the Dukes of Courland, the Swedes, the Poles and the Russians. Begun in 1443, the first section of the castle was completed in 1451. Reconstruction of the castle was begun in 1584, after the Livonian War. The Bauska Castle was blown up in 1706 during the Northern War. It was never rebuilt and only the ruins remain today.

In Bauska's old town section (currently undergoing major reconstruction) you can still see the one story wooden buildings characteristic of the 18th and 19th centuries. The 16th century Holy Spirit Church is also worth noting. The church steeple, which was struck by lightning in the beginning of the 19th century, has never been repaired.

POINTS OF INTEREST NEAR BAUSKA

The Castle of MEŽOTNE - northeast of Bauska.

Settlement in this area goes back to the early 1200's, when it was inhabited by Viesturs and his Semigallian tribe. The present Classic style castle was built between 1797 and 1813. The exterior of the castle has been restored, as well as portions of the interior. A stroll around the well-maintained grounds will provide you some lovely views of the Lielupe River.

The Castle of RUNDĀLE - 11 km. west of Bauska.

The castle served as the summer residence for the Dukes of Courland. It is considered an artistic monument, and is one of Latvia's most outstanding examples of Baroque architecture. The interior consists of Baroque as well as Rococo elements. Designed by the Italian architect Francesco Bartolomeo Rastrelli, construction of the castle was begun in 1736. The castle was completed in 1768 and restoration work was started in 1972. In addition to viewing the castle

The Castle of Rundāle

interior, be sure to check out the displays of European and Latvian decorative craftwork, and Latvian architectural and sculptural art from the 13th-19th centuries.

TĒRVETE - west of Bauska

Tērvete is the historic administrative center of the ancient Semigallian tribes. This area of forests, rivers and lakes was home to the mightiest of Latvian kings, Viesturs. Along with his 12 chieftains, Viesturs ruled the entire area from his wooden fortress. In 1280, his successor, Namejs, mounted an attack on Rīga. The following year, German warriors retaliated. Their overwhelming power - some 14,000 men - guaranteed a German victory. Against such odds, Namejs was unable to recapture his fortress. Namejs and his tribe chose exile in Lithuania over servitude to the German occupiers. The Semigallian wooden fortress was destroyed, and in its place, the Germans built a stone castle in 1339, the ruins of which can still be seen today.

Tērvete serves as the gateway to the beautiful Meža ainavu parks (Forest Landscape Park), which is within easy walking distance from the village. A good starting point is the Annas Brigaderes memoriālais muzejs (Anna Brigadere Memorial Museum) named Sprīdīši, after one of this author's most famous characters. Brigadere is the beloved writer of children's stories, plays and poems. Born in 1861, Brigadere spent her life in this area, drawing inspiration from the natural wonders around her. She lived in Sprīdīši from 1922 until her death in 1933. The rooms she lived and worked in have been well preserved. As you leave the museum, walk down to the stream from which the writer drew her daily water supply.

The park consists of several distinct areas, among them: Saules noskaņu parks (Moods of the Sun Park); Veco priežu parks (Ancient Pines Park) - where you will see some of the oldest and tallest pines in all of Latvia; Pasaku mežs (Fairytale Forest); and Rūķīšu mežs (Dwarf Forest). Within the park you will find, in addition to the pines, indigenous ancient, massive oaks, silvery-white birch groves, junipers, lindens, and European mountain ash, as well as a variety of introduced trees and bushes. There are numerous marked footpaths, bridges, and observation decks with names such as Sapņu Pilī (In the Dream Castle). This is truly an enchanting, and enchanted forest. There are a variety of wooden sculptures scattered within these woods, all contributing to the fairytale feeling you are sure to experience as you stroll along. Be sure to see Sprīdītis, and milzis (giant) Lutausis, as well as Meža ķēniņš (The Forest King), and Rūķītis (The Little Dwarf).

The Anna Brigadere Memorial Museum, Sprīdīši

CĒSIS

The numerous castle mounds and archeological excavations give evidence of just how ancient the settlements are in Cēsis. The site of modern Cēsis, located near the banks of the Gauja River in the central highlands of Vidzeme, was first reported as a settlement back in 1224. By 1383, historical documents described it as a walled fortress. Because of its strategic location on the Gauja River, Cēsis rapidly developed into a commercial center. It was a member of the Hanseatic League as early as the late 14th century. In 1577, Ivan the Terrible inflicted incredible atrocities on those trying to defend Cēsis against his attacks. One legend from this period claims that the residents of the castle filled the cellar with powder and blew themselves up rather than surrendering to Ivan the Terrible. Repeatedly devastated by wars, Cēsis nearly burned to the ground in a major fire in 1671. During the War of National Liberation (1918-1920), Cēsis was the site of a decisive battle (June 19-23, 1919) fought and won against German forces by a combined Latvian-Estonian regiment.

By the 1930's, Cēsis had developed into a tourist center. Today, Cēsis is at the very center of the Gauja National Park. Walk around the narrow little streets in the old town, as well as the numerous parks. Then check out the ancient cemetery by the railroad station, and Riekstu kalns (Nut hill). Don't miss St. John's Church, which was built in 1281, or the Cēsis castle and castle park.

Latvian poet Eduards Veidenbaums was born in Cēsis, and is buried in nearby Liepa cemetary. A museum dedicated to Veidenbaum's life is located in Kalači, outside of Cēsis. Other notable Latvian writers and cultural figures having ties to Cēsis include the brothers Kaudzītis, Kronvaldu Atis, Auseklis, Jānis Poruks and others. Kārlis Skalbe, poet, and author of fairy tales, is honored in a memorial museum at nearby Vecpiebalga.

Cēsis is also considered the birthplace of the maroon-white-maroon Latvian flag. According to legend, Latvians were fighting against invading crusaders. The mortally wounded Latvian chieftain was placed on an all white flag captured from the enemy in a previous battle. The warriors gathered around their dying leader, who told them they must continue to defend their homeland, and drive the enemy away. The chieftain died, and his body was removed from the enemy flag upon which he had lain. The flag was soaked in blood everywhere but the very center where the chieftain's body had been. Saddened and enraged by his death, the warriors tied the maroon-white-maroon flag to a spear, attacked the invaders, and drove them from their land. Historical chronicles mention 1279 as the date when this Latvian flag made its first public appearance, as it were. Warriors from Cēsis carried it with them when they arrived in Rīga for another battle.

The Cēsis Castle

DAUGAVPILS

The first historical record of Daugavpils appeared in 1275, but archeological digs have shown that the banks of the Daugava River in the Daugavpils region have been inhabited since the Stone Age. Daugavpils received its charter in 1582 and by the 1860's, it was connected by rail to Petersburg, Rīga, and Warsaw among others. This made it an even more important trade and commerce center. It has always been of great strategic importance to the Latvian nation due to its proximity to Russia, Poland, and Lithuania.

The city has always had a multi-national character because of its location at the crossroads between East and West. But the massive industrial growth forced by the Soviets has resulted in a population explosion of a foreign work force so immense, that only 10% of the population is made up of Latvians. This influx of non-Latvians has also elevated Daugavpils to the status of second largest city in Latvia after Rīga.

Points of interest include the 19th century Daugavpils castle and fortress, which are considered to be the only examples of this kind still intact in all of Latvia. You might also want to check out the city high school, built in 1835. The Regional Studies and Art Museum on Lenina st. might be enlightening. The Latgale Applied Arts Studio turns out interesting ceramics reflecting the style of the Latgale region. And there is also the ancient Grīvas cemetary.

Approximately 3 kilometers upstream on the Daugava River is the site of the proposed Daugavpils hydrolectric power station. Due to massive public opposition, the building of the dam was halted in 1987.

The spiritual center of Latvia's Catholic community lies 46 km. northeast of Daugavpils. Situated in the scenic lake region, the Aglona Baroque style Cathedral-Basilica attracts 50,000 pilgrims during mid-August religious holidays.

JĒKABPILS

Jēkabpils takes its name from Duke Jacob himself. This area was settled in the 13th century, and is associated with the Duchy of Courland. The city grew up on the left bank of the Daugava River. Jēkabpils was a popular stopover point for the Vikings and other travelers along the Daugava trade route. The city was officially founded in 1920. Jēkabpils, along with Krustpils, right across the river, is primarily a river town. But sugar refineries and manufacturing plants for building materials make it an important industrial center as well.

Jēkabpils has several historically significant sites. Among the oldest structures is the Krustpils castle built in the 13th century. Not quite as old is the Krustpils church, which dates back to 1683. And from the 18th century there is the Jēkabpils Church (1769) as well as the Nikolaja Cloister Church. Be sure to check out the Regional Studies Museum for a bit of insight about the area. And the Maritime School makes sense in light of the fact that the Daugava carries seabound river traffic.

233

The Jēkabpils region also has a memorial museum to the beloved poet Jānis Rainis. The house - called Tadenava - in which the museum is located was built by the poet's father, shortly after the birth of his son on September 11, 1865. Rainis spent the first four years of his life in this house. Although memories from such tender years are few and far between, Rainis, according to his later writings, always retained a very vivid impression of the sun from his life at Tadenava. And this motif can be found again and again throughout his works.

Two of the rooms in the museum are dedicated to Rainis' parents and his sister. Also on display are a loom, work tools, and housewares from the mid 1860's. Call 77251 when you're in Jēkabpils for directions to Tadenava. The museum is open from May 15-October 15 every day except Monday and the hours are from 10-17:00.

JELGAVA

Situated on the banks of the Lielupe River, Jelgava is the provincial capital of the Zemgale region. It was first mentioned in historical documents in 1265. At one time Jelgava was the stronghold of the Semigallian tribes. Officially founded in 1573, Jelgava became the capital of the Duchy of Courland.

Since the Lielupe River served as a major transportation route between Rīga and Lithuania, as well as a major postal route between Russia and Western Europe, over the centuries Jelgava developed into a trade and manufacturing center. Today, Jelgava is the only inland maritime harbor in Latvia. It is also the site of textile mills, agricultural machinery plants, food processing factories, and a sugar refinery, thereby making Jelgava the most significant industrial center of the Zemgale region.

During the second half of the 18th century Jelgava was known as a major printing center. "Latviešu avīzes" (Latvian Newspapers), the first Latvian language newspaper was printed in Jelgava. At one time, a full half of all Latvian language books in Latvia were also printed here.

Jelgava has also been home to numerous Latvian patriots. Kārlis Ulmanis, independent Latvia's last president, was born near Jelgava and educated in Jelgava's school system. Jānis Čakste, Latvia's first president, and Alberts Kviesis, Latvia's third president, both graduated from the Jelgava high school. Even a former Lithuanian president, A. Smetonas, was educated in the same school. Quite an alumni list!

While in Jelgava, be sure to see the Jelgava Castle, which was designed by Italian architect F.B. Rastrelli. It took over 30 years to complete and is located on the site of the original castle built by the Livonian Order in 1265, near the river. This castle served as the residence of the dukes of Kurzeme and Zemgale, and the French King, Louis XVIII held court here as well. Destroyed in 1919, the 300 room Baroque building was reconstructed during Latvia's independence. During this period, it was, and still remains today, home to the Latvian Academy of Agriculture. The building was reconstructed one more time, after it was gutted during World War II.

Because Jelgava suffered extensive damage during both of the World Wars, numerous historically significant buildings are gone forever. One that remains is Annas baznica (church), built in 1619. The altar painting was done by Latvian artist Jānis Rozentāls. Also worth noting are the City Hall and the Freemason Lodge. The Academia Petrina is an excellent example of how the Baroque and Classic styles of architecture can be skillfully integrated.

Historical Note: Approximately 28 km. from Jelgava, up the Lielupe River is Ložmetējkalns (Machine Gun Hill). This is the site of a famous battle fought by Latvia's Riflemen against the invading Germans in 1917. One year later, Latvia declared independence.

KULDIGA

Kuldīga is situated in the heart of Kurzeme, where the Venta River is met by one of its tributaries, Aleksupīte. The Cour, Lamekins, ruled the area in the 12th century. The castle hill, where his fortress once stood, is less than 3 km. from the center of Kuldīga. It eventually became a stronghold for the Teutonic Knights, and by the middle of the 14th century was incorporated as a city. In 1561, Kuldīga served as the first capital to the Duchy of Courland. Kuldīga evolved into a significant trade and manufacture center in the 17th century. But by the time the Northern War ended in 1721, Kuldīga lagged well behind both Liepāja and Ventspils in this area. Nonetheless, the city continued to grow and flourish. In 1886, the Baltic Teacher's Academy was transferred here from Rīga, and operated til 1915. By the 1930's Kuldīga was a popular vacation spot and remains one today.

Kuldīga's old town section is an eclectic combination of buildings in the Renaissance, Baroque and Gothic architectural styles, standing alongside Germanic looking living quarters and trade buildings.

The Alekšupīte River flowing through Kuldīga is reminiscent of the canals of Venice

Start your tour at the town hall square, which was mentioned in historical documents in the early 17th century. It has been a popular staging area for numerous Latvian films. The new town hall was built in 1860 in Italian Renaissance style. The original town hall, built in the 17th century is across the square at number 5 Padomju st. The basement of the building served as the town jail. Up the street at number 7 is the oldest residential building in Kuldīga. It was built in 1670, and reconstructed in 1742. The building's weather vane, decorated with a mythical unicorn is displayed in the museum, which is housed in St. Katrīna's church.

Turn into Raiņa st., and at number 10 is the Holy Trinity Catholic Church. Built in 1640 in Italian Renaissance style, the interior is ornately decorated and sculpted in 17th century Baroque with a strong

Rococo influence. Note the Madonna and Child sculpture, which dates back to the early 16th century, and the confessional from 1691. The altar was a gift from Tsar Alexander I in 1820.

On the next block, Leņina st., number 3 is an 18th century granary, reconstructed in 1970. Today it houses the Kuldīga Photo Studio and Kocis Applied Arts Studio. Continue along Padomju st. toward the Venta River. At number 33 is St. Katrīnas church. Mentioned as far back as 1252, the present-day structure was built in 1655. The early Baroque style building was remodeled in 1866, and again in 1968. Note the masterfully sculpted wooden altar and pulpit that date back to 1660. The 996-pipe organ was made in 1712. Go up to the top of the 25 m. high tower for a spectacular view of the town and the Venta River.

Kuldīgas rumba - waterfall on the Venta River at Kuldīga

As you head toward the river, notice the mill built in 1807. Beyond the mill sluice, is the scenic Alekšupīte waterfall. It is the highest natural waterfall in Kurzeme. Continuing on, note the Roman style bridge spanning the Venta. At 4 Pils st. note the castle keep. It was built in 1735 from Kuldīga's castle rocks. Across the street is the site of the castle built in 1242. It collapsed in 1735, was never rebuilt, and is now a park with numerous stone and bronze statues. At number 5 is the Art Museum, founded in 1935. Open from 12-17:00 Tuesday, Thursday & Friday, 11-18:00 Wednesday, Saturday & Sunday, closed Monday.

By now you will have noticed the scenic, 2.5 m. high waterfall - the Kuldīgas rumba. An old folk tale explains its creation in the following way. Long ago, a sorcerer lived in the castle keep. He so angered the devil, that one night the devil decided to get even. Having filled a huge sack with rocks, he intended to dump the contents on the castle keep. As soon as the devil appeared over the Venta, the sorcerer bellowed a loud rooster crow. When a real rooster responded in kind, it so frightened the devil, that he dropped all of the rocks in the Venta, and thereby created the waterfall.

Outside of Kuldīga, about 20 km. away, lies the little town of Ēdole. Ēdole boasts a 13th century castle, which is currently being restored and transformed into a cultural center with convention facilities by the Environmental Protection Club of Latvia. The town of Ēdole also boasts a 17th century church typical of the Kurzeme region, as well as Latvia's first library.

LIEPĀJA

Liepāja sits at the entrance of the waters from Lake Liepāja into the Baltic and was originally a fisherman's village. Mentioned in historical chronicles as early as the 9th century, it was known as Liva Portus because of the numerous lime trees which grow there. In 1253 it was conquered by the Teutonic Knights. By 1625 it was incorporated. An artificial harbor was built between 1697-1703. Between 1860-63, the harbor was deepened, the facilities improved and a naval base was established. Charles the XII of Sweden captured it in 1701 during the Great Northern War, and it was taken by French and Prussian armies in 1812 during the Napoleonic campaigns. The British held the city in 1854 during the Crimean War. In 1919, Liepāja was the seat of the Provisional Government of independent Latvia.

Today Liepāja is the largest urban center in western Latvia. As a gateway to the West, it became an important communications center in 1869 when it was linked with Copenhagen by an undersea cable. In 1906 a passenger line to New York and Halifax was established. In 1889 Liepāja became the first city in the entire Russian Empire to have electric streetcar service. The Tosmāre Works in Liepāja built railroad cars, agricultural equipment, and KOD type airplanes prior to World War II. There were also large dry-dock facilities for ship repairs. Since the occupation, the Soviets monitor the Baltic Sea from the naval base in the ice-free harbor.

Liepāja suffered heavy damage during the second world war. At one time, the Trinity Lutheran church, consecrated in 1758, had a beautiful organ with 131 pipes. Peter the Great lived in Liepāja and his house has a commemorative plaque.

Today Liepāja is an important center of both political and cultural activity. Liepāja was the birthplace of the Latvian Social Democratic Party back in 1904 and today, almost every political movement - the Popular Front, Independence Movement, and Environmental movement - has an active chapter in Liepāja. Liepāja also boasts some of the best rock and roll groups of the country, the most notable being the heavy metal group, Līvi. And for all you rock devotees looking for some live action, there is the annual Rock Festival held in August, as a benefit for the city.

SIGULDA AND THE GAUJA NATIONAL PARK

Strategically situated as it is on the banks of the Gauja River, Sigulda has been inhabited since the beginning of the 2nd millenium B.C. Archeological excavations have unearthed weapons and other articles which indicate that the Finno-Ugric residents were hunters and fishermen. Up until the end of the 12th century, the area was a stronghold of Liv tribes, with wooden fortresses occupying the highest hills. The Teutonic Knights began to take over in the beginning of the 13th century, and they erected stone castles at Sigulda, Krimulda and Turaida. By 1207, historical chronicles refer to Sigulda as a town. During the 16th century, Sigulda was occupied by the Russians, Poles, and Swedes. Only one-third of the town's population survived the devastation of the Northern War and ensuing plague in the early 1700's. But Sigulda quickly rebounded. By the 1880's, it began to develop as a resort area.

Today, Sigulda is the gateway to the Gauja National Park, which was founded in 1973, and encompasses 920.5 sq. km. It is also a renowned winter sports recreation area. A world class bobsled run is located a few hundred meters from Sigulda's center, and another is currently under construction within the Gauja National Park. Latvians have emerged as world class bobsledists, particularly since their Olympic medal winning performances at the 1988 Winter Olympics in Calgary, Canada.

The Gauja National Park embraces some of the most beautiful scenery in all of Latvia. You will quickly understand why it is referred to as the "Switzerland of Vidzeme". The ancient Gauja River valley with its numerous tributaries, caves and cliffs, the over 200 giant ancient oaks with a circumference of 2 to 3 meters, the lakes, unique vegetation, and abundant wildlife, make the Gauja National Park a marvelous place to visit any season of the year. This area is less than an hour's drive from Rīga on the Rīga-Pskov highway. Be sure to stop at the Sēnīte (mushroom) restaurant (about 12 km. before the park) for a bite to eat, or for some liquid refreshment.

The Gauja National Park is divided into 7 zones, 3 of which are open to the public: Siguldas, Ligatnes and Araišu. All three offer a wealth of natural wonders and historical monuments, while retaining their own unique character. Whether you're a sports enthusiast, nature lover or a history buff, you will be richly rewarded by your visit to the park. For those of you without a car, Intourist can make arrangements for you.

Siguldas Zona

Points of Interest on the Sigulda Side of the Gauja River.

-Monument to Latvian folklorist Krišjānis Barons located at the corner of K. Barona and Līvkalna sts.

-The Sigulda church, built in 1225, reconstructed in 1673, and again in 1701.

-The Sigulda castle ruins. The castle, built by the Teutonic Order between 1207-1226, had 2 forts occupying neighboring hilltops. A deep moat, spanned by a drawbridge, separated the two. The castle structures were surrounded by fortress walls containing several watchtowers, which were connected by an underground passage, and also by a moat. The castle was demolished during the Northern War (1700-1721). The walls of the main building, and of 2 watchtowers, are all that remain today.

-The new Sigulda castle, built in 1878. In the courtyard is a monument to Latvian linguist Kronvaldu Atis. The castle houses a sanatorium.

The new Sigulda Castle

-The Sigulda cemetery, with a chapel built in 1856.

-Gleznotāju kalns (Artist's hill). From this location 93 m. above sea level, you can see a breathtaking 12 km. panorama of the Gauja

River valley. This was a favorite painting spot for Latvian artists J. Feders, J. Rozentāls and V. Purvītis.

-Kraukļu ala (Raven cave), 5 m. deep by 11 and a half m. high, is located in a ravine of the tributary Vējupīte.

-Pētera ala (Peter's cave), approximately 6 m. deep by 5 m. high, is found in a steep bank of the Vējupīte.

-Satezeles castle mound, a Liv settlement dating back to 1212.

-Ķeizara krēsls (The Tsar's chair) - a scenic look-out point.

-Bobsled run facilities.

-Ferris wheel which gives you a great view of the entire area.

To cross over the Gauja River, you have a choice. You can take the 153 m. bridge, built in 1936 and rising 16.5 m. above the river, or the funicular railway, which takes approximately 3 minutes and rises 40 m. above the river valley. The boarding point for the latter is located at the end of Baumaņa st.

Points of Interest Across the Gauja River.

-The Krimulda castle ruins. Located by the tributary Vikmeste, this castle was built between 1255-1273, and served as a residence for visiting dignitaries. It was destroyed in the beginning of the 17th century.

-The Krimulda castle was built in 1854 and today houses a children's sanatorium.

-Lielā Velnala (Big Devil Cave), is 11 m. deep, by 5 and a half m. wide, by 2 and a half m. high. This devonian period cave has an interesting legend explaining the name. It seems the devil was flying over the Gauja when he heard a rooster crowing. Frightened, he hid in the cave, and slept until the following evening. His breath turned the cave walls a sooty black color.

-Mazā Velnala (Little Devil Cave), is about 10 m. deep. The water from Gudrības avotiņš (Wisdom spring), which flows from this cave, was long ago used by mothers to bathe their babies. It was believed that the water had properties which would make the children smart and lucky in life.

-Taurētāju kalns (Horn blower hill). In ancient times, sentries watched the movements of approaching enemies from this mountain and would signal their whereabouts with horns.

-Tourist Center Sigulda, where you can rent a boat for a peaceful ride on the Gauja River.

-Dainu māja. Krišjānis Barons, father of the daina (see literature section), lived in this house in the summer of 1922.

-Dainu kalns. This site of ancient Liv settlements, known as Jelgavkalns, was renamed in 1985 on the 150th anniversary of the birth of Krišjānis Barons. Latvian sculptor Indulis Ranka created 15 works to honor Barons. The sculptures are displayed on Dainu kalns.

-Turaidas Rozes kaps. The gravesite of Maija, the Rose of Turaida (1601- August 6, 1620). The following is the beautiful but sad legend, based on a true event, associated with this maiden.

In 1601, during the Polish-Swedish War, the Swedes captured Turaida castle. When the 3-day battle ended, the old castle scribe went down to the valley to see if there were any wounded in need of help. He found a little girl wandering among the wounded. He adopted her and named her Maija. Twenty years passed, and Maija grew up to be a hard-working, kind hearted, beautiful young woman. Her beauty was so legendary, that she became known as the Rose of Turaida. All the young men in the area wanted to marry her. But Maija loved Viktors, a gardener at Sigulda castle, and they soon became engaged. The two would often meet at Gūtmaņa cave, mid-way between the two castles.

One day a Polish officer, named Jakubovskis, came to Turaida castle. He was so smitten by Maija's beauty that he wanted to make her his mistress. But neither the officer's expensive presents nor his threats could persuade Maija. He finally forged a letter in Viktors' handwriting to lure Maija to the cave. Trapped and desperate, Maija told Jakubovskis that the scarf around her neck (a present from Viktors) was magic, and would protect the wearer from any harm. Maija offered the scarf to the officer in exchange for her honor and freedom. To prove the legitimacy of her claims, she told Jakubovskis to strike her with his sword. He did just that, and the murdered girl fell to the ground. Jakubovskis fled from the cave and disappeared from Turaida without a trace.

That evening, Viktors went to the cave to meet Maija. When he found her lifeless body, he called some peasants to help him move her. When they lifted her up, they found Viktors' garden hatchet, and charged him with Maija's murder. Viktors was taken to Turaida castle where he was sentenced to death. But a witness was found - a friend of Jakubovskis - who explained the officer's devious plan to lure Maija to the cave.

Viktors was cleared, and he buried his beloved in the Turaida church cemetery. After planting a lime tree over her grave, Viktors left for parts unknown, never to be seen again. All he took with him was some earth from Maija's grave.

-Turaidas baznīca. This church was built in 1750 by Latvian craftsmen. The Baroque turret crowning the church, the unusually carved wooden pews, and the ancient altar painting are well preserved. It is the oldest wooden architectural monument in the Vidzeme region. The church houses a branch of the Sigulda History Museum.

-The Turaida Castle mound and Turaida Castle complex. The original wooden fortress was built by Liv chieftain, Kaupo, in the 12th century. It was destroyed by German crusaders in 1212. Traces of the wooden fortress, which are under the present day buttress foundations, along with work implements and other tools, were unearthed during archeological excavations. The stone castle was built in 1214, and remained intact until 1776, when a fire destroyed parts of it. The original castle was surrounded by high stone walls and 5 towers. There has been a lot of restoration work done on the castle to recreate many of the lost features, including the main tower, the northern and western towers, parts of the outside wall, and the domestic building, which today houses the Sigulda Local History Museum. Be sure to climb the stairs to the top of the tower, where the lovely scenery of the surrounding area will make up for the energy you expended getting to the viewing platform!

The Gauja River valley as seen from the Turaida Castle tower at Sigulda

-Viktora ala (Victor's cave), is approximately 6 m. deep by 7 m. high. Rumor has it that Viktors created this cave for his beloved Maija, so that she would be able to see the Sigulda castle gardens, where he worked.

-Gūtmaņa ala. This is the largest and most popular cave in Latvia. It is 18 m. deep, 12 m. wide and 10 m. high. Located at the foot of Taurētāju kalns (Horn blower hill), it is actually a grotto, eroded by a small underground spring, and the waters of the Gauja River, before it changed its course by almost half a km. at the end of the 18th century. The cave takes its name from a man named Gūtmanis, who lived in the area and healed the sick with water gathered inside the cave. This is the cave where Viktors and Maija often met, and where he found her dead body. The walls of the cave are covered with countless inscriptions, the oldest dating back to 1668.

Ligatnes Zona

This is actually an educational and recreational area, established in 1975. Its purpose is to acquaint visitors with the animal and plant life of the area, and also with the geographical aspects of the park. There are several walking trails which describe the wide variety of plant life found in the park. Another section will familiarize you with animals frequently seen in the park, including elk, boar, deer, fox, rabbit and beaver. There are also several sandstone outcrops, among them Gavilu iezis (rock), Jumprāviezis, and Katrīniezis. You can climb the viewing platform, or drive the 5.2 km. auto trail. You can even rent a horse and go on a guided trail ride down along the shores of the Gauja River.

Araišu Zona

This zone is a miniature version of an ancient Vidzeme rural district. Here you will find peasant homes, noblemen estates, taverns, windmills and the characteristic rural landscape consisting of birch groves, hills, rivers and lakes. Archeological excavations on an island in Araišu ezers (lake) have unearthed a 9th-10th century dwelling complete with work tools, weapons, jewelry, and housewares. Don't miss the 18th century minister's home next to the lake. There is also the Lielstraupes pils (castle), dating back to the 13th century. The castle has been restored, and the church is being used as a concert hall. And finally, there is the 18th century Ungurmuiža (Ungur estate), built of wood. Check out the unique wall decorations, as well as the little tea house, barn and chapel.

TUKUMS

Tukums is an ancient Liv settlement. The name derives from the Finno-Ugric words Tukku mägi - which means a row of hills. The natural beauty and abundance of resources in this entire area makes it clear why the name was chosen. Tukums first appeared in historical chronicles in 1445. The town was formally founded in 1798.

Check out the Tukums castle mound and Karātavu or Kapu (Cemetery) hill. Then look for the rooster and cross topping the steeple of the Lutheran church built in 1670. Nearby is the Durbes castle, which was built in 1820 by the Swiss Janis Berlics. Then go on to Milzu (Giant) hill, the highest elevation in the region. The view of the Baltic Sea is superb.

Back in town, the Tukums Regional Studies and Art Museum has collected notable works by Latvian artists from the 1920's and 1930's. The collection was established in the 1930's and fortunately, escaped the destruction of World War II. On display are the works of many famous Latvian artists, including Vilhems Purvītis, Voldemārs Tone, and Jānis Rozentāls. Contemporary artists - Leo Svempa, Kārlis Neile, Otto Skulme, Jānis Pauluks, and others are also featured.

While you're in the the Tukums region, stop by the Jaunpils castle, built at the end of the 14th century, and the Lutheran church complex that dates back to the 15th/16th centuries. Restoration work is underway on both. The roof of the church was rebuilt in the summer of 1987, and a rooster sculpture was replaced on the steeple. The castle is presently being used as a restaurant, dormitory, and movie theater.

VALMIERA

Valmiera occupies an important place in the commercial and intellectual history of Latvia. The city on the banks of the Gauja River has been inhabited since the 11th century. The first mention of it in historical chronicles is in 1283. Valmiera evolved into a major link along the Gauja River trading route, eventually becoming a member of the Hanseatic League.

In 1802 a major peasant revolt took place at nearby Kauguri. A monument honoring the victims can be seen on the highway leading to Ainaži. Also in the area are the Bestes and Deidera taverns.

14th century Jaunpils Castle

Peasant meetings took place in these taverns, which resulted in the uprising.

Valmiera has been the location of the Teacher's Academy since 1902. Numerous Latvian social leaders were educated here. Around the time of Latvia's independence - 1918 - Valmiera was known as Latvia's "most Latvian" city, boasting a population that was 95% Latvian. The demographics of the city have changed dramatically since World War II. Even though Valmiera is located in an agricultural region, the city itself has rather rapidly developed into an industrial center focusing on the manufacture of glass fibres.

Stop by the Sīmaņu church, which was build in 1283 and reconstructed in 1729. The church was used as a concert hall until the revival of the Valmiera parish under glasnost. Since the beginning of 1989 it is again being used for services, and locals are petitioning for the ownership of the church to be transferred from the Valmiera museum back to the congregation. Currently, however, the church still serves as an annex to the Valmiera museum, which often has exhibits there. The museum is located right next to the church, at 3 Bruņinieku st. In front of it stands a statue bringing to life a popular Latvian novel written about the city and the rambunctious students that attend the Teacher's Academy. Walk over to the Valmiera castle ruins located just beyond the church. And definitely climb the observation tower on Valterkalniņš. You will be rewarded by a great panoramic view of the Gauja valley.

While you're in the Valmiera area, immerse yourself in the natural beauty of this river valley. Zilais kalns (Blue mountain), and Burtnieku ezers (lake) are especially lovely. And don't miss the most picturesque section of the Gauja River, with its rapids, cliffs and steep banks. These natural wonders can be found between Valmiera and Strenči, approximately 4 km. below Strenči.

Ērgļu klints - Eagle Cliff on the Gauja River near Valmiera

VENTSPILS

The natural, ice-free port of Ventspils is a major historical and current center of commerce. Like Rīga, Ventspils was also a member of the Hanseatic League. In ancient times, it was inhabited by the Vend tribes, who successfully repulsed a number of attacks by the Vikings. The castle built by the Livonian Order in 1290 has been fairly well preserved. In 1378, Ventspils was incorporated as a city.

Eventually, Ventspils became the headquarters for Duke Jacob's naval fleet, and thus evolved into a major shipbuilding center. Remnants of the old dock built at that time can still be seen. Duke Jacob launched his ships to colonize Tobago and Gambia from here.

Ventspils and its populace suffered heavy devastation during both the Northern War and the plague. But in the beginning of the 20th century, it experienced a rebirth when a rail link to Russia was established. This in turn revived the port facilities and commerce in general.

Today, Ventspils is a major manufacturing and trade center. But many Latvians believe that Ventspils is presently suffering through a second plague - this time of man-made origins. In 1961, the Soviets built a gas refinery in Ventspils and erected a pipeline to the harbor facility. The U.S. firm, Occidental Petroleum, built a facility for the manufacture of liquid ammonia and fertilizer (potassium salts). As a result of the manufacturing facilities, the city has become both overcrowded and heavily polluted. Since the 1950's, the population has quadrupled. The bulk of this population explosion consists of a non-Latvian work force. Both the industrial facilities and the large housing projects erected to accomodate the foreign workers, were designed with little regard for the local environment. This results in Ventspils being one of the most polluted and environmentally hazardous cities in all of Latvia. In recent years, gas masks have been distributed to the children of the city to protect them against frequent industrial accidents.

Although Ventspils is an open city, it is not recommended to tourists because of the health risks.

USEFUL WORDS AND EXPRESSIONS

Hello	Sveiki
Good morning	Labrīt
Good evening	Labvakar
Good night	Ar labu nakti
Goodbye	Atā
Yesterday	Vakar
Today	Šodien
Tomorrow	Rītdien
Please	Lūdzu
Thank you	Paldies
Yes	Jā
No	Nē
You're welcome	Lūdzu
Excuse me	Atvainojiet, lūdzu
I'm sorry	Atvainojos
My name is...	Mani sauc...
Do you speak English?	Vai jūs runājiet angliski?
I don't speak Latvian	Es nerunāju latviski
Please speak slowly	Lūdzu runājiet lēnāk
I don't understand	Nesaprotu
I would like to go (by car) to...	Vēlos braukt uz...
I would like to go (by foot) to...	Vēlos iet uz...
Where is...	Kur ir...
I would like...	Vēlētos...
How much does it cost?	Cik maksā?

At a restaurant

I would like to order...	Vēlētos...
Some more, please	Lūdzu, vēl
That's enough, thank you	Pietiek, paldies
coffee (with milk)	kafija (ar pienu)
sugar	cukurs
tea	tēja
juice	sula
mineral water	minerālūdens
beer	alus
wine (red, white)	vīns (sarkans, balts)
bread	maize
butter	sviests

Locations

street	iela
square	laukums
hotel	viesnica
castle	pils
church	baznīca
restaurant	restorāns
hospital	slimnīca
drug store	aptieka
movie theater	kinoteātris
theater	teātris
museum	muzejs
post office	pasts

Days of the week

Monday	Pirmdiena
Tuesday	Otrdiena
Wednesday	Trešdiena
Thursday	Ceturtdiena
Friday	Piektdiena
Saturday	Sestdiena
Sunday	Svētdiena

Cardinal numbers

1	viens	16	sešpadsmit
2	divi	17	septiņpadsmit
3	trīs	18	astoņpadsmit
4	četri	19	deviņpadsmit
5	pieci	20	divdesmit
6	seši	25	divdesmitpieci
7	septiņi	30	trīsdesmit
8	astoņi	40	četrdesmit
9	deviņi	50	piecdesmit
10	desmit	60	sešdesmit
11	vienpadsmit	70	septiņdesmit
12	divpadsmit	80	astoņdesmit
13	trīspadsmit	90	deviņdesmit
14	četrpadsmit	100	simts
15	piecpadsmit		

Ordinal numbers

1st	pirmais	8th	astotais
2nd	otrais	9th	devītais
3rd	trešais	10th	desmitais
4th	ceturtais	11th	vienpadsmitais
5th	piektais	20th	divdesmitais
6th	sestais	100th	simtais
7th	septītais		

PRONUNCIATION GUIDE

The Latvian language belongs to the Baltic branch of Indo-European languages, which also includes Lithuanian and the now extinct Old Prussian. The alphabet is as follows:

a/ā, b, c, č, d, e/ē, f, g, ģ, h, i/ī, j, k, ķ, l, ļ, m, n, ņ, o, p, r, s, š, t, u/ū, v, z, ž.

The letters b, d, f, g, h, k, l, m, n, p, s, t, v and z are almost identical to their English counterparts in pronunciation.

The letter c is pronounced as ts; č as ch in chalk; ģ as gy in Hungarian; j as y in yes; ķ as ty in Hungarian; ļ as gl in Italian; ņ as ñ in Spanish; š as sh in show; ž as s in vision. The letter r is trilled.

The short and long vowels are: a as the o in hot; ā as in father; e as in bet; ē as the a in bare; i as in pit; ī as the ee in feet; u as the oo in foot; ū as the oo in food. The ai combination is pronounced as the i in bike. The ei combination is pronouced as ey in hey. The letter o is a dipthong as in the r-less pronunciation of pour; and ie as in the r-less pronunciation of beer.

ESTONIA

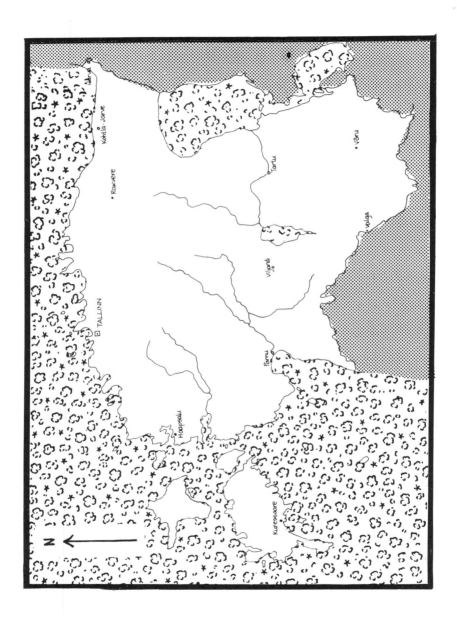

ESTONIA

While it shares both political and historical ties with its southern Baltic neighbors of Latvia and Lithuania, Estonia has always distinguished itself by its independent spirit and culture. The Estonian people trace their roots to the Finno-Ugric family of nations, and have more in common, culturally and linguistically, with the Finns to the north than the Indo-European Balts to the south.

The ancestors of modern-day Estonians first settled their homeland well over 6,000 years ago. By the time the Germans, Danes and Russians invaded their land in the 13th century, the Estonians had already established a highly developed, and fiercely independent society of loosely federated states.

This national consciousness served them well during the ensuing centuries of Swedish, Polish and Russian rule. In 1918 the Estonian people resumed control of their historical homeland and enjoyed a return to independence that lasted until the Soviet invasion of 1940. The last 50 years of Soviet rule, however, have not dampened the Estonian spirit. If anything, it has strengthened and invigorated it. As the 1990's begin, the Estonian love of their land, language and culture is once again emerging as a powerful political force throughout the land.

For the Estonian people today, Estonia is an exciting, exhilarating place to be. It is an excitement that every visitor will want to share.

ESTONIAN HISTORY

The history of human settlement in Estonia, like that throughout the Baltic Sea region, is believed to date back to the closing of the Ice Age 10,000 years ago. Whereas in Latvia and Lithuania the early nomadic tribes were replaced around 2000 B.C. by Indo-European peoples, archeological discoveries suggest that Finno-Ugric tribes from South-Eastern Europe migrated to Estonia as early as 6,000 B.C.

These early semi-nomadic hunters occupied the river valleys and began settling in villages during the Bronze Age, from 1300-500 B.C. By 400 A.D. the people that emerged as forebears of modern Estonians enjoyed a rapid economic and cultural development. Hunting and fishing were increasingly replaced by agriculture and cattle breeding, while trade with neighboring nations along the Baltic Sea flourished. Over the next eight centuries, the Estonians developed into the most progressive and prosperous branch of the Finnish family of nations. Although divided into a number of independent states during this period, the rulers of the various Estonian tribes succeeded at times in uniting into a loose federation. Between 1000 and 1200 A.D. combined Estonian forces successfully repulsed Russian invasions, while Estonian sailors completed several expeditions to Sweden and Denmark.

Estonia's early independence came to an end when it was besieged by the Germans, Russians and Danes in the 13th century. The German crusaders, having established a base in Rīga, conquered southern Estonia, while the Danes retained control of Tallinn and the northern regions. This German-Danish rule of a divided Estonia lasted until the 16th century. The Russians once again made an unsuccessful assault on Estonia in 1558, leaving Estonia in Swedish and Polish hands. In 1625, Estonia was annexed in full by Sweden, and remained under Swedish rule until the Russians, under Czar Peter I, finally subjugated Estonia and its southern Baltic neighbors in the early 18th century.

As in Latvia to the south, Russian rule in Estonia was shared by the Baltic-German nobility, which owned most of the land in the country. The native Estonian peasantry lived in a state of serfdom under German and Russian political and cultural domination.

The rise of Estonian national consciousness began in the early part of the 19th century with the liberation of the peasants and the acquisition of the right to own property. By the mid 19th-century the Society of Estonian Literati was formed, greatly contributing to the development of the written Estonian language and the collection of Estonian folklore. Perhaps the most symbolic turning point in Estonian cultural history was the first all-Estonian song festival, held in Tartu in 1869. This newly established tradition served as a focal point for growing Estonian national consciousness over the next three decades, enabling the Estonians to withstand a harsh Russification campaign, and set the stage for Estonian political assertiveness in the beginning of the 20th century.

One of the first major turning points in modern Estonian history came in 1904, when a growing Estonian national movement successfully assumed political control of the city of Tallinn, replacing its Baltic German rulers. Spearheaded by a vigorous press and national literary movement, and fueled by national and democratic ideas in Western Europe, the Estonian people began laying the foundation for national independence.

The collapse of the German Empire and onset of the Russian Revolution provided the Estonian people with the opportunity they had long sought. In 1917, over 40,000 Estonians held a demonstration in Petrograd, forcing the Provisional Russian government to grant self-government in the Estonian region. With the ascension of Bolshevik rule in Russia, Estonia initially became an autonomous part of the new Soviet Russian federation. Yet when elections for an Estonian Constituent Assembly were held in November 1917, the Bolsheviks only managed 35.5% of the vote.

Within three months, on February 24, 1918, Estonia declared its national independence and a provisional government was created. On the following day, German troops entered Tallinn, forcing the new government into exile. With the defeat of Germany by the Western powers in November, Soviet Russian troops invaded the country, hoping to return Estonia to Bolshevik control. Thus began the Estonian War of Independence. Soviet Russian troops overran the country but were finally defeated by the Estonians in February of 1919. This success, however, was followed by a second German attempt to seize control of the Baltic region. Estonian troops defeated the German mercenaries in two battles in northern Latvia. One more attempt by Russian forces to seize Estonia was repulsed in November 1919, and on February 2, 1920, the Soviet Union finally conceded, signing the Peace Treaty of Tartu.

With the Soviet recognition of Estonian independence in 1920, other nations, such as Finland and Poland, soon followed suit. Estonia, together with Latvia and Lithuania, was admitted to the League of Nations in 1921, and was granted de jure recognition by the United States on July 28, 1922. A parliamentary democracy and a constitution, patterned after that of Switzerland, was formed.

The Estonian government immediately set out to rebuild its economy following the long, destructive war years. Land reform was initiated and an economy, based on agriculture, forestry and shale-oil was rapidly developed. In the 1920's the first shale-oil distilleries in the world were founded in Estonia, and the shale-oil industry became the cornerstone of the nation's economy.

Independent Estonia also became notable for establishing one of the most liberal ethnic minority policies in the world. Legislation guaranteed minority rights, and government subsidies ensured that all ethnic groups could maintain schools in their own native languages. Both culturally and economically, the new nation flourished and prospered.

The parliamentary structure of Estonia's government was unable to cope with the global economic depression of the late 20's. This situation led to the adoption of a new constitution in 1933, which gave Estonia's president, Konstantin Päts, near dictatorial powers. A third constitution, balancing the executive and legislative branches was adopted in 1937, and appeared to prepare the way for long sought economic and political stability.

This stability was shattered by the onset of World War II and the 1939 Molotov-Ribbentrop Pact between the Soviet Union and Nazi Germany. Estonia, like its neighbors, Latvia and Lithuania, was secretly handed over to the Soviets.

On June 16, 1940 the Estonian government was given eight hours to comply with an ultimatum from the Soviet government, demanding the free entry of Soviet troops into Estonian territory. Within days the democratic Estonian government was deposed and replaced by handpicked Communists from Moscow. In a series of events identical to those in Latvia and Lithuania, rigged elections were held, a Communist government was installed, and independent Estonia was annexed to the Soviet Union as a Soviet Republic. Over the next year, the new Moscow-controlled government deported over 60,000 Estonians, including entire families, to Siberia.

Soviet rule in Estonia was interrupted in 1941 by a Nazi German invasion and annexation. Estonia's Communist rulers were replaced by Nazis, who proceeded to expand their Europe-wide reign of terror against Jews, Gypsies and nationalists in Estonia as well. The Soviets returned once more in 1944. Although Estonian partisans took to the forests to battle the Soviet invaders, they were no match for the Soviet army.

The Sovietization of Estonia, interrupted by the German occupation, resumed at an accelerated pace after the war. Independent Estonia's agricultural reforms, which had fostered the development of private farming, were destroyed by mass collectivization. All aspects of

Estonia's economy were put under Moscow's direct control. The cultural and linguistic Russification that the Estonian people had endured at the turn of the century while under Czarist rule, was systematically reimposed on Estonian society. Religious activities were sharply curtailed and Estonian history was rewritten. Estonian national symbols, such as its blue, black, and white flag, were outlawed and replaced by newly created Soviet symbols, intended to wipe out all traces of the nation's independent past. The sovereign Estonian state was transformed into one of fifteen Soviet republics, while democratic traditions were replaced with totalitarian Communist Party rule.

Despite the repressive nature of Soviet rule, Estonian national consciousness remained strong in the ensuing years. Within Soviet-ruled Estonia, national rights activists kept the hope of independence alive despite the threat of arrest and imprisonment. Well over 80,000 Estonians had fled the country in the wake of the second Soviet invasion, and formed organizations in the West, dedicated to restoring Estonian independence. This hope was strengthened by the position of Western governments who refused to recognize the legitimacy of Soviet rule in the country. Even after 40 plus years of Soviet rule in Estonia, an Estonian Consulate, representing the last legal, independent government of Estonia, continued its diplomatic activities in New York.

Recent History - Moving Toward Independence

The long repressed Estonian desire for a return to national independence was finally released in a dramatic and public way in 1987. On August 23, Estonians in Tallinn held a mass demonstration to demand the publication of the 1939 Molotov-Ribbentrop pact and its secret protocols. Simultaneous rallies marking the 48th anniversary of the signing of the Stalin-Hitler pact which led to the Soviet absorption of the Baltic States were also held in Latvia and Lithuania.

Mikhail Gorbachev had opened up the possibility of free expression in the Soviet Union with his policy of glasnost. The first thing the Estonians chose to express was their desire for freedom from Soviet rule. In January of 1988, former Estonian political prisoners announced the creation of the Estonian Independence Party. In addition to endorsing the restoration of a free and independent Estonia, the new group - openly opposed to the Communist Party - called for a total reconstruction of Estonian society, including multi-party elections, the restoration of Estonian as the official language of the republic, and economic, environmental, and social reforms.

Another new group, the Estonian Heritage Society, set out to support Estonia's drive toward independence by resurrecting the symbols of its pre-Soviet era. Estonian national monuments, destroyed and buried by Soviet troops over 40 years ago, were being dug up, restored and rededicated.

Despite initial harassment and expulsion of national leaders, the independence movement continued to gain momentum and began to extend into all aspects of Estonian life. In Estonia, a powerful national consciousness was evident even among its Communist leaders. By April, Communist Party officials in Estonia joined with other national leaders in forming the Popular Front of Estonia. In June, over 150,000 Estonians held a rally in Tallinn in support of the Popular Front, openly displaying the outlawed blue, black and white national flag of independent Estonia. In September, over 300,000 Estonians waved flags and sang patriotic songs during an all-day political rally in an outdoor amphitheater in Tallinn. Shortly thereafter, the 48-year ban on the flag was lifted.

As popular support continued to grow for the anti-Communist Independence Party, the officially sanctioned Popular Front, and the Communist-ruled government in Estonia continued to take increasingly bolder steps. The first congress of the Popular Front of Estonia in October ratified a demand for Estonian autonomy and called upon Moscow to admit that Estonia had been forcibly incorporated into the USSR in 1940. In the following month, the Communist-controlled Supreme Soviet of Estonia declared Estonia's sovereignty and asserted its right to veto any laws imposed upon it by Moscow.

In 1989 the re-emerging symbols of Estonian independence were accompanied by a broad-based political campaign, designed to realize that independence in fact. By February, the blue, black and white national flag of Estonia was hoisted atop the 13th century Pikk Hermann tower in Tallinn. Simultaneously, a citizen's registration campaign was begun, with the purpose of creating a political base for the restoration of an independent government of the pre-Soviet Republic of Estonia. By the end of 1989 nearly half a million Estonian citizens were registered. A citizen's congress was scheduled for early 1990.

The mass public support for Estonian indpendence was dramatized even further on August 23, 1989, as Estonians joined Latvians and Lithuanians in a 430-mile long human chain, extending from Tallinn in the north to Vilnius, Lithuania in the south. Over 2 million Balts participated in the call for independence in the Baltic States.

It has been said that independence is not an act, but a process. This process continues to unfold in Estonia at an accelerated pace. On February 2, 1990, representatives of Estonia's various

Soviet-installed governmental bodies - local councils, the Supreme Soviet Estonia and delegates to the USSR Congress of People's Deputies - held a joint convention where they approved an Estonian Declaration of Independence, based on the 1920 Tartu Peace Treaty between the Soviet Union and the independent Republic of Estonia. The declaration called for immediate negotiations between the Estonian people and the government of the USSR, in order to reestablish the independence of the Estonian Republic.

What the ultimate status of Estonia will be when you read this, or visit Estonia, remains to be seen.

GEOGRAPHY

Northernmost of the three Baltic Republics, Estonia is situated on the east coast of the Baltic Sea, and is bordered by the Gulf of Finland on the north, the Baltic Sea on the west, Russia on the east, and Latvia on the south. Estonia covers 47,549 square kilometers (18,370 sq. mi.), making it approximately the size of New Hampshire and Vermont combined, and larger in land size than either Denmark or the Netherlands. Included in this territory are over 1500 coastal islands. The largest of these is Saaremaa at 2,710 sq. km., followed by Hiiumaa, Muhamaa and Vormsi.

Estonia is part of the great East European plain, and can be divided into two distinct regions. The higher part of the plain runs north to south through the eastern part of Estonia, and consists of the Pandivere plateau in the province of Virumaa, the Otepää plateau in the province of Tartumaa, and the Haanja plateau in the province of Võrumaa. The average elevation is 50 m. (164 ft.) above sea level, with only 10% of the territory reaching over 100 m. in height. In spite of this, the highest point in the Baltic States is found within Estonian territory on the Haanja plateau at Suur Muna Mägi (Big Egg Hill), with an elevation of just over 317 m. (1,040 ft.). Thanks to retreating glaciers, the landscape is quite varied and the soil is fertile.

The lower portion of Estonia encompasses the western and northern coastal regions, including the islands, and also the areas around Lake Peipsi and Lake Võrts (which, by the way, are the two largest of Estonia's more than 1500 lakes. Peipsi is also the fourth largest lake in Europe). These areas tend to be mostly flat, often marshy, and strewn with boulders, especially in the north.

Numerous rivers (420 of them are longer than 10 km.) run through

Estonia's limestone, dolomite and sandstone plains. Among them, the Emajõgi (209 km.), the Võhandu (159 km.), the Pärnu (153 km.), the Kasari (99 km.), the Pirita (98 km.), and the Narva (78 km.).

Forests make up approximately 38% of Estonian territory. Pine forests dominate along the Baltic coast and the Gulf of Finland, while inland forests are mixed, with pine, spruce and birch species dominating. Northwestern Estonia (including the islands) is covered by meadows and junipers forests. Marshlands make up almost 50% of the land.

The vast forests of Estonia are populated by elk, deer, wild boar, badger, fox, squirrel, and beaver. The brown bear, wolf, and lynx are much rarer, but still seen. Over 300 species of birds also call Estonia home, among them migrating flocks of geese, swans, and ducks. But the national bird is the graceful barn swallow. It is believed that good fortune will follow if one decides to nest in your rafters.

The inland and coastal waters of Estonia boast over 80 species of fish. Although Estonia's economic history, as well as social lore, is closely linked with fishing, the present polluted state of the Baltic Sea has forced the Estonian fishing industry to send its ships to points all over the globe.

Climatically, Estonia falls in the temperate zone. Winters tend to be milder than in corresponding latitudes due to the Baltic Sea and the Gulf Stream. The coldest month is February, with an average temperature of 23° F. It is generally warmer in the western coastal regions and islands than in the eastern portion of the country. July is the warmest month of summer, averaging in the mid-60's. Annual precipitation ranges between 21-26 inches.

LITERATURE

Although Estonian literature is a rather modern phenomenon, going back to the mid-1800's and the time of the national awakening, there is nonetheless an extraordinary wealth of folk poetry dating back to ancient times. Through the years of occupation by foreigners, Estonian folklore imbued the Estonian people with a sense of national identity. As the only outlet for poetic imagination, the Estonian oral tradition remained strong.

In the early 1500's, the written Estonian word began to appear in the form of both a Catholic and Lutheran catechism. An Estonian language

New Testament appeared in 1680. But the first known example of secular Estonian literature, written by a native Estonian, is a poem by Käsu Hans. Written in 1708, the poem bemoans the destruction of Tartu, and the deportation of its citizens by the Russians in the Great Northern War. Kristjan Jaak Peterson (1801-1822) is considered the first real Estonian poet. His career was cut short by tuberculosis. But this gifted young man, who proudly wore native folk dress, delved into Estonian mythology and helped to set the scene for the national awakening which was only to blossom some 40 years after his death.

The emergence of an Estonian intelligentsia in the mid 1800's coincided with the development of a national consciousness among the Estonian people. The outstanding literary figure of this period was Friedrich Reinhold Kreutzwald (1803-1882). The first Estonian writer to garner a reputation outside of Estonia, Kreutzwald wrote and compiled the national epic Kalevipoeg (Son of Kalev). He combined traditional Estonian folklore, along with his own verse in portraying the mythological adventures of Kalevipoeg. The epic story symbolically describes the life and tragic fate of the Estonian nation at the end of the 13th century, at which time Estonia became an arena for both foreign powers and foreign religions. The tragic ending of this epic finds the hero chained to the gates of Hell, having lost both of his legs by his own sword. But the final lines of this epic poem promise that Kalevipoeg will be freed when Estonia is freed, and an era of happiness for the Estonian people will follow. The impact of this uniquely Estonian saga was an affirmation of the historical existence of the Estonian nation.

Another great literary figure of this period was Johann Voldemar Jannsen, who was the first to publish an Estonian-language newspaper, Perno Postimees, in 1857. It later became the Eesti Postimees (Estonian Postman), and played a large part in conveying the ideas of nationhood to the Estonian masses.

Jannsen's daughter, Lydia (1843-1886), is considered the major poet of the national awakening. Her chosen pen name, Koidula, means Land of Dawn. Emajõe ööbik (The nightingale of Emajõgi) written in 1867 is considered her most important work. The depth of sentiment and power of expression in her verse is unsurpassed in its patriotic evocations. Married to a Latvian doctor, Koidula spent many years living outside of Estonia. This only served to inflame her passion for Estonia. She died at an early age of cancer, and her remains rest at Metsakalmistu (Forest Cemetery) in Tallinn. Numerous prominent Estonian cultural figures are also buried in this beautifully landscaped cemetery.

Romanticized historical novels, as well as socially critical realism came into vogue at the end of the 1800's. The best example of the former is Eduard Bornhöhe's Tasuja (The Avenger). Written in 1880, it depicts the Estonian struggle against German invaders. The best writers of the realism genre are Ernst Peterson-Särgava (1868-1958) and Eduard Vilde (1865-1933). A novelist of great stature, Vilde had a profound political, as well as literary, influence on his contemporaries. In his writings he touched upon all aspects of national life, from the ridiculous to the tragic. Külmale maale (Banished), written in 1896, was a landmark in the development of Estonian realistic fiction. Vilde was also a playwright. Two of his finest works in this genre include Tabamata ime (The Unattained Miracle) written in 1912, and the comedy, Pisuhänd (The Fire Dragon) written the following year. These two plays display Vilde's sarcasm and wit to the hilt.

The turn of the century saw the emergence of another great poet, Juhan Liiv (1864-1913). Although he struggled with schizophrenia, his works contain both subtleties, and intensity of feeling and imagery. Although he remained largely unknown to his contemporaries, Liiv's patriotism established him as a great Symbolist poet ahead of his time.

During this same period, the Noor-Eesti (Young Estonia) literary and cultural group emerged, which was to lay the foundation of modern Estonian literature. The major figures in this group were Gustav Suits (1883-1956), Friedebert Tuglas (1886-1971), and Johannes Aavik (1880-1973). This new generation of writers, all under the age of 25, sought to emancipate Estonian culture from its narrow world. Each of these giants influenced the movement in their own ways. Suits' first volume of poetry, Elu tuli (The Fire of Life), in 1905, displayed his youthful enthusiasm through his inflammatory and tempestuous verse. Tuglas established modern Estonian literary criticism, while Aavik modernized the Estonian language and expanded its range of expression.

The independence era saw the emergence of a new literary group, Siuru, which took its name from a mythical songbird. Members of this group shocked conventional tastes by exploring sensual and erotic themes in Estonian literature. Without a doubt, the most gifted member of this group was Marie Under (1883-1980). She burst on the scene with a powerful, exciting, highly emotional impressionism that had heretofore been unknown in the world of Estonian literature.

Another giant of this period was A. H. Tammsaare (1878-1940). His five volume prose saga, Tõde ja õigus (Truth and Justice) was written between 1926-1933. This epic work explored three decades of Estonian social and political life from the 1870's to the 1920's. The story weaves realistic details about rural and urban life within the framework of philosophical issues and the human condition.

The most popular playwright in this period was Hugo Raudsepp (1883-1952). A master of cynical comedies, his best works included Mikumärdi (Mikumardi farm, 1929), and Vedelvorst (Lazybones, 1932), both commentaries on rural life.

The Soviet invasion wreaked havoc on Estonian literary development. As an independent nation, Estonia had one of the world's highest literacy rates, over 98%, and ranked second only to Iceland in per capita book publication. The Estonian literary heritage had reached vast and varied proportions. The Soviet takeover stopped the creative flow, which had been unleashed during the national awakening. Many authors left the country, and those that remained were not allowed to publish their works, as they were not ideologically correct. The works that came from this period reflected Soviet style socialist realism.

The 1960's saw a rebirth of sorts. A new generation of writers and poets came on the scene. Betti Alver, August Sang, Jaan Kross, Ain Kaalep, and Artur Alliksaar stand out among the poets, while on the prose side Arvo Valton, Mati Unt, Enn Vetemaa, J. Smuul, Paul Eerik Rummo, and Mats Traat are worth noting.

Today, with the advent of glasnost, and the loosening grip of censorship on creative thought, Estonian writers, poets and playwrights are again poised and ready to burst forth with creative energy.

MUSIC

Estonian music has its roots in the regivärss. These folk songs are characterized by the extensive use of alliteration and assonance, and the continual repetition of a theme. Subject matter covers family life, important events, such as weddings, mythology, and agricultural work. It is widely believed that these songs were created exclusively by women. In 1904, systematic research of regivarss was undertaken by philologist Dr. O. Kallas. The collection process resulted in over 16,000 melodies, which were filed in the Estonian Folklore Archives.

Folk music instruments include the kannel, which is in the lyre family, and consists of taut gutstrings pulled over a wooden sounding board. The kannel figures prominently in folklore as the musical symbol of the Estonian soul. Other instruments include primitive but sonorous fiddles and whistle-pipes.

Kannel

Estonian music came into its own during the time of the national awakening in the mid-1800's. The first all-Estonian song festival was held in Tartu in 1869, and the tradition is attributed to J. V. Jannsen. Jannsen, who organized the song festival, was the publisher of the first Estonian language newspaper. This first song festival had 845 performers singing to an audience of 15,000 people. By the sixth song festival in 1896, there were over 5500 performers and the audience had grown to 50,000!

The first Estonian composers were closely connected with the national song festivals. Some of the names associated with the choral and symphonic music of this period are J. Kappel, M. Härma, A. Lemba, R. Tobias, M. Saar, N. Võrk and A. Vedro.

The song festivals continued to play an important role during the independence years as well. New choral and orchestral music was needed, and Estonian composers were certainly up to the task. In addition, concerts which coincided with the national song festivals became showcases for the best works from all musical genres.

During World War II, the poem, "My Fatherland is my Love", written by Lydia Koidula (Jannsen's daughter), was set to music by composer-choir director Gustav Ernesaks. The song has been adopted as the unofficial Estonian hymn and solemnly closes every song festival.

If the first national awakening was exemplified, in part, by the 1869 song festival, then the summer of 1988 marked the beginning of a second national awakening. During that summer, there was a great surge of Estonian national political activity, with the goal being the elimination of Soviet occupation and the re-establishment of a free and independent Estonia. This goal was clearly reflected in spontaneous song fests which popped up throughout Estonia. Referred to as the "summer of song" or the "singing revolution", these events demonstrated the sense of selfhood and unity that song brings to the Estonian people.

The Song Festival Amphitheater

The song festival tradition continues to this day. If your visit to Estonia happens to coincide with the first week of July in 1990, be sure to head for the Song Festival Amphitheater outside Tallinn. The amphitheater can accomodate over 100,000 spectators. The sound of 30,000 voices joined in choral harmony is an amazing and powerful experience.

Estonian music is by no means limited to folk, choral and symphonic. Rock music, especially in the 1980's, has proved to be a potent force in Estonian demands for independence. In 1980, the Estonian punk rock band, Propeller, was scheduled to perform during half-time, and again after a soccer match in Tallinn. Over 7,000 people showed up for the match. This amounted to more spectators than any soccer game had ever had in Estonia. The half-time program was so volatile, that Russian officials cancelled the after-game show. Rather than preventing trouble, which was the intention of the announcement, quite the opposite happened. The mostly teenage audience went on a rampage: smashing store windows, wrecking busses, overturning cars, all the while shouting anti-Russian slogans. The bewildered Russified Tallinn bureaucracy became acutely aware of the deep seated resentment Estonians have for the occupiers of their country. In response, officials disbanded Propeller, and prohibited them from performing.

The Song Festival Amphitheater during the three day Rock Festival in June, 1989

Rock music continued to play a large role in demands for independence during the "summer of song". In June, 1988, a crowd of 80,000 people had gathered in Tallinn to sing the rock songs of Estonian composer Alo Mattiisen. To the rhythm of a driving rock beat, the once-banned independent Estonian flag was raised over the city, while the crowd repeated the refrain from one of Mattiisen's most powerful songs: "I was born Estonian. I am now Estonian, and it is Estonian I shall ever remain".

For rock music lovers, or those merely interested in viewing political change in progress, there is the Tallinn Rock Festival. The three-day festival is held at the Song Festival Amphitheater. The 1989 fest was a huge success. Another is planned for June, 1990. For this festival, organizers are hoping to include western, as well as Estonian rock groups. In any case, music lovers will be well rewarded!

FINE ART

Estonian folk art goes back thousands of years. By the 18th century wooden household utensils were decorated with geometrical designs, and carved animal heads. The color and quality of Estonian woven goods was of an exceptionally high level. While northern Estonians favored floral ornamentation, southern Estonians preferred geometric designs. This love of color and design is evident in Estonian paintings as well.

The first prominent Estonian painter was J. Köler (1826-99), who did beautiful landscapes, as well as portraits. Equally talented was P. Raud (1865-1930), who specialized in portraits, and his brother Kristjan Raud (1865-1943). The latter was best known as the illustrator of the Estonian national epic, Kalevipoeg.

Other painters of note from this period were T. Grenzstein (1863-1916), who concentrated on religious subjects, and A. Laipman-Laikmaa (1866-1942), who worked in pastels and was equally skilled at landscapes and portraits. K. Mägi (1878-1925) introduced modern tendencies into Estonian art. He was primarily influenced by the French post-impressionists. N. Triik (1884-1940), a portraitist, and P. Burman (1888-1934) also showed non-Estonian influences in their works.

The beginning of the 20th century (1906) marked the first formal exhibition of Estonian painting and sculpture. In 1909, the Estonian

National Museum was established in Tartu. It was based on extensive ethnographic collections gathered in 19th century.

The years of independence saw the establishment of the Pallas Art School in Tartu in 1919. During the next 20 years, the school graduated 64 artists in sculpture, painting, and the graphic arts. In 1938, the State School of Industrial Arts was divided into the State School of Industrial Arts, and the Higher State Art School, which had programs in painting, sculpture, and the industrial arts.

During this period, artistic expression was highly differentiated, but realism prevailed as the dominant influence. The Pallas Art School was beginning to have a profound affect on the painters of the day. Among the more notable names are A. Vabbe, A. Johani, V. Ormisson,E. Ole, M. Laarman, A. Akberg, and J. Vahtra.

As with all of the arts, the Soviet occupation hampered freedom of expression. But in this area, too, the creative flow is starting a comeback. The art lovers among you should check out the Fine Arts Museum in Kadriorg Palace for a good overview of Estonian art through the ages. You might also want to stop in a bookstore to pick up a survey of Estonian art.

Old Town Tallinn

270

HISTORY OF TALLINN

In the early summer of 1219, Voldemar II of Denmark attacked what was then the town of Lindanissa, inhabited by the Revele Estonians. Faced with awesome Danish naval power, the natives garnered their forces and put up a mighty struggle. But Voldemar II saw a vision: coming down from the heavens was a white cross on a red field (the Danerog, or the Danish flag). This vision inspired Voldemar's victory, and shortly thereafter the Danes built a fortress-style seat of power on Toompea (Cathedral Hill), which is a huge chunk of rock almost 50 meters high left by the receding Ice Age glaciers. The seat of the bishopry was also established, and more than a century of exploitative Danish rule followed. Interesting to note that the Danish flag, born in Estonia, is the oldest national flag in continual use.

During this period Tallinn gained the rights of a city (1248), with a Council of 24 burghers meeting in the present Town Hall. The Lubeck law, which stated that all legal matters could be referred to the Lubeck Court for final adjudication, was in effect, and remained in effect for over 600 years through countless wars and foreign invasions. In 1285, Tallinn succeeded in joining the Hanseatic League, which strengthened the city's position as a major European trade center. Active trade with German, Dutch, and Scandinavian cities brought great prosperity, and Tallinn experienced a spurt of growth with the building of guild halls, warehouses, and churches as well as homes for the wealthy merchants.

There were, however, numerous peasant rebellions. As a result of large-scale uprisings in 1343, the Danes sold the duchy of Estonia, including the towns of Narva, Rakvere and Tallinn, to the Teutonic Order for 19,000 silver marks.

With the advent of the Lutheran Reformation, the Teutonic Order lost power. Iconoclasts destroyed works of art, and demolished churches and monasteries. Antagonism between the burghers and the nobility broke into open hostilities, precipitating the intervention of the Russians, who wanted to protect their trade routes. After a lengthy Russian siege, Tallinn swore an oath of allegiance to the King of Sweden. The Livonian War (1558-83) devastated Tallinn's economy. In 1577, Tallinn endured still another Russian siege, which was brilliantly ended by the famous Swede, General Pontus de La Gardie, whose remains are buried in Cathedral Church. As a result, all trading with Russia ended, and the fortunes of Tallinn began to decline. Several plagues added further destruction by decimating the population.

Estonia also suffered from Sweden's war with Poland (1626-29), which

Gustavus II Adolphus waged after capturing lands south of Lake Ladoga in Ingeria, presently Leningrad. Domestically, Gustavus II Adolphus instituted great social, judicial, and educational reforms in Estonia. He established gymnasia (secondary schools) in Tartu (1630) and Tallinn (1631). Tartu's gymnasium has since become Tartu University, and Tallinn's still functions as the 21st Secondary School. Estonians refer to this relatively humanistic era as the "good old Swedish period".

Tallinn capitulated to Peter the Great in 1710, during the Great Northern War, which Sweden lost to Russia. This city, once an important Hanseatic commercial center, had became a provincial town.

In the 19th century, a railroad was built between Tallinn and St. Petersburg, tying the two cities economically. While there were several peasant uprisings against German barons who had remained over the centuries, large-scale revolutionary uprisings did not occur until 1905 and 1917, when the workers rebelled. By this time, Tallinn had become an industrial city.

On February 24, 1918, in Tallinn, The Committee of Elders of the Maapäev declared Estonia an independent republic, with Tallinn as its capital city. The seat of the parliamentary government was located high on Toompea. While this declaration was being made, Estonia's territory was in the midst of Soviet-German fighting. Many of the Elders were executed or jailed by the occupying German forces. After the World War I armistice, Estonia still had to fight a War of Independence against Soviet forces from November, 1918 until January, 1920. On February 2, 1920, Estonia and Soviet Russia signed the Treaty of Tartu, in which the Soviet Union renounced all sovereign rights to Estonian territory in perpetuity.

TALLINN

The capital city of Estonia dates back to the 12th century. Give yourself adequate time to get a feel for this medieval marvel. Excellent, well-preserved examples of craftsmanship can be seen at every turn. The student of vaulted ceilings and art historians interested in altarpieces and religious artifacts will be especially well rewarded strolling through Tallinn. Much of the restoration of the Old Town was done a decade ago when the Soviet Union hosted the 1980 Olympic Games. Since Tallinn was the location for the regatta, it was spruced up for all the world to see. Townspeople still mention that event as a turning point with ethnic pride.

To set the scene for your visit to Tallinn - a bit of background mythology! In Finno-Ugric mythology, all things of nature have their own spirits. The lake which sits on the plateau above Tallinn is no exception. It has the old man/spirit of Ülemiste järv. Centuries ago, as the builders of Tallinn ended their workday, this old man/spirit would query them as to their progress. "Is the city finished yet?" Every day the answer was the same: "No, not yet." To this day, the city is not considered finished, and the reason is very simple. Residents know that once the city is finished, the old man/spirit will pull the plug under Ülemiste and flood Tallinn. Based on this myth, its easy to understand why Estonians feel that complacency, boredom and decay set in once something is finished. What gives Tallinners their natural buoyancy is knowing they will never finish building their city. So as you look at the 2000 acre Ulemiste jarv, remember that supplying Tallinn with water since the 14th century is not its sole purpose!

If you arrive in Tallinn by the water route from Helsinki, you will have met the Estonians' closest relatives - the Finns. The first sightings of land will be on your left. This is the suburb of Merivälja. Originally a fishing collective, Merivälja has become a legend in its own time. It has been called a "state-within-a-state" because its citizens believe that, "if you need something, build it yourself."

Dominating the horizon further along will be the triangular west gable of the Pirita Cloister ruins. The compound, completed in 1436 under the auspices of the Order of St. Birgitta in Sweden, included a church, monastery and convent. Although it was destroyed by fire in 1577, the remaining ruins are magnificent. Be sure to climb to the top of the tower for a beautiful view of the sea, the towers of Tallinn, Naissaar Island and the Olympic complex.

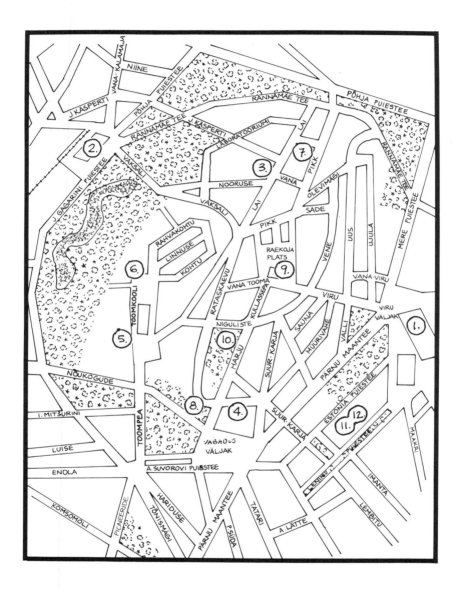

OLD TOWN TALLINN

1. Hotel Viru
2. Baltic Railway Station
3. Museum of Natural History
4. Theater and Music Museum
5. Toompea Castle
6. Toome Church
7. Oleviste Church
8. Kiek in de Kök
9. Raekoda - Town Hall
10. Niguliste Church
11. Estonia Opera and Ballet Theater
12. Estonian Philharmonic Society Concert Hall

The St. Birgitta Cloister ruins

The Georg Ots at dock in Helsinki

As the ship moves toward its berth in Tallinn Harbor, on the left you will see the semi-circular shell of the laululava (Song Festival Amphitheater). This shell accomodates 30,000 singers and seats an audience of 100,000. The tree-covered grounds above the amphitheater provide ample room for several thousand more. The shell was built in 1960. It was the site of the centennial song festival in 1969, as well as the location of the spontaneous song fests which took place in the summer of 1988.

The Old Town

The Tallinn skyline is dominated by medieval church spires. Until you spot Paks (Fat) Margareeta, a wide, round bastion completed in 1529, and part of the Suur Rannavärav (The Great Sea Gate), which sits squarely on the bluff overlooking the harbor, you may have the impression that you will be mooring under the buttresses of Oleviste Kirik (St. Olaf's Church). Built between 1241-1250, the Gothic style chapel was added to the church in 1500. Destroyed by fire in 1819, it was rebuilt shortly thereafter. Today, the church is home to one of the largest Methodist congregations in the world.

All of the towers and bastions of the walled city are named. Some are named after prominent people, others simply bear nicknames of endearment. Directly opposite Paks Margareeta, is the tower of Pikk (Tall) Hermann, the flag-bearer, which guards Tallinn land-side. Pikk Hermann stands 45 m. high, with 3 m. thick walls. The Landskrone and Pilstiker corner towers have also survived to this day. The fourth tower was demolished in 1773. The old defensive structures of Toompea Castle, dating back to the early 1200's, were rebuilt in the second half of the 14th century.

Just south of Pikk Hermann on Toompea is Hirve Park, the site of the Statue of Linda (Kalevipoeg's mother). This was the site of the first and many subsequent demonstrations against Soviet occupation, the Molotov-Ribbentrop Pact, and the mass deportations of Estonian citizens in 1941 and 1949. On June 14, 1989, the Muinsuskaitse Selts (Cultural Preservation Society) dedicated a plaque honoring those who died or were deported on June 14, 1941. The flowers at the base of the plaque which sits in front of the Linda Statue are placed by Estonians who wish to honor the memory of the dead and deported.

By far the most personable of the towers is Kiek-in-de-Kök (Peek-into-the-Kitchen), which bears a striking resemblance to a good-natured uncle. Built in the mid-1400's, this red-roofed artillery tower is 49.5 m. high and has walls that are 4 m. thick. Iron cannonballs dating back to 1577 are embedded in the walls and

Pikk Hermann

attest to the function of the tower. The name comes from the fact that from the tower, one could literally peek into the kitchens of the houses below.

Restoration of the bastions is in progress. Many have been turned into museums. Kiek-in-de-Kök has a fine collection of medieval armaments and relics on display. Paks Margareeta and her side-kick on the other side of the Suur Rannavärev house a maritime museum well worth visiting, since Estonia has developed and maintained a strong seafaring tradition.

The medieval churches still used for religious services are maintained by the congregations. Oleviste Kirik, for instance is

Kiek in de Kök

used by both Baptist and Methodist congregations. Niguliste Kirik (St. Nicholas' Church) has been transformed into a museum. It was built in the 13th century in honor of the patron saint of seamen, and rebuilt in the 15th century after a fire demolished it. After the bombing of Tallinn in March, 1944, only a shell of the original building remained. Reconstruction of the building has returned it to its original form. Owing to the excellent acoustics, Niguliste Kirik is used for concerts and recordings.

The noblest of Tallinn's churches, the elegant Toome Kirik (Cathedral Church), sits atop Cathedral Hill and is the seat of the bishopry. The Danish king himself was its patron until Danish rule ended in 1346. First mentioned in 1233, the church has been expanded and

Niguliste Church as seen from Kiek in de Kök

rebuilt over the years. A fire in 1684 destroyed much of the building, although some tombstones and monuments from the 13th-17th centuries did survive. Among the more notable tombstones is that of Pontus de la Gardie - the famous Swedish field marshall who, after having driven the Russians out of Estonia, drowned in the Narva River in 1585. Coats of arms of aristocratic congregation members can be seen on the walls and embellish the sarcophagi.

Dearest to the Estonian people is the Pühavaimu Kirik (Church of the Holy Spirit), which dates back to the early 14th century. The church has retained its 14th century appearance despite numerous repairs. The present-day steeple was reconstructed in 1630. Although representing different periods, the interior artifacts are particularly tasteful. Don't miss the suspended pulpit - the oldest in Tallinn, dating back to the late 16th century, and the carved wooden pews - also 16th century. The altar, in triptych style typical of the period, was commissioned from Lubeck master Bernt Notke in 1483. It is adorned with wooden sculptures and paintings. Be sure to note the azure-faced wall clock, dating from 1684, which is set in the outer facade.

Easily mistaken for a church spire is the tower of the Raekoda (Town Hall). Construction of Tallinn's oldest civic building was begun in 1371 and completed in 1404. Atop the tower is a replica of Vana Toomas (Old Thomas) - the original, which dates back to 1530, is on display in the Museum of the City of Tallinn. Looking at Estonia's social history, it is hard to distinguish whether the Church brought with it commerce, or vice-versa. Both co-existed intransigently since the days of the Teutonic Order. As a matter of fact, the Raekoda has a large money-counting room, money vault and a meeting hall which was used by the captains of commerce. The local population was expected to support both the Town Council and the Church. Today, the Raekoda is a museum and has a busy concert calendar.

Raekoda plats (Town Hall Square) is surrounded by numerous restored buildings which date back to the 15th century, and currently house small businesses. Behind the Raekoda, across a narrow alleyway, stand two buildings. One was the debtor's jail and the other the jailkeeper's house. If the money counted up in the Raekoda was not sufficient, the payer was marched across the alley to jail. Artifacts associated with the Raekoda are on display in both of these buildings. Across from the Raekoda is an apothecary which dates back to 1422, and has been in continuous operation since that time.

As you stroll through Old Town Tallinn, don't hesitate to step into one of the old buildings that catches your fancy. Many of them are offices, and no one seems to mind that the occasional tourist comes in to admire the craftsmanship. Almost all of the medieval buildings have a large fireplace in the front room, and most have fine dolomite carvings on interior window casings and high quality woodcarvings. With a bit of luck, someone just may offer to give you a tour of the whole building!

Conclude your visit to Old Town Tallinn by climbing up Toompea (Cathedral Hill) to survey the red tiled roofs of the city below. The look-out site is located at the end of Kohtu Street. While you're on Toompea hill, check out Lossi Plats, where you can see Toompea Loss (Palace). The Aleksander Nevski Cathedral is also located on this square, and is a fine example of Russian Orthodox architecture. Although numerous wars and plagues have left their mark on Tallinn, the city goes about its business with great creative energy and a fierce pride and determination to remain Estonian.

Raekoda in Tallinn's town square

Toompea Palace

Around Town

With the intent of pushing Tallinn headlong into the circuit of Western tourism, the city fathers and Intourist commissioned Finnish architects and contractors to build a luxury-class western hotel outside the town's Viru Gate in 1969. Hotel Viru has gained a reputation far beyond the original intent. For the townspeople, it is a symbol of Westernism and everything which that implies. Another modern hotel, the Olümpia, was built for the 1980 Olympic Games, but does not seem to enjoy the reputation of the Viru.

Bordering the Viru on the west is a peaceful little park, which is home to an enormous sitting statue of the writer Anton H. Tammsaare. He is the beloved author of Estonia's classic opus "Truth and Justice", and many other works. On the far side of the park lies the Estonia Performing Arts Center, built in 1910-13, and designed by Finnish architect Armas Lindgren. On its left, is the Ooperisaal (Opera House), and on the right is the Kontsert saal (Concert Hall), where the first constituent assembly of the young Estonian Republic met on April 23, 1919. The artistic direction of the small opera company has always been ambitious and the standards are high. They have no trouble scheduling renowned guest artists. The Opera House was the first in the Baltic States and the Soviet Union to stage "Porgy and Bess." Included in the company's repertoire are standard international, as well as Estonian operas.

MUSEUMS

Tallinn has an abundance of museums. You're sure to find one that coincides with your particular interests. Others will serve to enlighten you about the rich history and culture of Estonia. The open-air ethnographic museum at Roc al Mara, is an absolute must-see for getting a real feeling for Estonia's rural life in the 18th-19th centuries.

Linnamuuseum
17 Vene st., tel. 446553.
Open daily 10:30-17:30, closed Tuesdays.

The Museum of the City of Tallinn is housed in the 15th century home of a wealthy merchant. Among the numerous exhibits you will find: municipal caskets, tapestries, silverpieces, 1800 pieces of earthenware and porcelain, 400 tinpieces, glassworks numbering in the

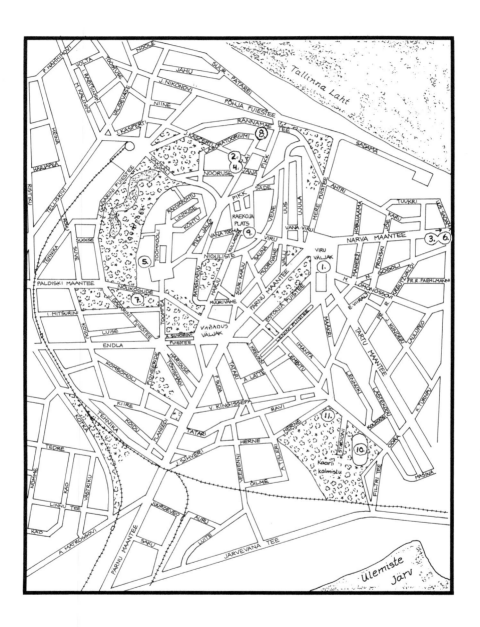

TALLINN

1. Hotel Viru
2. Museum of Natural History
3. Fine Arts Museum at Kadrioru Loss
4. Estonian Youth Theater
5. Toompea Castle
6. Song Festival Amphitheater
7. Linda Statue in Hirve Park
8. Suur Rannavärav - The Great Sea Gate
9. Raekoda - Town Hall
10. Komsomol Stadium
11. Kalev Sports Hall

thousands, and 350 pieces of furniture from various periods. In addition, the museum owns 1700 graphic works representing all of the important Baltic masters of the 19th-20th centuries, as well as 40,000 photographs and negatives. On permanent display is a pictorial history of Tallinn since the Northern War (1700-1710).

Tarbekunstimuuseum
3 Aida tanav.

The Museum of Applied Arts is cleverly tucked away inside an old store-house, which is just one of the buildings lining the inside of the ramparts on the western edge of the old town. Inside are 3 floors of high quality crafts, totalling 1800 pieces of glass art works, ceramics, metals, weavings, leather and wood.

Kadrioru loss
Kadriorg Palace, tel. 426240.
Open daily 11:00-18:00, closed Tuesdays.

The Fine Arts Museum is set in a park on the eastern end of town. This Baroque style pink stucco building with white trim was originally built by Peter the Great in 1718 for his wife Catherine. It was designed by Italian architect Nicolo Michetti. As it was erected on a hillside, the front of the building consists of 2 stories, while the back is only one story. Kadrioru loss (The Palace of Catherine's valley) also served as the residence of independent Estonia's president, Konstantin Pats. The museum's holdings include 5300 paintings dating back to the earliest of art periods in Estonia, 3700 pieces of sculpture, and over 1200 graphic works. Beyond the palace is the museum's sculpture garden.

Museum of the Baltic Fleet
44 Narva rd., tel. 426114.
Open daily 10:00-18:00, closed Fridays and Saturdays.

Open-Air Museum at Roc al Mara
12 Vabaohumuuseumi rd., tel. 559176.
Open daily from 10:00-16:00.

Located in a picturesque spot on the Kakumae Peninsula, this ethnographic museum opened to the public in 1964. There are more than 60 buildings from all over Estonia, as well as some 40,000 artifacts on display, offering a glimpse at Estonian rural life in previous centuries. Folk ensembles often give performances of Estonian dancing and music.

Kadrioru loss - home to the Fine Arts Museum

<u>Meremuuseum</u>
70 Pikk st., tel. 601275.
Open daily 10:30-17:30, closed Saturdays and Sundays.

The Nautical Museum located at Paks Margareta is filled with exhibits from Estonia's maritime past. Ship models, artifacts from wrecks, and large sections on fishing and trade give the visitor an idea of Estonia's prominence as a maritime state.

<u>History Museum</u>
17 Pikk st., tel. 443446.
Open daily 11:00-18:00, closed Wednesdays.

<u>Museum of Natural History</u>
29 Lai st., tel. 444223.
Open daily 10:00-17:30, closed Tuesdays.

The Estonian State Open-Air Museum. This building is a restored example of a northern Estonian village tavern.

Paks Margareta - site of the Maritime Museum

Kiek-in-de-Kok Tower
1 Nõukogude st., tel. 446686.
Open daily 10:30-17:30, closed Mondays.

The museum houses a great collection of medieval armaments and relics.

Theater and Music Museum
12 Müürivahe st., tel. 442132.
Open daily 10:00-18:00, closed Tuesdays.

Home Museum of Friedebert Tuglas
12 Vaike-Illimari st., in the suburb of Nomme, tel. 510104.
Open daily 09:00-17:00, closed Saturdays and Sundays.

Tuglas was a prose writer known for establishing modern Estonian literary criticism.

Ed. Vilde Memorial Museum
34 L. Koidula st., tel. 426300.
Open daily 11:00-18:00, closed Tuesdays.

The author is best known for his historical trilogy on peasant life in the mid 19th century.

Anton Hansen Tammsaare Memorial Museum
12 L. Koidula st., tel. 427208.
Open daily 11:00-18:00, closed Tuesdays.

Writer of the epic, five volume novel Tode ja Oigus (Truth and Justice), which is a realistic examination of Estonian rural and urban life, as well as a philosophical look at the human condition.

THEATERS AND CONCERT HALLS

When you're in the mood for a concert, play, or ballet while visiting Tallinn, just check with the service desk in your hotel to find out what is currently playing in town. Prices are reasonable by Western standards, and you will get a great taste of Estonia's cultural life. Concerts and theater are very popular among the Estonians, and many events are sold out well in advance. Intourist and the Estonian Tourist Bureau can arrange tickets for you.

Estonia teater (Estonian Opera and Ballet Theater)
4 Estonia blvd., tel. 444709.

Drama teater (V. Kingissepp Drama Theater)
5 Pärnu rd., tel. 443378.

Morsoo teater (Estonian Youth Theater)
23 Lai st., tel. 609624.

Muku teater (Estonian Puppet Theater)
1 Lai st., tel. 601633.

Russian Drama Theater
5 Vabadus sq., tel. 443716

Estonian Philharmonic Society Concert Hall
4 Estonia blvd., in the right wing of the building.

Concerts are also held in Kadriorg Palace, the Town Hall, and the Kiek in de Kók Cannon Tower. During the summer, you will find open-air concerts on the Harju Hill Concert Grounds. Estonians love music and singing. Be sure to attend at least one performance...

MOVIE THEATERS

Documentaries, films based on popular novels and foreign films are popular fare in Estonia. You will find that most movies are dubbed into Russian, but have Estonian captions.

Kosmos	45 Pärnu rd.	682093
Sõprus	8 Vana Posti st.	441143
Eha	49 Tartu rd.	427326
Oktoober	4 Viru st.	444143
Rahu	96b Kalinini st.	474374
Kaja	118 Ed. Vilde st.	539830
Voit	326 Pärnu rd.	510186
Lembitu	8 Kalinini st.	444067
Koit	1 Rannaku blvd.	518269

SPORTS

The Olympic Center at Pirita has facilities for kayaking, sailing, rowing, etc. You can rent row boats and power boats, and if sailing is your preference, that, too, can be accomodated. But if you prefer to view rather than do, check with your hotel service bureau for sporting events around town.

Just east of the Olympic Center is Pirita Beach, one of the most popular beaches around Tallinn. The Pirita Restaurant and Bar at 5 Merivalja St. offers a delightful view of the Gulf of Finland, as well as of the bathers, sail-boarders and the boating traffic thereupon.

Dynamo Stadium	24 Roheline aas st.	421533
Dynamo Sports Hall	3 Toompea st.	446709
Komsomol Stadium	3 Staadioni st.	661623
Kalev Sports Hall	12 Liivalaia st.	661687

Olympic Sailing Center

Pirita Beach

WHERE TO STAY

Western tourists, whether on individual or group trips, usually stay in the modern Hotel Viru, 4 Viru sq., tel. 652070, built and furnished by a Finnish company. This Intourist hotel provides guests with a variety of services. The Viru has saunas, several restaurants and bars, as well as personal services such as hairdressers.

The Estonian Tourist Bureau uses the Olümpia and Palace Hotels. The Palace Hotel opened in September, 1989, and is geared toward business travelers, and individuals, not groups. A Sheraton Hotel is scheduled to open in 1992. The Estonian Tourist Bureau can also arrange for you to stay in dormitories or private homes during major events like the Song Festival.

For help in arranging your trip to Estonia, turn to:

Enterprise World Travel
1150 Connecticut Av NW
Suite 515
Washington, DC
(202) 296-7050

They have arranged numerous Estonian tours and work in conjunction with Baltic Tours of Boston.

EAT, DRINK AND BE MERRY

When its time to eat, be sure to check out one of the restaurants or cafes listed below to get a taste of Estonian fare. To eliminate hassles, it's best to make reservations through the service desk at your hotel.

A visit to Estonia would not be complete without sampling some of the fine locally canned fish. The delicately smoked Forrell (trout) is the best, and consequently the hardest to find. Forrell is usually available at the better quality restaurants, where it is traditionally served with a loaf of praetud sai (fried white bread). The trout are farmed in small reservoirs formed by damming some of the cleanest streams in Estonia. Also worth sampling are numerous varieties of salted and/or smoked herring, sprats and anchovies. These fish are eaten with bread and boiled potatoes, and washed down with shots of ice cold vodka. Viru Valge (Viru White) is made is Estonia and is one of the finest vodkas you will come across anywhere. Don't forget to buy a bottle to take home with you!

If beer is more to your liking, you are in luck! Estonian beer is generally strong and of good quality. Saaremaa is the brand most highly praised by the locals. Although difficult to find, it is most definitly worth asking for. Estonians are proud of their beer and will try to accomodate the thirsty tourist. Rosolie (beet salad), sült (head cheese) and the wonderful Estonian leib (bread) are nice accompaniments to the beer.

Ice cream lovers might want to stop off at the ice cream shop on Saiakang St., just off of Raekoja Plats. 40 kopeks will buy you a large portion of excellent quality ice cream. For an additional 5 kopeks you can get cookies for some added crunch.

Restaurants:

Viru	4 Viru sq.	650773
Euroopa	24 Viru st.	444769
Pärnu	3 Turi st.	557495
Tallinn-Balti	39 Gagarini blvd.	442421
Vana Toomas	8 Town Hall sq.	443905
Pirita	5 Merivälja st.	439130
Kannu Kukk	75 Ed. Vilde st.	536250

Cafes:

Harju	4 Suur-Karja st.	446666
Kullus	15 Lauristini st.	441316
Narva	20 Narva rd.	424459
Pärl	1 Pikk st.	440710
Tallinn	6 Harju st.	449204

Bars:

There are several bars, including foreign currency only bars, in the Hotel Viru, Hotel Tallinn, Olümpia Hotel and Hotel Palace. You might also like to try the Fox Burrow in the basement at 3/5 Rataskaevu st., tel. 448591.

WHERE TO SHOP

Foreign Currency Stores

Valuta arid are open to non residents, since they only accept foreign currency, not rubles. You may also use traveler's checks and major credit cards. Here you will find everything from automobiles to electrical appliances, clothing, beverages, including alcohol, cigarettes, amber, food products, books, and souvenirs. There are 4 locations:

2 Tehnika st., tel. 446347.
29 Gagarini blvd., tel. 446344.
31 Gagarini blvd., tel. 443461.
6 Narva rd., tel. 421081.

If you're looking for that perfect Estonian souvenir, however, then you should head for one of the stores listed below. You can find beautifully photographed books, amber jewelry, mittens, place mats and leather jewelry. Many of the items utilize traditional motifs.

If you are planning to buy Estonian handcrafts, you might want to check out the Tarbekunstimuuseum (The Museum of Applied Art) at 3 Aida st. There you will see the finest examples of ceramic, glass, leather, wood, and other works. Its a good way to educate yourself on the quality of hand made versus mass-produced souvenirs.

Book Stores:

Areng	16 Narva rd.	430494.
Lugemisvara	1 Harju st.	443565.
Rahva Raamat	10 Pärnu rd.	443682.

Jewelry Stores:

Juveel	8 Pärnu rd.	444216.
	1 Viru st.	449938.

Gift Stores:

Heli (records)	16 Town Hall sq.	442503
Kingitused	3 Mundi st.	441556.
Soprus	225 Sopruse blvd.	538026.
Uku	9 Pikk st.	443280.

Arts and Crafts:

6 Vabadus sq.
19 Viru st.
2 Hobuse st.
14 Kingissepa st.

GETTING AROUND

Tallinn's public transportation system makes it possible to move around the town. There are numerous bus, tram, and trolley lines which go to all parts of the city. Tickets are available at kiosks, and shops. A tram ride costs 3 kopeks, a trolley is 4 kopeks, and a bus ride is 5 kopeks. A single ride requires one ticket, which you validate upon entering the vehicle. Express buses require two tickets. A monthly bus/tram pass is available for the low cost of 3 rubles. If you plan on using public transportation during your stay in Tallinn, the monthly pass is recommended, as it eliminates the need for buying individual tickets. Be sure to carry the monthly pass with you, as you may be asked to show it. Upon leaving Tallinn, a still valid pass can serve as a much appreciated parting gift or tip. For information, call 440486.

If you prefer to get around by taxi, there are two options. You can order a state run taxi by calling 603044, or the taxi depot at 511649. Taxis are usually available in front of hotels. The cost is 20 kopeks per kilometer. Also available are set route taxis. There are 10 different routes, all originating from Viru Square. They operate between 3PM and 2AM, from 3PM to 3AM on Fridays, Saturdays and holidays.

The Central Railway Station is located at 39 Gagarini blvd. For information, call 446756. You can book your tickets at the Intourist office in your hotel, or by calling 448087.

GAS STATIONS

#3	141 Pärnu rd.	552264
#5	58 Leningradi rd.	212160
#7	83 Leningradi rd.	211568
#8	96 Paldiski rd.	559191
#9	66a Kadaka st.	532134

SERVICE STATIONS

54 Veerenni st.	556579
7 Turi st.	556532
1 Ülemiste st.	422985
1 Kauba st.	557756
232 Pärnu rd.	557094

TELEPHONE, TELEGRAM, POST OFFICE

To make a local call from a pay phone, drop in a 2 kopek coin, wait for the dial tone, and dial the number. When your party answers, wait for the coin to drop and start your conversation.

There is no direct dialing of long distance calls. You can order a long distance call through your hotel service bureau, or go to the Long Distance Telephone Exchange at 10 Lomonossovi st. This is also the place to go to if you want to send a telegram.

The Central Post Office is located at 1/3 Narva rd., tel. 448913. There are numerous brance offices, a few of which are listed below.

4 Skala st.
3 Nekrasovi st.
At the Baltic Railway Station
24 Narva rd.
22 Merivälja st.
116 Mustamae st.
33a Gagarini blvd.
137 Tammsaare st.

PERSONAL SERVICES

When it's time for laundry, a hair cut, shoe repair, etc., check with the service desk at your hotel. For the more independent minded, listed below are some of your options.

Dry Cleaning:

26 Müürivahe st.	446563
13 Tatari st.	443075
285 Parnu rd.	495225
18 L. Koidula st.	421209

Laundry Service:

17/30 Müürivahe st.	444578
3 Nekrassovi st.	495225
73 Ed. Vilde st.	531252

Shoe Repair:

1 Anveldi st.	424480
5 Town Hall sq.	444979
18 Tombi st.	425178

<u>Hairdressers for Men and Women</u>:

      5 Harju st.
      61 Kingisseppi st.

<u>Saunas/Public baths</u>:

23 Gogoli st.	424901
240 Pärnu rd.	510064
122 Sihi st.	510345
3 Tulbi st.	443216
9a Vana Kalamaja st.	445912
3 Paldiski rd.	446982
4 Viru sq.	652070

WHERE TO TURN FOR HELP

Emergency phone numbers:

Fire: 01
Police: 02
Ambulance: 03

Lost property: 444305

Pharmacies and medical attention

Medicines are not readily available in Estonia, so that it is very important for you to take any medication you regularly use with you. This is also true of non-prescription drugs, and personal care items. If you are in need of medical attention, check with the service desk in your hotel. Below are some centrally located pharmacies.

5 Tõnismägi st., tel. 442282.
10 Pärnu rd., tel. 442262.
Rae Apteek in Town Hall square

LAHEMAA NATIONAL PARK

Within easy reach of Tallinn are points of interest for the tourist who wants to see more of Estonia than just its capital. One of the more interesting places is the Lahemaa National Forest, situated on the Gulf of Finland, just 40 km. east of Tallinn. Founded in 1971, the 65,000 hectare park encompasses beautiful and unique natural landscapes, as well as recreational areas and villages. Although there are several reserves which are off-limits to the public (they have been set aside for scientific research), there are ample areas open to the tourist. Whether you're interested in history, geography, and cultural anthropology, or you just want to be surrounded by natural beauty, you are sure to be delighted by Lahemaa.

The Baltic Sea has carved 4 peninsulas into the coastal line and has created today's dunes, beach barriers and terraces. The pine dominated forests are broken up by numerous rivers, which are spawning grounds for trout and salmon. As the rivers flow through terraced limestone, they form picturesque waterfalls and rapids. The southernmost of the park's 14 lakes were formed by retreating glaciers, while the younger coastal lakes were once sea bays. Several underground brooks and springs are also situated within the park.

Lahemaa has a wealth of huge boulders: The Tammispea is the highest at almost 8 m., while the Majakivi has the largest volume (580 cu. m.) Stone fields - the most notable ones are found on the Käsmu Peninsula - cover large areas of the park. Sandstone and limestone outcrops are also visible throughout the area.

The park's flora cosists of more than 800 species of higher plants, with over 30 of them classified as rare. Fauna is equally well represented with some 37 mammal, 213 bird and 24 fish species. Lynx, brown bear, and European mink are common in Lahemaa Park, as are the black stork, crane, and mute swan.

The cultural heritage within the park's boundaries is as rich and varied as the natural. Hundreds of stone covered mounds - the remnants of ancient settlements - can be found at Kahala, Palmse and Vihula. The seaside villages of Altja, Naturi, Käsmu, and Virve evoke images of their seafaring past. Throughout the countryside you will come upon moisad (manor houses). Many have been restored, and if they are not being used as schools or hospitals, they are open for tours. The most notable and well preserved of these is the moisad at Palmse. A walk around the manor house itself, as well as the surrounding buildings, will provide you with a glimpse of how the German Barons lived. Restoration work on the complex is nearly

Palmse mois - the manor house in Lahemaa Park

complete. All of the buildings - including greenhouses, farm structures, guesthouses, etc. - are open to the public. The distillery was still being worked on in late 1989, and is expected to be completed soon.

The Lahemaa National Park has a wide range of nature walks of varying lengths and degree of difficulty. Camping, open fires and fishing are allowed only by permission of the park directorate. For detailed information on the park, contact the Lahemaa Tourist Center in Viitna, tel. 202128. The park can be accessed via the Tallinn-Narva Highway, or check with the service desk in your hotel regarding public transportation.

ESTONIA'S ISLANDS

Over 800 islands dot the shoreline of Estonia. The two largest are Saaremaa and Hiiumaa. If you happen to be in Estonia on June 24th, definitely set out for the islands to experience the mid-summer's eve festival. Although these celebrations take place all over the country, the one on Saaremaa is especially popular. Saaremaa has retained it's independence era flavor, i.e., doors are never locked, there is very little industry, and therefore very little Russification has occurred.

Saaremaa officially opened as a tourist destination in the summer of 1989, and therefore information on lodging and transportation is at best, scarce. Check with the service desk at your hotel for latest details. Because it is such a popular vacation spot for Estonian vacationers, it would be wise to arrange for ferry tickets to the island upon arrival.

Saaremaa was part of a feudal church-state created in 1228. There are numerous architectural monuments from this period on Saaremaa. The Kuressaare Castle dates back to the 13th century, and so do 3 of the island's gothic-style churches: Valjala, Kaarma and Poide. Construction of the Kihelkonna Church was begun in the 14th century. You might also want to check out the 18th century Telluste manor house as well as the 19th century Keljala manor house and adjoining park. Saaremaa even has an ethnographic museum in Viki.

TARTU

Archeological evidence indicates that the area around present-day Tartu has been inhabited since the 5th century. It was first mentioned as a settlement in 1030. In 1224 it became the seat of the Tartu bishopric, and in 1248 Tartu was granted city rights. Situated along the east-west waterway linking southern Estonia with the Russian hinterland, Tartu was an important trade center by the mid-16th century, and was the second largest city in Estonia after Tallinn. By the mid-1800's, during Estonia's national awakening, Tartu had become the cultural center of Estonia.

Located in southeastern Estonia, this medieval town is nestled between Cathedral Hill and Estonia's longest river, the Emajõgi. These natural barriers, however, did not provide sufficient protection from enemies. Historical records show that Tartu has been burned to the ground 55 times. Only two buildings, both in ruins, date back to the middle ages: the 13th century St. Peter and St. Paul Cathedral on top of Cathedral Hill, and the 14th century St. John's Church at the foot of the hill. The rest of Tartu is built in Classical and Baroque styles.

One of the two most imposing structures in Tartu is the Raekoda (Town

Hall), which was built in 1789 and dominates Town Hall Square. It is the third Town Hall to occupy that particular spot. The other is the main building of Tartu University, which proudly displays its gleaming white Corinthian columns.

Tartu Town Square as seen from across the Emajogi River

Cathedral Hill itself is a splendid park which incorporates a delightful array of sightseeing wonders, including a pagan sacrificial stone, a gunpowder magazine - now a restaurant-cafe, and a once world-famous astrophysical observatory which has been turned into a museum. A new observatory was built in 1964 and is located 20 km. southwest of Tartu.

Spanning a slight incline is the Inglisild (Angel's Bridge) - a footbridge with a nice view of the city - built in honor of the first chancellor of the University after it re-opened in 1802, G.F. Parrot. Nearby is the Kuradisild (Devil's Bridge). There are various statues in honor of noteworthy university scholars scattered throughout the park.

Monuments dedicated to numerous literary figures who made significant contributions to the national awakening are located around the city.

Perhaps the most moving is the monument erected in 1983 to Kristjan Jaak Peterson (1801-1822), showing him with a book in one hand and a walking stick in the other. He walked back and forth from Riga, where his parents lived, to Tartu to attend the university. In his short lifetime - he died of tuberculosis - he was the first poet to write in Estonian. Among his inspiring words to the Estonian people, "why shouldn't we enjoin our voices to other voices..."

Undoubtedly, the vitality of this city comes from its enormous student population. Tartu University has 9 faculties of study, 87 separate chairs, several scientific institutions employing more than 110 Doctors of Science and 500 graduate students, and a student body of 7500. The medical college is the largest, with 200 lecturers and 1800 students. Founded in 1632, the University celebrated its 350th anniversary with more than 300 events. The chancellors of the Universities of Uppsala, Stockholm (both in Sweden) and Helsinki (Finland) attended the ceremonies and were awarded honorary doctorates.

Across town, standing on a rise is the Eesti Põllumajanduse Akadeemia (Estonian Agricultural College) with its Corinthian columns. The Academy has 7 faculties of study with 4000 undergraduates majoring in 11 specialties. A vast amount of research is carried out by 20 Doctors of Science and 155 graduate students. The Academy stresses the scientific approach to agriculture through both theory and intensive hands-on practice. The students of the two universities can be distinguished by the caps they wear: green for the Academy and blue for the University.

You might want to check out one of the 9 museums in Tartu, or the botanical gardens dating back to 1803. There is also the Vanemuine Music and Drama Theater, which occupies a prominent position on a hillside. The tradition of Estonian language theater was born in Tartu, which claims to be the repository of the Estonian nation's soul. Walking through the streets of the city, you just might sense the justification for this claim. Tartu is both youthful and serious.

PÄRNU

Pärnu is located in southwestern Estonia, on the shores of the Pärnu River where it empties into the Pärnu Bay in the Gulf of Rīga. It is both a major port and a resort city. Its silver-sanded shoreline is blessed by gentle winds and softly undulating waves.

The city was first mentioned in 1154 by an Arabian geographer, al-Idrisi. The streets were laid out in the 13th century, and it was officially founded in 1251. From the 15th-18th century, Pärnu was controlled in turn by the Livonian Order, Poland, and Sweden. During the Swedish period the city was surrounded by a green belt, the remainders of which you can see in Vallikaar, Koidula Väljak and Vana Park. Toward the first half of the past century, the main recreation area was the old park, known as Badesalon, where townspeople relaxed by playing billiards and reading newspapers. They took their meals in the salon and danced to a live orchestra in the park.

The city changed radically when, in 1837, several merchants got together to build an inn. Seeing no great economic opportunities in the existent leisure pastimes, they undertook the building of a full-scale spa modelled after the one in Rīga. By 1889, the city was in the resort business, promising rest and rehabilitation through restorative and pacifying mud baths. A rail connection to St. Petersburg-Tallinn-Rīga in 1896 was a definite boon.

The mud-bath sanatorium in Pärnu

Both of Pärnu's museums are worth visiting. One is the home of Lydia Koidula (1843-1886), the beloved poet of Estonia's national awakening period, and daughter of the first Estonian language newspaper publisher. To get to the museum from downtown Pärnu, proceed northwest on Tallinn Road and take a left onto Silla Street after the bridge.

The Folk Art Museum is located in the center of town on Lenin Avenue and Aia Street. Much of the local history, as well as crafts and work implements, are on display. Archeological excavations have revealed that the Pärnu area has been inhabited since the early Stone Age. Artifacts from that period are also on display.

Pärnu is also home to the Lydia Koidula Drama Theater. The origins of the theater date back to a theater association called Endla, which was founded in 1875. The professional drama theater was founded in 1911 under the same name. In 1953, the name was changed in honor of Koidula.

USEFUL WORDS AND EXPRESSIONS

Hello	Tere
Good morning	Tere hommikut
Good evening	Head õhtut
Good night	Head ööd
Good bye	Nägemiseni
Yesterday	Eile
Today	Täna
Tomorrow	Homme
Please	Palun
Thank you	Tänan väga (or) Aitäh
Yes	Ja
No	Ei
You're welcome	Võtke heaks
Excuse me	Vabandage
I'm sorry	Andke andeks
My name is...	Minu nimi on...
Do you speak English?	Kas Teie räägite inglis keelt?
I don't speak Estonian	Mina ei räägi eesti keelt
Please speak slowly	Palun rääkige aeglaselt
I don't understand	Mina ei saa aru
I would like to go to...	Mina sooviksin minna...se
Where is...	Kus on...
I would like...	Mina tahan...
How much does it cost?	Kui palju see maksab?

At a restaurant

I would like to order	Mina soovin tellida
Some more, please	Lisa palun
That's enough, thank you	Aitab, tänan
coffee (with milk)	kohvi (piimaga)
sugar	suhkur
tea	tee
juice	mahl
mineral water	mineraalvesi
beer	õlu
wine (red, white)	vein (punane, valge)
bread	leib
butter	või

Locations

street	tänav
square	plats
hotel	hotel
castle	loss
church	kirik
restaurant	söökla (or) restoraan
hospital	haigla
drug store	apteek
movie theater	kino
theater	teater
museum	muuseum
post office	post kontor

Days of the week

Monday	Esmaspäev
Tuesday	Teisipäev
Wednesday	Kolmapäev
Thursday	Neljapäev
Friday	Reede
Saturday	Laupäev
Sunday	Pühapäev

Cardinal numbers

1	üks	16	kuusteist
2	kaks	17	seitseteist
3	kolm	18	kaheksateist
4	neli	19	üheksateist
5	viis	20	kakskümmend
6	kuus	25	kakskümmendviis
7	seitse	30	kolmkümmend
8	kaheksa	40	nelikümmend
9	üheksa	50	viiskümmend
10	kümme	60	kuuskümmend
11	üksteist	70	seitsekümmend
12	kaksteist	80	kaheksakümmend
13	kolmteist	90	üheksakümmend
14	neliteist	100	sada
15	viisteist		

307

Ordinal numbers

1st	esimene	8th	kaheksas
2nd	teine	9th	üheksas
3rd	kolmas	10th	kümmnes
4th	neljaš	11th	üheteisküümnes
5th	viies	20th	kakskümmemd
6th	kuues	100th	sajandik
7th	seitsmes		

PRONUNCIATION GUIDE

The Estonian language belongs to the Balto-Finnic branch of the Finno-Ugric family. It is closely related to Finnish and bears a very distant relationship to Hungarian. Estonian and Italian have been singled out by the International PEN Club as the most beautiful languages. The beauty of Estonian comes from the numerous long vowel sounds and the lack of harsh consonants. The Estonian alphabet is as follows:

a, b, (c), č, d, e, f, g, h, i, j, k, l, m, n, o, p, (q), r, s, ś, z, ž, t, u, v, (w), õ, ä, ö, ü, (x), and (y).

The letters c, q, w, x, and y are only used in foreign words, and c, f, s, z, and z are used in foreign words to indicate pronunciation. Double letters indicate both long vowels and consonants. Dipthongs always have a short first vowel.

Vowels

The letter a is pronounced as the English u in but; aa is like a in father; e as in pen; ee as in the English eh or French de; i as in pin; ii as the ee in feel; o as in November; oo as eau in the French peau; u as in put; uu as the oo in food; ä almost as in cat, but with a less open mouth; ää is the same as a, but with a more open mouth; ö as ir in girl, but with rounded lips; öö as the oeu in the French voeu; õ is peculiar to Estonian and is pronounced with the lips in the position of a short e while the tongue is retracted; ôô is the same as o, but longer; ü is produced by pronouncing i with a protrusion of the lips and a narrow opening of the mouth; üü is the same as u, but longer and clearer.

Consonants

The letter b is voiceless, almost like the p in copy; d is voiceless as the t in city; g is voiceless as the ck in ticket; k, p, and t are stronger and longer than the voiceless g, b, and d; h is the same as in English, but less aspirated; j like y in you; l as in lily; m is the same as in English, but shorter; n as in English; r is trilled; s is voiceless and weaker than the English s; š as the sh in shoe; v as in English; f as in English; z as the s in was; ž as the s in pleasure.